How to Read a French Fry

and Other Stories of Intriguing Kitchen Science

With more than 100 recipes

Russ Parsons

"Parsons's affable voice and intellectual clarity make his lessons a pleasure, and there are excellent recipes to illustrate them."
— *New York Times*

"A book for both the left-brained and right-brained cook . . . Every recipe offers something to savor." — *Wall Street Journal*

"Dense with facts . . . rich with invaluable tips . . . The kind of book that any committed cook will want to have around."—*Atlanta Journal*

"Fascinating to read and totally useful in the kitchen . . . Parsons's scientific explanations are very satisfying." — Jeffrey Steingarten

"Those who have been clipping Parsons's articles for years will be thrilled to find them here in one volume." — *Gourmet*

"An engaging blend of professional reporting and amateur sleuthing."
— *Houston Chronicle*

"A book that gets us to think about the whys and hows of cooking."
—*Washington Post*

"Both fascinating science and a tasty collection."— *Charlotte Observer*

"Russ Parsons not only unravels some of the intrigue of the kitchen but, in entertaining fashion, shows us why this understanding matters."
— Mark Bittman

"Particularly useful . . . A book that can serve as an introduction to the high-level science that for a long time cooks have understood only intuitively." — *Boston Globe*

"With passion and enthusiasm, Russ Parsons explains the science behind kitchen common sense. As if that's not enough, the recipes are some of the most appealing ever." — Deborah Madison

"An enjoyable, variably paced read." — *Austin Chronicle*

"This is an unlikely creation: a kitchen-science book that makes you hungry, and it's also a cookbook that teaches, from an authority on food and cooking." — Thomas Keller

"[A] delightful book that is one part kitchen science and one part cookbook." — *Library Journal*

"Mouthwatering recipes, fascinating information and charming commentary." — Paula Wolfert

"Unique . . . A truly valuable resource for the serious cook, with excellent recipes to boot." — *Publishers Weekly*

"A book that is destined to be stained and dog-eared."
— *San Francisco Chronicle*

HOUGHTON MIFFLIN COMPANY

Boston   New York

how to read a french fry

Russ Parsons

and other stories of intriguing kitchen science ✦

First Houghton Mifflin paperback edition 2003

Visit our Web site: www.houghtonmifflinbooks.com.

Library of Congress Cataloging-in-Publication Data
Parsons, Russ.
    How to read a french fry : and other stories of
intriguing kitchen science / Russ Parsons.
        p.   cm.
    ISBN 0-395-96783-X
    ISBN 0-618-37943-6 (pbk.)
    1. Cookery. I. Title.
    TX651.P36 2001
    641.5 — dc21   00-054685

QUM 10 9 8 7 6 5 4 3 2 1
Printed in the United States of America

Book design by Melodie Wertelet
Cover photograph by Jim Scherer

The author is grateful for permission to reprint the recipes in this
book that originally appeared in the *Los Angeles Times*. Reprinted
with permission of the *Los Angeles Times*, copyright © 2000.

For my mom, who taught me to use words;

my dad, who taught me to think;

and Kathy and Sarah, who taught me almost everything else.

acknowledgments

Being a journalist means never getting to say thank you.
You work on a story, you talk to your sources, the story appears,
and then you move on to the next one. Most of what we do as
journalists is relay other people's knowledge to our readers. And
the only thanks we give is a brief mention in the newspaper. I've
got 25 years of thank-yous saved up.

The people who've helped me fall into three groups: cooks,
writers and scientists. The first group, of course, is closest to my
heart. They've fed me (come to think of it, so have many of the
writers and one or two of the scientists too). People like Andre
Diddy, Deborah Madison, Michel Mal, Rosa Rajkovic, Michael
Roberts, Nadia Santini, Ken Shoemaker and Trudy Baker, Martha
Rose Shulman, Nancy Silverton, Chris Smith, Zanne Stewart,
C. B. Stubblefield and Clifford Wright have taught me much of
what I know about the joys of cooking for other people. Special
mention goes to the two truly brilliant cooks I've known, Thomas
Keller of the French Laundry in Yountville, California, and Michel
Richard of Citronelle in Washington, D.C., my French brother.

A writer is a magpie, collecting bits and pieces of technique
from everyone he reads. Another, less polite way of putting it is
that we are a bunch of thieves, stealing anything that isn't nailed
down. The people I've robbed most happily include first and fore-
most Phyllis Richman and Matt Kramer, but also Toni Allegra,
Michael Bauer, Rose Levy Beranbaum, Mark Bittman, Amanda

Hesser, Charles Perry, Fred Plotkin, Bart Ripp, Jeffrey Steingarten, Sylvia Thompson and Paula Wolfert. And, of course, the queen mother of all food writers, Julia Child. Special mention must be made of the food staff at the *Los Angeles Times,* especially Ruth Reichl, who hired me in the first place and was by far the best boss I've ever had in any capacity, and Donna Deane and Mayi Brady, who tested most of these recipes.

Then there are the scientists. Anyone who writes about the science of cooking owes a tremendous debt to Harold McGee, who opened our eyes to the subject. His *On Food and Cooking* remains an incredible achievement; everything that has been written since only makes it more remarkable. But there are also many other books on food science that are worth investigating. Two authors I find extremely valuable are Belle Lowe, whose books, though published in the 1930s, remain remarkably up to date in many ways, and Margaret McWilliams. In addition, I relied on the expertise of many, many people, both in print and in person. These include: P. J. Bechtel of Colorado State University; Eric Block of State University of New York–Albany; Michael Blumenthal of Rutgers University (who handed me practically everything I needed for the frying chapter and, indirectly, gave me the title for this book); Carlos Chrisosto of the University of California at Davis; Terry Dockerty of the Cattleman's Beef Association; Janet Eastridge of the Department of Agriculture; Ray Field of the University of Wyoming; Gregory Gray of the Department of Agriculture; Arthur Grosser of McGill University; Arthur Maurer of the University of Wisconsin; Nell Mondy of Cornell; Leslie Norris of McCormick and Company; Jay Novakofski of the University of Illinois–Urbana; Louis Rockland of Food Tech Research; Daryl Tatum of Colorado State University; and Alan Sams of Texas A&M. There are many more whose contributions to papers or journals were useful. Whether they knew it or not, they all contributed to this book. Of course, any faults lie with my misinterpretations, not with their information.

I owe a tremendous debt of gratitude to my stalwart agent, Judith Weber, who was always there when I needed her and contributed many good ideas (including spotting the title!), but always knew when not to ask me, "How's the book going?" And finally, to the crew at Houghton Mifflin, especially my editor, Rux Martin, who never flinched when I asked to do "just one more rewrite." That we've come through this process and remain on as good terms as when we started is a testament to our long friendship.

contents

recipes x

introduction 1

one ✦ how to read a french fry 9

two ✦ the second life of plants 47

three ✦ miracle in a shell 123

four ✦ from a pebble to a pillow 149

five ✦ meat and heat 217

six ✦ fat, flour and fear 285

index 313

recipes

✦ APPETIZERS AND FIRST COURSES

tuscan potato chips *25*

stuffed zucchini flowers *27*

fried little fish *29*

goat cheese tart with caramelized
   onions and green olives *34*

roasted tomatoes with goat cheese *63*

trout mousse *142*

white bean crostini *191*

ceviche with shrimp and avocado *235*

dungeness crab coleslaw *238*

✦ BREAKFAST AND BRUNCH

cornmeal waffles with winter fruit compote *110*

strawberry preserves *119*

nectarine and rose geranium jam *120*

meyer lemon marmalade *121*

scrambled eggs with morels and asparagus *141*

✦ SALADS

roasted beet and orange salad *78*

celery salad with walnuts and blue cheese *135*

green goddess salad *136*

smoked tuna salad in tomatoes *137*

seafood rice salad *188*

calamari salad *236*

crisp salmon salad *237*

✦ SOUPS

smoky cream of corn soup *165*

cream of cauliflower soup *205*

squash soup with moroccan spices *207*

fish soup with shellfish *240*

✦ PASTA, RICE AND BEANS

orecchiette with prosciutto and peas *167*

pasta with broccoli rabe *168*

macaroni and cheese with green onions and ham *170*

broccoli lasagna *172*

free-form lasagna of roasted asparagus *175*

wild mushroom lasagna *177*

pasta with potatoes *179*

soft polenta with ragù *180*

artichoke risotto *184*

zucchini and porcini risotto *186*

pinto bean puree *192*

white bean and swiss chard stew *194*

pinto bean and squash stew *196*

pork and beans . . . and endive *198*

potato gnocchi *211*

✦ RED MEAT, CHICKEN AND FISH

crisp-skinned salmon on creamy leeks and cabbage *38*

country fried chicken *40*

pan-fried chicken breasts with fresh tomatoes,
   green olives and rosemary *42*

pork schnitzel with arugula salad *44*

ragout of shrimp and fava beans *84*

braised duck and lentils *200*

sausages and ribs with red wine–braised lentils *202*

salmon braised with leeks, prosciutto and mushrooms *242*

oven-steamed salmon with cucumber salad *244*

grilled salmon with chipotle-tequila butter *246*

grilled swordfish with salsa verde *248*

baked fish with potatoes and artichokes *250*

broiled sand dabs with brown butter *252*

recipes

roast brined turkey *255*

turkey tonnato sandwich *256*

real fajitas *258*

umbrian-style pork roast *259*

roast lamb with fresh peas and turnips *260*

chicken braised with green olives and thyme *266*

chicken in the pot *268*

mushroom pot roast *270*

lamb and lentils to eat with a spoon *272*

braised lamb shanks with green olives *274*

ragù napoletano *276*

wild mushroom meat loaf *279*

spicy garlic sausages *281*

lamb, orange zest and rosemary sausages *282*

smokerless smoked bratwurst *283*

✦ VEGETABLES

brussels sprouts and bacon *36*

sautéed green beans with garlic and sage *37*

butter-braised spinach *64*

belgian endive braised with cream *65*

radicchio al forno *66*

glazed zucchini *67*

california succotash of squash,
    lima beans and corn *68*

creamed onions with shiitake mushrooms *70*

market mix *72*

baked tomatoes stuffed with mozzarella *73*

rajas (grilled peppers and cream) *74*

ratatouille *76*

potato gratin *209*

butternut squash puree
    with balsamic vinegar *213*

gratin of sweet potatoes and bourbon *214*

puree of winter squash and apples *215*

✦ VEGETABLE MAIN COURSES

spring vegetable stew of snap peas, lettuce,
     new potatoes and artichokes *80*

stew of charred tomatoes, pasta
     and cranberry beans *82*

grilled vegetable sandwich *86*

stuffed zucchini *88*

eggplant and goat cheese casserole *91*

✦ DESSERTS

peach fritters *30*

strawberry soup *95*

sliced melons in lime-mint syrup *96*

fall fruit compote *97*

quince applesauce *98*

dreamsicle oranges *99*

candied citrus peel *100*

ultimate strawberry shortcake *102*

perfumed strawberries in meringue baskets *104*

mango crepes with mexican cream *106*

cornmeal crepes with spiced plum compote *108*

vanilla-baked apples with bourbon sauce *112*

apricot-almond clafoutis *114*

berry ice cream *115*

stone fruit ice cream *116*

white peach and fig ice cream *117*

chocolate pots de crème *144*

lemon sponge pudding *146*

lemon curd tart *147*

recipes

➤

recipes

short-pastry crust *296*

flaky piecrust *297*

rustic tart crust *299*

rustic peach tart *300*

nectarine and almond tart *301*

lavender-fig tart *302*

apple crisp *303*

snickerdoodles *306*

New Mexican Christmas Cookies (biscochitos) *307*

gingersnaps *308*

grandma smith's christmas cookies *309*

sour cherry–stuffed almond cookies *310*

how to read a french fry

Wilder sat on a tall stool in front of the stove, watching water boil in a small enamel pot. He seemed fascinated by the process. I wondered if he'd uncovered some splendid connection between things he'd always thought of as separate. The kitchen is routinely rich in such moments.

Don De Lillo, *White Noise*

introduction

Have you ever noticed that a whole onion smells different from one that's been cut? Have you ever wondered why? Here's the answer: Physically, an onion is 90 percent water, trapped in a fairly flimsy network of cellulose. Within that network is a subnetwork of smaller cells, called vacuoles. These vacuoles separate a variety of chemical components suspended in the water. It's only when the vacuoles are ruptured, either by cutting or by smashing, that these chemical components combine and then recombine again and again in a cascade of chemical reactions, creating the smell and taste we associate with raw onions. Most simply put, what happens is that the contents of these separate vacuoles combine to form a variety of sulfur-rich compounds called sulfonic acids. These acids in turn combine to form still more compounds that provide most of the fresh-cut onion character. What's more, this chain of reactions happens in a flash. It's a little miracle. In fact, not until the 1970s had science advanced to the point that it could begin to decipher what happens in that fleeting instant between the time your knife touches the onion and the fumes reach your nose.

Think about it: the chopping of an onion is one of the most common acts in all of cooking. Any good cook has done it thousands, probably millions of times. Yet how many have ever stopped to think about what is really going on? All of this is neither trivial nor purely technical. For example, it's important to realize that these sulfonic acids are extremely unstable, meaning they go away quickly. One of the places they go, of course, is right up your nose, which triggers the crying response we associate with chopping onions (for this reason, these chemicals are called lachrymators, from the Latin word for tears). More critically, they are both water-soluble and heat-sensitive, which means that the chemicals will dissolve in water and will vaporize when heated. In short: soak an onion or cook it and those acrid flavor characteristics go away. By the same token, and perhaps just as useful, chill an onion or rinse it under cold water and you won't cry as much when chopping it. Also, a sharper knife will damage far fewer cells than a dull one.

And what about those so-called sweet onions, the Vidalias or Mauis or whatever you want to call them? Though sweet onions cost significantly more, they usually contain no more sugar than plain five-pounds-for-a-dollar yellow storage onions. They taste sweeter because they are much lower in the acrid sulfuric compounds (as well as in the enzyme that produces much of the onion flavor). The practical application of this is that while raw sweet onions are delicious on hamburgers or in salads, it is spendthrift to cook one. Take away those sulfuric acids by cooking, and a yellow storage onion will actually taste much sweeter than the so-called sweet. You can even make raw storage onions taste sweeter by soaking them in several changes of cold water (hot water is more effective at dispersing the acids, but even that small amount of heat will begin to cook the onion, breaking up the delicate physical framework and robbing it of its crispness). Each time you rinse the cut onions, you will note that the water becomes milky. That is the trail of the sulfurous compounds. Use vinegar to rinse them, as they do in Mexico, and your onions will seem even sweeter, because the remaining sulfuric acids are overshadowed by more palatable acetic acids.

There are other lessons for the cook in this little bit of onion chemistry. For example, now it should be clear why the size of the dice you cut is important. The smaller the pieces of onion, the faster the cellulose framework breaks down and the faster the sulfuric compounds go away. Chop an onion small and it will melt into the background, its residual sweetness forming an almost imperceptible harmonizing flavor. Leave it large if you want both texture and flavor to retain some bite. You can control the effect by how you cook the onion as well. In a hot pan, it will cook so quickly that some of the sharp flavor will remain, as will some of the crisp texture. Cook it slowly and, again, it will melt into the background, flavoring everything else without retaining much of its original identity. What's more, all of these things are equally true for the other members of the onion family: garlic, shallots, chives, green onions and leeks. They are all built the same way; the differences in flavor are due to subtle differences in the chemicals involved. Garlic, for example, follows the same process but breaks down into a slightly different set of chemicals.

The kitchen is full of such little miracles, from the browning of meat to the emulsion of a sauce. How are various meats different from one another? Why do you cook pork differently from beef? How do various cuts within the same type of meat differ? Why do you cook a leg of lamb longer than a rack? And what about chicken and fish? How is frying different from roasting, and how is steaming different from either of these? Why are some potatoes better for boiling and others for baking? Why can you stick your hand in a 450-degree oven but not in 212-degree boiling water? Cooking is full of questions that science can help answer—questions you might not have even thought about asking but that can make you a better cook.

In the good old days, you learned to cook in the kitchen. You worked at the elbow of a master—your mother, a great chef or the fry cook down the street—and you absorbed the basics. You learned by watching and repeating. You saw what they did and then you tried to do it yourself, mimicking as exactly as possible every act they performed. When you had absorbed a sufficient amount of knowledge, you then became the teacher, passing along exactly the same lessons in exactly the same way.

There is much to be said for tradition, but as a method of instruction, it has its drawbacks. In the first place, it puts an enormous burden on the talents of that one teacher. If your mom/chef/fry cook was, let us say, something less than supremely skilled, bad habits may have been passed along every bit as easily as good ones. It's a fairly limited way of cooking too. If you ever want to move beyond your teacher's range of dishes, you've got to find another mentor, or you're out of luck. There's the story about the daughter who is learning to cook. Her mother teaches her that when cooking a ham, you always cut off the shank end. She asks why, and her mother explains that that's the way her mother taught her and that it is done to tenderize the meat. She asks her grandmother why, and the grandmother tells her that that is the way *her* mother did it and it's because the meat tastes better that way. Puzzled, she visits her great-grandmother out on the farm and asks her for her story. "Well," she says, pointing at the little old wood-fired stove, "That's the only way I could get it to fit."

But perhaps the biggest drawback to tradition as a way of instruction is that it assumes there's someone around who is actually cooking. More and more, that seems to be a dangerous assumption. While microwave meals and TV dinners may be a boon to busy working families, they have been deadly to the tradition of home cooking. We are now three and sometimes four generations removed from the age of real cooks — those who made do using the raw ingredients at hand, without the aid of food industry shortcuts.

But by now this is an old song. What's rarely asked is whether we would be willing to listen even if those imaginary teachers of the past were still around. We've changed, and the unquestioning following of instructions no longer seems to be part of our makeup. Give an instruction, from "Work!" to "Duck!" and the immediate response is, "Why?" "Because" is not an acceptable answer. We want to know why something works. How it works. What happens if you do this instead. Really? I'll try it myself and see.

Even the way we approach a recipe — probably as close as we can come to those mentors of old — has changed. On the one hand, because of this lack of mentoring, the amount of detail required in a recipe has increased almost exponentially over the past few generations. At the turn of the century, it was perfectly understood for a writer to instruct, "Prepare in the usual manner." Today a recipe not only needs to explain what the usual manner is but needs to include how the ingredient is to be cleaned and cut before cooking (and in some cases what it looks like and where it can be bought), the size and type of pan it is to be prepared in, the type of heat it is to be cooked over and for exactly how long and, ideally, several indications of progress — and eventually doneness — along the way. The problem is, almost no recipe can be written in enough detail to cover every possible question that might arise.

That's not to say we know less about food today. In fact, maybe the opposite is true. No matter how uneducated most people are about the process of cooking, we tend to be extremely knowledgeable about eating. While it might have been possible for cooks in the past to master merely by rote the dozen or so regional specialties that would have been any cook's repertoire, things are different now. Today we eat — and, hopefully, cook — across regional and cultural boundaries. Not only is someone in Atlanta liable to fix Boston baked beans for dinner, he might try his hand the next night at pad Thai. Any reasonably proficient foodies can discuss the intricacies of dishes made in countries they may have trouble locating on a map. We can debate the provenance of almost any ingredient listed on a restaurant menu.

And we have developed very definite opinions about how we want our food to taste. We have eaten at the tables of the most creative chefs in the country, and we know what we like — even if we don't know how to roast a chicken.

The trick, then, is to provide the answers to basic cooking questions in a way that people can understand enough to follow them. The physical processes of cooking are, after all, universal. Browning a piece of meat works exactly the same whether it is being done in a wok in Sichuan or in a *padella* in Padua. That is where this book comes in. It is not intended to be a food science textbook. There are plenty of those, and if you are interested in what you find here, you can move on to them. Rather, this book is about getting you to pause for a minute to examine some of the important processes in cooking, to explain the science behind them and then to tell you how you can use that knowledge to improve your own cooking. You can think of it as a kind of modern cooking class, one that uses basic scientific principles to explain culinary truths — and does it with a minimum of technical language.

At this point, some of you are probably heading for the door. It's that "S-word" again. Science has gotten a bad name lately. We equate it with everything from sophisticated weaponry to Frankenstein-like experimentation with life itself. It has become synonymous with not just technology but technology run amok. What could be more ironic? As science becomes more and more an intrinsic part of our lives, we have come to loathe it as something completely separate and foreign. Yet at its most basic level, science is nothing more than a way of answering questions about the things that happen to us every day. It is not something separate from the natural world; it is a way of looking at the natural world and trying to understand it. Perhaps the problem is that science as most of us experience it — at second hand, through reading reports — has moved so far past the questions that concern most of us that we no longer see the connections. Trips to Mars and explorations of the gene code are doubtless fascinating, but neither has much application to life. Maybe what is needed is a return to real science, to questions that we laypeople ponder. Nowhere is there a better laboratory for this than the kitchen.

Some fear that turning toward kitchen science means turning away from the art of cooking, as if the two were contradictory. Nothing could be further from the truth. If it makes you more comfortable, think of this as an anti-cookbook. We'll begin with some science, then proceed on to practical advice. Finally, there are recipes that demonstrate the things you've read. Once you understand these basic processes, you will be free to cook well even without any recipes at all. You'll know how to get the results you want, and you'll be able to adjust the recipes to fit your taste and the ingredients you have on hand. The only limit will be your creative ability. In the same way, this book can also be read as an explication of other cookbooks. You'll no longer have to rely on the cookbook writer to tell you how hot the flame should be, how brown the meat should be or when something is done. You'll know for yourself. It's the next best thing to having mom — the scientist — there explaining everything.

In some cases, the connections between the recipes may seem a bit tenuous until you've read the chapters. For example, what exactly do a vinaigrette and a chocolate pudding have in common? Well, look at it this way: Vinaigrette is an emulsion — a combination of two ingredients that don't normally get along (oil and water). Mayonnaise is an emulsion made using eggs. Hollandaise is a hot emulsion made with cooked eggs. Puddings are nothing more than stiffened emulsions of cooked eggs. One thing leads to another. The kitchen is routinely rich in such unexpected connections.

how to read a french fry

Everyone loves deep-fried foods, as a glance at any fast-food menu will prove. Yet most people would sooner tune their own car or perform minor surgery on a family member before they would try to fry in their own kitchen. To say that we are ambivalent about frying is an understatement. On the one hand, it has become synonymous with minimum-wage labor ("You want fries with that?"). But hardly anyone will dare to try it at home. You can hardly blame them. Anyone doubting that cooking is a complex art (or perhaps "craft" is more accurate) need only consider frying. Perhaps no other type of cooking involves quite as many variables or requires as many decisions on the part of the cook. Oil, main ingredient, coating—not only does each of these things need to be carefully thought about, but each of them is also constantly changing throughout the cooking process, brief though it might be. No wonder most people never fry. But before you dismiss the technique entirely, remember two things: how delicious fried food is, and the fact that all over the country, it is done by people who are not yet old enough to vote.

The fundamental truth of frying is that it is one of the hottest forms of cooking there is. That is the reason fried foods have such a nice crunch, and it is also the reason so many people are afraid of it. To get to the first, you must overcome the second. But you need to understand a little about how heat works. Though higher temperatures might be reached in roasting—most home ovens go up to at least 500 degrees, while most oils begin to smoke at about 400 degrees—it is really a far cooler form of cooking.

That sounds contradictory, but only because we usually think of heat solely in terms of temperature, when in reality temperature is not really a reliable guide to how hot something is. Think about it: you can stick your hand in a 500-degree oven, but you'd never try that with even 200-degree oil. Why is that? Heat is energy, the movement of molecules. The hotter something is, the faster those molecules are moving. Something heats up—energy is transferred—when those speedy little molecules bump into it, setting its molecules in motion. Temperature measures how fast those molecules are moving. That is important, but equally—if not more—important is how many of those molecules there are in a certain space. Put most simply, the more molecules there are, the more quickly heat is transferred. This is called conduction. In a 500-degree oven, the air molecules are moving very fast indeed, but relatively speaking, there aren't very many of them. Your hand will need to be hit by many seconds' worth before it will begin to heat up to a temperature that feels uncomfortable. Because oil is so dense—it has so many more molecules in a similar space—it transfers heat much more quickly.

Water transfers heat more quickly than air as well, though not nearly so quickly as oil. Because water molecules are not bound together as tightly as those in oil, water not only conducts heat less efficiently, it self-regulates the heat. When it reaches a certain temperature, the molecules are moving so fast that the water isn't sticky enough to hold them together. When the molecules begin to escape into the atmosphere, the water can get no hotter. This is called the boiling point, and it is 212 degrees at sea level. Though oil will boil too, that happens only in theory. Practically speaking, oil begins to burn well before it reaches the boiling point.

So the first thing a cook needs to know about frying is that it is extremely efficient. It cooks foods very quickly. A slice of carrot that may take 20 minutes to cook by roasting or 10 minutes by boiling will fry in only 2 to 3 minutes. For this reason, fried foods are usually cut into fairly small pieces. Otherwise, they would never cook through to the center before those blistering-hot temperatures burned the outside.

Oils are fats, and all fats are not the same. They vary in composition according to their source. Chemically, all fats are composed of carbon, oxygen and hydrogen. This is the same combination that makes up carbohydrates like flour and sugar, but the ratio of the ingredients is different. Fats are much higher in hydrogen than in carbon and oxygen. How much higher in hydrogen is important. The amount of hydrogen a fat contains determines its saturation. Fats containing lots of hydrogen are said to be highly saturated. Since their chemical structures are more densely packed (containing more hydrogen), highly saturated fats are firmer at lower temperatures. Oils are generally among the least saturated fats — and, by definition, oils are liquid at room temperature. Animal fats are among the most saturated. At room temperature, they are solid. (But all animal fats are not equally saturated — chilled cooked beef is stiffer than chilled cooked pork because beef fat is more saturated.) Even liquid fats, though, vary greatly in saturation. For example, something like rapeseed oil (called canola in this country) contains only about 6 percent saturated fat, while corn oil, olive oil and soybean oil are between 13 and 15 percent saturated. Vegetable oils can be artificially altered to increase their saturation too. Shortening is hydrogenated vegetable oil — oil to which more hydrogen has been added — and it contains about 25 percent saturated fat. Some vegetable fats are as saturated as animal fats. Palm oil, for example, is more than half saturated fat — about the same as butter.

Saturated fat is something we hear a lot about because of its reputed role in heart disease. This has been demonstrated statistically (people whose diets are high in saturated fat are more likely to have heart problems), though the mechanism by which this happens is not clear. The theory is that saturated fats increase the level of cholesterol in the blood, which in turn increases the risk of heart disease. To cooks, saturated fats are important because, generally speaking, the more highly saturated the frying oil, the crisper the crust of the cooked food. This explains the popularity of lard and other animal fats as frying mediums (the Belgians, who are reputed to make the best french fries in the world, swear by horse fat).

Frying is further complicated by the fact that oil is not a static ingredient. It is constantly changing throughout the cooking process — indeed, even before it begins. The quality of the oil you start with is vital to the quality of the food you finish with. And that quality is affected by a variety of factors, ranging from things as obvious as contamination to things as subtle as light and air. Almost from the time oils are created, when they are ground from their originating seed or rendered from an animal fat, they are changing. The changes are subtle at first and with proper storage can remain undetectable for a long time. But eventually, even without ever being opened or even poured from the bottle, oil will begin to develop off smells and tastes.

The first step in rancidity is technically called reversion. You'll recognize it by a fishy aroma and flavor. Rancidity has many causes. Oil can turn rancid because it has absorbed outside odors. It can go rancid because of trace minerals and enzymes that occur naturally within the oil. It can go rancid because of microorganisms that are introduced from the outside. And it can go rancid because of exposure to oxygen, light and moisture. To avoid rancidity, use the freshest possible oil and store it in a dark, cool place. Try to keep oil in a container that is just big enough to hold it, to minimize exposure to oxygen.

These changes are exaggerated when oil is heated and used for cooking. When you add even a drop of water—which is the primary constituent of most foods—to heated oil, the oil begins to hydrolyze. Briefly put, the water begins to break the fat cells down into component parts. Some of these parts then re-form into new substances called polymers. They are responsible for the ring of plastic-like material you sometimes find around the inside of the pan just above the surface of the frying oil. Polymers can be the very devil to scrub out, but they can also be quite useful. The repeated slow heating of oil that's called for in the seasoning of a cast-iron skillet is really just a controlled buildup of polymers. In this case, they form a natural waterproof, nonstick surface.

Other changes happen as well. Each oil has a specific smoking point. This is the temperature at which the oil begins to break down into free fatty acids and a chemical called acrolein. Acrolein is almost immediately vaporized—it literally goes up in smoke. It is also extremely caustic. The smoke will burn your eyes, and food cooked in it will scorch and have a bitter flavor. This is a concern even with fresh oil, since most oils have smoking points in the 400-to-450-degree range, perilously close to the temperature at which most frying is done—350 to 375 degrees. As the oils break down during cooking, though, the smoking point drops even further. Obviously, at a certain point the oil must be discarded and replaced with fresh. Though these changes are natural and inevitable, you can preserve the quality of your cooking oil by making sure that it stays as clean as possible and by cooking in a pot that is narrower than it is tall—to limit the oil's exposure to oxygen.

On the other hand, this oily breakdown is not a wholly bad thing. In fact, to a certain extent, frying would be impossible without it. Have you ever noticed how something fried in absolutely fresh oil never completely browns? In fact, it may not cook through at all. It sounds crazy, but that's because the oil is *too* fresh. The reason goes back to the basic fact that oil and water don't mix. Since most foods are made predominantly of water, that poses an obvious problem. Odd as it may sound, frying is essentially a drying process. When a piece of food is dropped into hot oil, the heat evaporates any moisture on the outside of the food. Since the food is surrounded by oil, the moisture forms a very thin barrier between the oil and what is being fried. Fresh oil can't penetrate that barrier.

Fortunately, some of the by-products of the breakdown of oil are chemical compounds called soaps. These are not the same as the soap you use to wash your hands, but they are similar. Traditionally, soap was made from rendered animal fats. What hand soap does is enable water to penetrate grease so it can be washed away. The chemical soaps created in the frying process behave similarly. They penetrate the water barrier and bring the oil into direct contact with the food being cooked, allowing both browning and thorough cooking. For that reason, old-time cooks always saved a ladleful of old oil to add to the fresh batch when they fried foods. This is a habit worth copying. It doesn't take much, just a tablespoon or so of old oil per cup of new.

More is certainly not better, in this case. You can't have soaps without polymers, and we know what happens when you get too many of those. In fact, scientists who study frying have identified five particular stages of oil life. Break-in oil is brand-new — it won't cook well until it has broken down a little. Fresh oil cooks a little better. Optimum oil is, well, just what it says. Degrading oil is in the transition to being spoiled. Runaway oil is dark and smells bad; it is prone to smoking and even burning. By examining a piece of fried food, you can tell a lot about the oil's age. You can learn to "read" a french fry. A fry cooked in break-in oil will be white on the surface and raw at the center. It will be missing those delicious smells and flavors we associate with fried foods. If fried in fresh oil, the potato will have begun to brown at the edges and be slightly crisp. The center will be more thoroughly cooked. If the oil was optimum, the fry will be golden brown and crisp, with rigid edges. It will be completely cooked and soft at the center, and perhaps most important, it will have the fully developed smells of cooked potato and oil that we associate with a great french fry. If the oil had begun to degrade, the fry will be a little darker and may have spots of scorching. It will be limp and greasy to the touch. With runaway oil, the color will be really dark and the fry really greasy. You'll notice it has collapsed inward. It will smell and taste like bad oil.

You can see these changes in the oil while you're frying if you watch the bubbles that come up when the food is added. Very fresh oil is very sticky—in scientific terms, it has high surface tension. The bubbles that come up will be very small. As the oil breaks down, surface tension decreases (the oil becomes less sticky) and the bubbles become larger. This continues to the point that, in runaway oil, the bubbles may actually be so large and tightly stacked that they resemble foam.

When it comes right down to it, each of those effects is directly traceable back to that dance between oil and water. Pay attention the next time you fry something. When you drop the food into the hot fat, there will be a giant whooshing of boiling bubbles. Of course, this is not actual boiling—remember that oil can't boil before it burns. It is the rush of moisture leaving the food and evaporating on contact with the hot oil (if you look closely, sometimes you can even make out the moisture barrier when you are frying something that is really watery). This sudden evaporation is what forms the crisp crust on the outside of the food—frying is drying. As the crust forms, the oil penetrates the same little holes and tunnels from which the water evaporated. At the same time, the heat penetrates more deeply into the food. The moisture from within the food turns to steam. That steam tries to leave the food, traveling to the exterior. At a certain point, depending on the temperature and on the food being fried, the exiting steam and the penetrating oil collide and reach an uneasy balance. That is why food that is properly fried has a crisp exterior but a very delicate interior. In reality, the outside is fried, but the inside is steamed.

If the temperature is too low, the pressure from the steam won't be enough to push back the oil. You'll wind up with greasy food. If the temperature is too high, the food will burn on the outside before the steam has had a chance to cook the center. But within those temperature extremes, frying is actually a fairly forgiving process. Scientists have found that neither cooking time nor oiliness is affected as long as the frying temperature remains between 350 and 375 degrees. This is a good thing, because as any cook will tell you, regulating the heat of the oil is probably the hardest thing about frying.

When you add food to hot oil, it is common for the temperature of the oil to drop by as much as 50 degrees because of the enormous difference in temperature between the oil and the food. For this reason, it is best to begin cooking when the heat is in the upper range. That way, the oil will still be at a good temperature after the drop. This rule varies somewhat depending on the type and size of the pieces being fried. A chicken leg will take longer to cook through than a french fry, so a slightly lower temperature is necessary in order to avoid burning the outside before the inside is done. It is also important that you don't crowd the food in the oil during frying. The more food you add to the oil, the greater the temperature drop will be. This is why fast-food fryers have such an enormous oil capacity—you need that much fat to balance the amount of food being fried, to maintain good frying temperatures while processing pounds of fries at a time.

To get an idea of just how complicated all of this frying can be, consider the simple french fry. Start with the potato. Not only must it be a russet, or baking, potato, it is better if it is an old one. Really good fry cooks even test their potatoes' specific gravity (this involves floating potatoes in brine)—the ones that sink have the highest specific gravity and will make the best french fries. There are different schools of thought when it comes to the oil, but it is generally agreed that saturated fats make the best french fries, and the real specificists love horse fat in particular. Furthermore, a good french fry is fried twice. The first pass, at about 350 degrees, cooks the potato through and makes it light and fluffy. The second frying, right before serving, is done at a higher temperature — 375 to 385 degrees — and gives the fry its final browning.

While many vegetables and even some meats can be fried perfectly just as they are, others need some kind of protection. Let's not forget that frying is a pretty violent type of cooking. The very things that make a nice crisp french fry can ruin a delicate piece of fish. Such foods need to be dipped in some kind of protective coating before they are subjected to the cruel heat of the deep fryer. It is necessary both to create a good crisp crust and to keep the interior from drying out. The crust, as we've said, is the dried-out surface of fried food. But it is more than that. To get a good crust, it is imperative that all the moisture be removed, not only because that provides crispness but also because the caramelization of sugars and the set of reactions that create browning in food cannot begin until the temperature has passed 300 degrees. Remember that water self-regulates its temperature to the boiling point — 212 degrees. Boiled food will not brown, so for any browning to happen, all the water must be evaporated.

The kind of coating you use depends on both the food being fried and the final result you want. Coatings can be as simple as a dusting of flour, or they can be complicated. Cornmeal, ground nuts, different kinds of flour and bread crumbs are a few of the choices cooks have at their discretion, depending on what kind of dish is being prepared. In addition, many coatings also include a liquid of one kind or another, both to help the coating stick to the food and to provide a more interesting texture (after the moisture is driven off, there are many more little nooks and crannies to get crisp).

Wet coatings are called batters. A thin paste of flour and water makes a batter that gives a delicate, barely perceptible crispness yet still protects the surface of the food being fried. Beer is frequently used as a liquid in batters because its sugars and proteins add a pleasant flavor and help to make a beautiful golden brown coating when fried. More complicated batters include eggs as well. Eggs not only provide moisture but contain proteins that aid in the browning process. Many times, coatings are layered. For example, one of the most common ways to fry food is to dust it lightly in flour, dip it in a mixture of beaten egg and water and then roll it in flour or bread crumbs. This produces an even thicker, crisper coating. Sometimes leavening agents, such as beaten egg whites or baking soda or powder, are added to make the cooked coating lighter and puffier.

Whatever type of coating you're using, make sure that it is firmly attached to the food. Nothing breaks oil down faster than particles of batter floating free and burning. Many cooks refrigerate food briefly before frying to firm up the batter. At the least, you should give the food a vigorous shake to break free any loose bits. And don't salt batters. The salt can fall out of the batter and speed the breakdown. Instead, salt food before the batter goes on and then again after the food has been fried.

So far, we've been talking about deep-frying, which is what most people think of first. But there are other types of frying that use less fat and can be grouped under the label "shallow frying." In this country, there is a popular form of cooking called panfrying. This is the way some fried chicken is cooked (and why a piece of meat cooked the same way is called chicken-fried). Panfrying uses less oil than deep-frying, about an inch deep. That's not enough to cover the food completely, so the process is actually a combination of frying (the part of the meat that's covered) and a moist kind of roasting (the part that's above the oil). In essence, the hot moisture created by the cooking process is driven upward through the food, from the part that is bathed in oil to the part that is not, where it can evaporate. Because this is a somewhat more moderate type of frying, it is useful for things that need to be cooked longer, like thicker or tougher cuts of meat. They can brown nicely and form a good crust but still cook all the way through.

Things can be fried in only a tablespoon or two of oil as well. We usually call that sautéing, which comes from the French word *sauter* ("to jump"). This derivation has nothing to do with the actual act of frying but rather with the way the food is stirred, with a quick jerk of the pan that pops it up in the air. Typically, we sauté something for one of two reasons. Sometimes sautéing is part of what could be thought of as "precooking." When we cook onions and garlic together in olive oil, for example, we rarely stop there. Usually we then proceed to make a sauce or a stew or a soup. The onions and garlic are sautéed to combine and mellow their flavors. Taste a raw onion and then a piece of onion that's been sautéed, and you'll see the difference. That brief initial cooking in just a little bit of hot oil evaporates the heat-volatile acidity in the onion. In other words, it takes away its sting. If you taste some of the oil in which the onion was cooked, you'll find that it has picked up some of the onion's flavors as well.

Depending on the recipe and how you want the onion cooked, sautéing can be done either quickly and lightly or slowly and deeply. Usually, though, even when we say we're "browning" an onion, we're really just wilting it — softening it so its flavors develop from the sharp bite of raw to the more mellow and developed tastes we think of as cooked. At this point, the onion will be translucent, not browned. But you can also cook an onion until it is, quite literally, brown. This takes low heat and special care. Rather than 5 minutes, deeply browning onions can take from 45 minutes to an hour. Throughout the cooking, the onions must be stirred frequently and the heat monitored closely. Here's why: what you're doing when you're browning onions this way is caramelizing them. In other words, you're browning the onions' natural sugars. The process begins at a temperature of about 300 degrees, but if the temperature goes too much above that, you run the risk of scorching the sugars. That will give the onions — and the dish — a powerfully bitter flavor. This degree of controlled heat obviously could never be accomplished by deep-frying. The onions would be either scorched on the outside or raw on the inside. Most probably, they would be both. That's why when you deep-fry onions — as in onion rings — you must first cloak them in a thick batter.

In this kind of shallow-frying, the oil serves two purposes: to transmit heat and to contribute flavor. In fact, though, some low-fat extremists do away with the fat entirely. If you are patient and have heavy pans, you can cook vegetables over very low heat, covered, with little or no fat at all. This is called "sweating," and it relies on the direct heat of the pan to cook the vegetables. Metal is a less efficient transmitter of heat than oil, and in order to avoid scorching, the vegetables must be cooked over very low heat and stirred constantly — kind of like an extreme version of sautéing. Of course, since there is no oil involved, there is also no mingling of flavors.

Sautéing can also be a final step in the cooking process. Vegetables that have been blanched in boiling water are frequently sautéed to finish. You can think of this as being almost akin to making a salad — the cooked vegetables are being dressed with flavored oil. In fact, they are often blessed with a final squirt of lemon or vinegar too, strengthening the analogy. Almost always, the actual cooking — the softening of the tough cellular material and the mellowing of the harsh raw flavors — is done by the boiling, not the frying. Sometimes, though, the frying is extended to allow the caramelization of some of the sugars in the vegetables.

Of course, sautéing is not limited to vegetables. Some of the most basic dishes in almost any cuisine are sautéed meats. In this case, only the most delicate cuts are used, since the cooking will by necessity be brief. This is frequently a two-stage process. First, the meat is browned, to develop flavor, then other ingredients (usually including a liquid) are added to finish the cooking. We'll talk more about this in the chapter on cooking meat. It's as far from the simple french fry as you can get, but many of the basic principles are the same.

✦ **Because of the intense heat involved,** deep-frying is best used for small pieces of food. Big pieces take too long to cook through and will burn on the outside before they are done. Because the cooking goes so quickly, only very tender foods should be deep-fried.

✦ **A simple flour dusting** is intended mainly to absorb excess moisture from the surface of the food being fried. It gives a thin, delicate coating that is barely perceptible as a crust. Because of the lack of sugars and amino acids in flour, it won't brown much either. Neither does it provide much protection to the food being fried.

✦ **Adding water to flour** to form a batter allows more flour to adhere to the surface of the food. This results in a thicker crust; how thick depends on how much water you add. A thin batter spreads the flour more thinly than a thick one. A thicker batter will be crunchier and will provide better protection for delicate foods. But water by itself does not add the sugars or amino acids essential for browning. This coating will be pale.

✦ **To get a really browned crust,** use a batter that contains amino acids and/or sugars. Eggs are high in protein and will work well. Beer has both protein and sugars — it will brown even better.

✦ **Keep liquid batters ice-cold** to improve their stickiness — their ability to adhere to the food.

✦ **Some batters include leavening agents** — baking powder or baking soda, yeast or beaten egg whites. These cause the batter to puff and expand when heated, providing the thickest, most protective coating for delicate foods, though they may not be as crisp as others.

✦ **Bread crumbs,** being larger and more irregularly shaped than flour, increase the surface area of the crust and will be crisper than flour. On their own, they will not stick to food, though, so you'll need to use a series of coatings: flour to dry the food, beaten egg to provide the "stickiness" and bread crumbs to give the crust.

* **Salt will drop out** of a batter and break down oil faster than almost anything else. Salt food to be fried *before* applying the batter and then *after* the frying.

* **Really fresh oil** will not cook food as well as oil that has broken down a little. If you're using fresh oil, be prepared to toss out the first batch of food. It will probably be lighter in color than you want and may not have cooked all the way through. If you deep-fry a lot, it's worth keeping a little old oil in the pantry. Adding a tablespoon or so of old oil per cup of fresh oil will improve the way it cooks remarkably.

* **Highly saturated fats,** such as animal fats or shortening, give the crispest crusts.

* **Use more oil** than you might think necessary. Technically, you need only enough oil to float the food being fried, but the more oil you use, the more retained heat you will have (20 pieces of potato will absorb the available heat from 1 cup of oil faster than from 2 cups), giving you a bigger "cushion" for cooking. On the other hand, do not overfill the pot with oil—one-half to two-thirds full is about right. When cold food is added to hot oil, there is a giant "whoosh" of foaming oil that could spill over the sides of a pot that is too full.

* **Use a deep-frying thermometer** to check the temperature of the oil. Some experts claim to be able to see a haze forming over the surface of the oil when the temperature is right. That may be so, but a deep-frying thermometer is the only way to be sure. Be careful to set it up so the bulb at the bottom rests just above the bottom of the pan and is not touching it. Then it will be taking the temperature of the oil, not the metal. If you don't have a deep-frying thermometer, you can drop in a small piece of bread for a cruder estimate. It should begin sizzling immediately and will become light brown in 5 to 10 seconds.

✦ **Be patient.** Do not add too many pieces of food to the oil at the same time. Remember that each one will absorb some of the heat and lower the temperature a little. Because of the spread in effective deep-frying temperatures (between 350 and 375 degrees, results will be largely the same), there is some margin for error, but that will disappear quickly if too much food is added to the pot.

✦ **Serve fried foods** as soon after cooking as possible. This is especially true for batter-coated foods, because the batter will begin reabsorbing moisture from the food immediately after it is removed from the hot oil and will quickly become soggy.

tuscan potato chips

These are neither Tuscan nor potatoes nor chips. But you'll get the idea. The intense drying action of frying gives these fresh pasta strips crunch. The pasta can, of course, also be rolled out by hand, but that is a special skill that takes lots of practice. A pasta machine — you can get one for less than $40 — is a very good investment.

1½ cups all-purpose flour

Salt

1 tablespoon olive oil

2 large eggs

2 tablespoons finely chopped
     fresh rosemary leaves

Vegetable oil for deep-frying

Put the flour in a food processor, add ¼ teaspoon salt and the olive oil and pulse to combine. Add the eggs and continue pulsing until the mixture forms a ball of dough that rides around on top of the blade, 1 to 2 minutes. Remove the dough and press it to flatten it slightly. Wrap it tightly in plastic wrap and set it aside at room temperature for 30 minutes, or refrigerate as long as overnight. (This will relax the gluten and make the dough easier to roll out.)

Cut the dough into quarters and cover 3 of the quarters with a damp tea towel. Working with one-quarter at a time, feed the dough through the widest setting of a pasta machine to form a sheet. Fold the sheet in thirds, like a letter, and feed it through the machine again, on the same setting. Continue until the dough feels satiny. Lightly flour the sheet between rollings if it begins to feel sticky.

Adjust the machine to the next setting and feed the dough through it again. Repeat until you have rolled it through the next-to-thinnest setting. Lay out the dough sheet and sprinkle evenly with one-quarter of the rosemary. Fold it lengthwise in half and run it through the machine once more. Set it aside on a floured surface and repeat with the rest of the dough.

Once all the dough has been rolled out, cut the sheets into fettuccine-width strips and then cut the strips into three-to-four-inch lengths.

Heat the vegetable oil to 375 degrees. In 4 or 5 batches, fry the pasta strips until puffed and golden, 1 to 2 minutes. Remove and drain on paper towels. Salt lightly and serve immediately.

6 servings

stuffed zucchini flowers

Fried zucchini flowers are one of the classic uses of *pastella,* the Italian flour-and-water batter. The mixture should be thin enough that it barely coats the flowers; you should be able to see the orange of the petals through the crust. The flowers can also be fried without a filling. This version came about on a day when I was planning to serve a mozzarella salad for another appetizer and accidentally added too much garlic to the bocconcini. When encased in a fried flower, the flavors, too strong on their own, were just right.

----

1 (8-ounce) package small fresh mozzarella balls (bocconcini, ciliegini or ovalini)

2 garlic cloves, minced

¼ teaspoon crushed red pepper

2 teaspoons olive oil

Salt and freshly ground black pepper

24 zucchini flowers (about 1 pound), preferably male flowers that don't have the zucchini attached

2 cups all-purpose flour

Approximately ½ cup water

Vegetable oil for deep-frying

1 bunch arugula

Grated zest of ½ lemon

Cut the mozzarella balls in half. Combine them with the garlic, crushed red pepper, olive oil and salt and pepper to taste. Marinate at room temperature for at least 30 minutes.

Soak the zucchini flowers in a large bowl of cold water to clean and freshen them. Remove them one at a time, gently pat dry, and open the blossoms with the tip of your finger. Carefully place a mozzarella piece deep inside each blossom. Place the blossoms on a tray.

When all the flowers are stuffed, whisk together in a large bowl the flour and enough water to make a batter as thick as heavy cream.

Preheat the oven to 200 degrees. Heat the vegetable oil to 375 degrees. Dredge the blossoms one at a time in the batter, turning the flower so the top seals itself, and immediately place the blossom in the hot oil. Do not crowd the pot. Cook until the oil stops bubbling and the flowers begin to brown, 5 to 7 minutes. Turn the flowers over and cook for another 2 to 3 minutes, browning the second side. Remove the flowers from the oil, drain well and place on a baking sheet lined with oil-absorbent paper (a brown paper bag works well). Salt lightly and keep them warm in the oven until all the frying is done.

Wash and dry the arugula well. Arrange it on a serving platter. Place the fried zucchini flowers on top and sprinkle with the lemon zest. Serve immediately.

8 to 10 servings

fried little fish

In this dish, a batter forms when the milk-drenched fish are tossed with flour. If you need proof that deep-frying involves drying, try these. The fish turn into crisp little bites almost instantly. Whitebait are very small fish, the size of minnows. If you can find them (probably in Asian markets), use them whole; they don't need to be cleaned. If you can't find whitebait or other minnow-sized fish, substitute the tiny white fish sold in Asian fish markets as "rice fish" or use pieces of squid.

½ pound whitebait, left whole,
   or calamari (squid), cleaned
   and cut into ½-inch pieces

1 cup milk

Vegetable oil for deep-frying

Salt and freshly ground black pepper

All-purpose flour for dredging

1 lemon, cut into 6 wedges

Soak the fish or calamari in the milk for at least 1 hour in the refrigerator.

Heat the oil to 375 degrees. Drain the fish or calamari well and season lightly with salt and pepper. Dredge them, a small handful at a time, in the flour. Immediately add them to the hot oil and fry until they are crisp and brown, 30 to 60 seconds, turning as needed. Remove them from the oil and drain on a baking sheet lined with oil-absorbent paper (a brown paper bag works well). Sprinkle the fish or calamari with salt and serve with the lemon wedges.

6 servings

peach fritters

These fritters are fried at a slightly lower temperature than savory foods to avoid scorching the sugar. The macaroon-like Italian cookies called amaretti are available at Italian delis and grocers and some supermarkets. This is an adaptation of James Beard's recipe for fruit fritters in *Theory and Practice of Good Cooking*. To make the cinnamon sugar, combine ¼ cup sugar and 1 teaspoon ground cinnamon.

----

  2 cups all-purpose flour

  2 large eggs, beaten

  2 tablespoons butter, melted

  1 cup light-flavored beer,
     at room temperature

  ¼ teaspoon salt

  1 tablespoon Cognac

  4 large peaches

  1 tablespoon sugar

     Vegetable oil for deep-frying

  2½ cups crushed amaretti
     (Italian almond cookies)

     Cinnamon sugar (see above)

Sift the flour into a bowl. Beat in the eggs, butter, beer and salt until smooth. Stir in the Cognac. Cover and refrigerate for 2 to 3 hours.

To peel the peaches, dip them briefly in boiling water, from 30 seconds to 2 minutes (ripe peaches will take a shorter time, firmer peaches will take longer). Remove from the boiling water and immediately place in an ice-water bath to stop the cooking. The skin should slip off easily. If it doesn't, return the peaches to the boiling water for another 15 to 30 seconds.

Slice the peeled peaches fairly thick (about ½ inch) into a large bowl. Add the sugar and toss to mix well. Set aside for 30 minutes.

Heat the oil to 350 degrees. Put the amaretti crumbs in a shallow bowl. Dip the peaches in the batter, a few slices at a time, then roll them in the amaretti crumbs and fry until golden brown on all sides, 4 to 5 minutes. Remove from the oil, drain on paper towels and serve hot, dusted with cinnamon sugar.

6 to 8 servings

✦ **For a crisp surface,** it is important to remove as much moisture from the surface of the food to be fried as possible. A dusting of flour will absorb the last bit. For the crispest crust, use the classic flour/egg wash/bread-crumb coating used for deep-frying.

✦ **Because there is little or no added moisture** present in tougher vegetables during shallow-frying or sautéing to break down their tough cellulose walls, they are usually blanched in boiling water first so they will cook through.

✦ **Because shallow-frying cooks so quickly,** use only very tender cuts of meat.

✦ **Fish is a good candidate for sautéing,** dusted only in a little flour. Make sure the fat is very hot.

✦ **Always salt meat before sautéing;** this draws juices to the surface, where they can caramelize and brown. If possible, let the meat sit for 5 minutes after salting to absorb the flavor.

✦ **Use more oil** than you may think is necessary. Though you can sauté something in just a film of oil, you'll get a better, more even crust if you use enough oil that the entire bottom surface of the food being fried comes into contact with it.

✦ **Though temperature** is not as critical for sautéing as for deep-frying, make sure the oil is hot enough that when you add the food, you get a good sizzle.

✦ **Let the food remain in contact** with the oil long enough to brown. Resist the temptation to move the food around too much. A good shake at the start will keep it from sticking; after that, don't touch the food until you're ready to turn it.

+ **If food sticks,** it is probably because either there is not enough oil or the oil is not hot enough.

+ **A good indicator that it is time** to turn meat that is being sautéed is when you see beads of what looks like blood appear on the top. These are meat juices that have been driven from the center by the heat from below.

+ **You can make a simple sauce** by adding a little liquid to the pan after you've removed the cooked food. Pour off all the oil, then return the pan to the heat to brown the bits of food that have stuck to the bottom of the pan. When they're brown, add the liquid of choice (water, stock or wine) and scrape the bottom of the pan with a spoon or spatula to release the flavorful browned bits. When most of the liquid has evaporated, leaving behind just a glaze, stir in a couple of tablespoons of butter or cream to add richness, if desired.

---

goat cheese tart
with caramelized onions and green olives

Cook the onions long and slowly to caramelize them so they turn sweet without scorching. Covering them during the first part of the cooking helps to wilt them more quickly, but you'll want to remove the lid for most of the process to allow the moisture to evaporate so they can brown. Bell peppers can be roasted under a broiler or over a gas burner: cook them, turning frequently, until the skin is evenly blackened, then set them aside in a zipper-lock plastic bag for 10 minutes to steam and cool. The papery outer skin will peel right off.

CRUST

- ¾ cup bread flour
- ¾ cup all-purpose flour
- ½ teaspoon salt
- 6 tablespoons (¾ stick) unsalted butter, chilled and cubed
- 2 tablespoons olive oil
- 3 tablespoons ice water

CARAMELIZED ONIONS

- 8 yellow onions, thinly sliced
- ¼ cup olive oil
- 1 small sprig fresh rosemary

- Salt and freshly ground black pepper
- 1 (5½-ounce) log fresh goat cheese
- ¼ cup chopped pitted green olives
- 1 red bell pepper, roasted (see above), peeled, cored, seeded and sliced into strips

Make the crust: Put the bread flour, all-purpose flour and salt in a food processor and pulse to combine. Add the butter and oil and process until the flour resembles coarse cornmeal. Add the water and process just until the dough forms a ball. Remove from the food processor and press into a disk. Wrap tightly and refrigerate at least 1 hour to allow the dough to relax.

Meanwhile, prepare the onions: Combine the onions, oil and rosemary in a large skillet. Cover and cook over medium-low heat until the onions release their water, about 15 minutes. Stir, reduce the heat to low and cook, stirring frequently, until the onions begin to brown, about 1 hour. Remove the lid and continue cooking over low heat, stirring frequently, until the onions are deep brown, 30 to 45 minutes. Do not let the onions scorch.

Set a strainer over a bowl. Remove the rosemary and turn the onions into the strainer. Let stand until the onions are thoroughly drained.

Assemble the tart: Preheat the oven to 400 degrees.

Remove the dough from the refrigerator. On a floured surface, roll it out to a 1/4-inch-thick round. Fit it into a 9-inch tart pan with a removable bottom. Fold the excess dough over itself to make a sturdy rim.

Spoon the onions across the bottom of the crust. Season lightly with salt and pepper. Dot the goat cheese over the onions. Scatter the olives over the goat cheese and arrange the pepper strips over all.

Bake until the edges of the crust are browned and the cheese is melted, about 45 minutes. Cool briefly to allow the cheese to set, then cut into wedges and serve.

6 servings

brussels sprouts and bacon

The brussels sprouts are first steamed, to keep them from developing that nasty mustardy smell, and then sautéed. Their pan sauce is almost like a hot vinaigrette, with the oil coming from the bacon fat. It's important to cook the bacon slowly over medium-low heat so that it renders as much fat as possible without burning.

- - - - - - - - - - - - - - - - - - - -

2 pounds brussels sprouts

3 strips bacon

½ cup red wine vinegar, plus
     1–2 tablespoons more, if desired

   Salt

¼ cup pine nuts, toasted

Trim the brussels sprouts, removing any outer leaves that are very dark or are damaged. Trim the dried-out base of each sprout and cut a ¼-to-½-inch-deep X in each.

Steam the sprouts over rapidly boiling water just until tender, about 5 minutes (no longer than 7 minutes). Let cool, then cut them into quarters. Set aside.

Meanwhile, cut the bacon into thin strips. Cook in a skillet over medium-low heat until crisp. Raise the heat to high, add the ½ cup vinegar and cook until the vinegar loses its raw smell, about 3 minutes.

Reduce the heat and add the brussels sprouts. Cook until the sprouts are heated through. Season to taste with salt and add the additional vinegar, if desired. Stir in the pine nuts and serve.

6 servings

sautéed green beans
with garlic and sage

Finishing the beans in the hot oil allows the flavorings to penetrate more than they would if you added cold oil, as for a salad. This is a simple recipe, but there are a lot of variations. You could use mint or basil to taste instead of the sage. You could substitute any kind of vinegar for the lemon juice. But the main variable is the garlic. Not only can you change the flavor by adding more or less than is called for, you can also change it by varying *when* you add the garlic. The recipe as written will give you a moderately strong, bright garlic flavor. If you cook the garlic in the olive oil first, it will be more developed but somewhat muted.

----

1   pound green beans,
      stem ends trimmed

2   tablespoons olive oil

1   garlic clove, minced
      Salt

3   fresh sage leaves, chopped
      Juice of ½ lemon

Cook the beans in plenty of rapidly boiling salted water until they are a vibrant green and have softened to the point that there is just a thread of crispness left at the center, about 5 minutes. Drain and immediately plunge the beans into a large bowl of ice water to stop the cooking. As soon as they are cool, remove them from the ice water and drain on a kitchen towel. Pat dry.

In a large skillet, heat the oil over medium heat. Add the beans, give them a toss and then add the garlic. Cook until the garlic is fragrant and the beans are cooked through, about 5 minutes. Season to taste with salt. Add the sage and lemon juice, toss to combine well and serve as a side dish.

4 servings

crisp-skinned salmon
on creamy leeks and cabbage

If you don't cook salmon properly, the skin winds up moist and slimy—something you peel off and push to the side of the plate. But the skin can be one of the starring features. The secret is to cook it so it crisps and renders the fat just underneath it. That way, the skin becomes crisp and flavorful—the perfect counterpoint to the rich flesh. Cutting shallow slashes in the skin allows it to render the fat. To make the skin even crispier, here's a trick I learned from French Laundry chef Thomas Keller: rub the back of a knife over the skin, not cutting it, but using it like a squeegee. This compresses the skin and drives moisture to the surface, where it can be wiped off with a paper towel.

Since I learned this technique for cooking salmon from Patricia Wells and Joel Robuchon's *Simply French,* I have served crisp-skinned salmon in many ways, often on a bed of stewed white beans. It truly is one of those kitchen basics you can use again and again in many different forms. Here, cooking the cabbage in stages keeps some of it fairly crunchy, while the rest melts into a near puree.

- 2 large leeks
- 1 (3-pound) cabbage
- 1 slice bacon
- ½ teaspoon cumin seeds
- 4 tablespoons (½ stick) butter
- 3–3½ pounds salmon fillet, preferably center-cut, in 1 or 2 pieces
- Salt and freshly ground black pepper
- ¼ cup heavy (whipping) cream
- 2 tablespoons vegetable oil

Trim the tough green tops from the leeks, leaving only the white and pale green parts. Leaving the leeks attached at the root end, slice lengthwise into quarters. Rinse well under cold running water until all the sand and any mud are gone. Thinly slice crosswise.

Quarter the cabbage, remove the tough white core and thinly slice. Slice the bacon into thin crosswise strips.

Toast the cumin seeds in a dry pan over medium heat, shaking frequently, until fragrant, about 5 minutes.

Combine the bacon and 2 tablespoons of the butter in a large skillet and cook over medium-high heat until the bacon has rendered its fat and is crisp, about 5 minutes. Reduce the heat to medium, add the leeks and the toasted cumin and cook until the leeks soften, about 5 minutes. Add half of the cabbage and cook, stirring, until soft, about 10 minutes. Add half of the remaining cabbage and cook until that is soft, 10 more minutes.

While the cabbage is cooking, prepare the salmon: Using the back of a knife, "squeegee" the skin of the salmon until you see moisture come out and collect on the knife. Wipe the knife and the salmon dry with paper towels. Repeat until moisture no longer appears. Cut the salmon into 8 equal pieces. Season with salt and pepper to taste on both sides and set aside.

Add the remaining cabbage to the skillet, along with the cream. Cook, stirring occasionally, until liquid is no longer visible when the pan is tilted. Season to taste with salt. Add the remaining 2 tablespoons butter to the cabbage and cook just until the sauce thickens, less than 1 minute, and keep warm.

Meanwhile, heat the oil in a wide nonstick skillet over high heat. Add the salmon fillets skin side down and cook until the skin is very crisp and the flesh has lightened about one-third of the way up the side, 2 to 3 minutes. Turn the fillets over and remove the skillet from the stove to finish cooking off the heat while you assemble the plates.

Divide the leek-and-cabbage mixture evenly among 8 plates or shallow bowls. Place a salmon fillet skin side up on top of each. Serve immediately.

8 servings

country fried chicken

This is the ultimate panfry. The intense heat of the oil browns one side of the chicken pieces while the other more or less steams. The result is chicken that has a crisp crust but is moist inside. A heavy cast-iron skillet is best, as it retains heat, which prevents the oil from cooling down very much when the chicken is added. You can substitute buttermilk for the milk.

1   (3-to-4-pound) chicken, cut into 8 serving pieces
    (2 legs, 2 thighs, 2 wings and 2 breasts)

Salt

2   cups milk

1½ cups all-purpose flour

1½ teaspoons freshly ground black pepper

½   teaspoon cayenne

Peanut oil, lard or vegetable shortening
    for shallow-frying

Season the chicken lightly with salt and place in a zipper-lock plastic bag. Pour the milk into the bag, seal and refrigerate for at least 1 hour.

Preheat the oven to 225 degrees.

Combine the flour, 1 teaspoon salt, the pepper and cayenne in a large brown paper bag.

Add enough oil, lard or shortening to come halfway up the sides of a large heavy skillet and heat over high heat until it is about 350 degrees (a piece of chicken dipped in the fat will sputter noisily).

Remove the chicken legs and thighs from the milk and gently shake off most of the excess liquid. Add to the flour mixture and shake well to coat thoroughly. Remove from the flour and place skin side down in the hot oil, being careful not to burn yourself with splatters. Fry until the chicken is browned on the first side, about 15 minutes. Keep a close eye on the heat; once you've added the chicken to the pan, you'll probably want to wait 3 to 5 minutes for the oil to heat, then reduce the heat to medium-high. Turn the chicken and cook until browned on the second side and nearly cooked through. When the dark meat is done, transfer it to a rack set on a cookie sheet lined with paper towels and keep it warm in the oven while you cook the white meat.

Remove the chicken breasts and wings from the milk, shake gently, add to the flour mixture and shake to coat well. Add the chicken skin side down to the hot oil and cook until well browned on the first side, about 10 minutes. Turn and continue cooking on the other side until browned and cooked through. When all the chicken is done, serve immediately.

2 to 4 servings

pan-fried chicken breasts
with fresh tomatoes, green olives and rosemary

This dish differs from fried chicken in that the bird finishes cooking with some liquid (in this case, from the tomatoes). It's a trade-off. The skin won't be crisp, but you'll wind up with a deeply flavored sauce that marries the tastes of the chicken and the other ingredients. Serve with steamed rice or buttered noodles.

Salt

4 chicken breasts

⅓ cup all-purpose flour

½ cup olive oil

1½ pounds plum tomatoes (about 6 tomatoes)

½ cup whole green olives

½ pound mushrooms, cleaned and quartered

2 garlic cloves, minced

1 tablespoon red wine vinegar

1 teaspoon minced fresh rosemary

Freshly ground black pepper

Salt the chicken breasts lightly. Place the flour in a large bowl and dredge the chicken breasts in the flour, tapping them against the side of the bowl to knock off any excess. Put on a plate.

Heat the oil in a large skillet over high heat until the chicken sizzles when you touch a piece to the oil. Add the chicken skin side down, reduce the heat to medium and cook, without disturbing, until well browned on the first side, about 10 minutes.

While the chicken is cooking, cut off the stem end of the tomatoes, then cut them crosswise in half. Squeeze out the seeds. Chop the tomatoes into large dice and set aside.

Turn the chicken over and cook until you see juices begin to break through the top crust, about 5 more minutes.

Meanwhile, place the olives on a cutting board and press down firmly with a large chef's knife to crush them. Once they're crushed, pick out the pits and discard.

When the chicken is done, transfer it to a plate and cover loosely with aluminum foil to keep warm. Pour off all but 1 to 2 tablespoons of the fat from the pan, turn the heat to high and add the mushrooms. Cook, stirring, until they begin to brown, 2 to 3 minutes. Add the tomatoes and garlic and cook, stirring, until the tomatoes begin to fall apart. Add the olives, vinegar and rosemary and cook for another 2 to 3 minutes. Season with salt and pepper to taste.

Return the chicken to the pan skin side down, cover and cook until hot and cooked through, about 5 minutes. Serve hot.

4 servings

pork schnitzel with arugula salad

This panfry is a great simple supper—hot crisp crust, tender meat and cool greens. The salad is served on top of the pork so that it warms slightly, releasing its perfume, but doesn't wilt. You can make this recipe with many cuts of meat, including veal cutlets or slices from pork tenderloin or butt or turkey breast. The important thing is to slice the meat against the grain so that it won't shred into pieces when you pound it thin.

- - - - - -

4   pork cutlets or thin-cut loin chops
        (about 1½ pounds)

    Salt

½   cup all-purpose flour

2   cups fresh bread crumbs

1   ounce Parmigiano-Reggiano cheese, grated
        (about 2 tablespoons)

1   large egg

2   tablespoons water

1   bunch arugula

2   tablespoons olive oil

2   tablespoons fresh lemon juice

⅓   cup peanut oil

Rinse the pork but do not pat it dry. Place 1 piece in a heavy-duty zipper-lock plastic bag and pound with a rolling pin until it is about ½ inch thick. (If you're using loin chops, be careful not to pound the bone; it splinters easily.) Remove the pork from the bag and season with salt on both sides. Dredge well in the flour, shake off excess and set aside. Repeat with the remaining pork.

Combine the bread crumbs and cheese in a large mixing bowl and set aside. In a shallow bowl, beat the egg with the water until smooth. Set aside.

Place the arugula in a salad bowl and dress it with the olive oil and lemon juice. Season with salt and set aside.

Heat the peanut oil in a large skillet over high heat. Dip 1 piece of pork into the egg bath and then into the bread crumbs. Pat the crumbs to coat the pork well, then gently shake off any excess. Dip 1 corner of the pork cutlet into the oil. If the oil is hot enough, the pork will sizzle loudly. Add the pork to the pan and repeat with the remaining pork. Fry the cutlets until they are well browned on the bottom, 2 to 3 minutes. Turn them over, salt the cooked side and fry for another 1 to 2 minutes. Transfer to paper towels to drain, then turn and salt the unsalted side.

Place each cutlet on a plate, with the best-browned side up, then place a handful of greens on top. Serve immediately.

4 servings

the second life of plants

Most of the ingredients we buy to cook with are long dead. Thankfully. The meat and dairy products in your refrigerator, the bins of sugar, flour, rice and grains in your pantry, all of the various spices and condiments in the cupboard — none of them is going anywhere, metaphorically speaking. Except for that rare block of wild mold–ripened artisanal cheese, any physical changes these foods go through while waiting for us to prepare them are restricted to bacterial spoilage. The exceptions to the rule are fruits and vegetables. Though we may think of them as cheerfully inanimate, their lives don't stop at harvest. Fruits and vegetables continue to change — and even to breathe — long after we've popped them into our shopping bags and taken them home. In the case of many fruits, they even continue to improve. In fact, you could make the argument that the most important physical process in the preparing of fruits and vegetables has nothing to do with the kitchen, but rather with this second life. Anything else is merely hurrying the process along or accentuating it.

Both fruits and vegetables come from plants, of course. But what makes one part of a plant a fruit and another a vegetable? Technically, fruits are the seeds and ovaries of plants. Vegetables are any edible parts of plants that are not fruits. In other words, vegetables are leaves, stems, roots (though some parts that grow underground are actually classified as tubers or bulbs) and even, in the case of artichokes, flower buds. Vegetables are not necessarily all of one thing or another. Though spinach is clearly mainly a leaf, chard is emphatically both a leaf and a stem. And sometimes things are not what they seem. Radishes, carrots and turnips are roots, but a potato is not, even though it grows underground. A potato is a swollen subterranean stem (its roots are in its eyes!). In the kitchen, though, the difference between fruits and vegetables is not as clear-cut as in science. We tend to call plant parts that are not distinguished by a noticeable sweetness vegetables, botany be damned. Therefore, while such things as tomatoes, cucumbers, green beans and peppers are all technically fruits, culinarily they are treated as vegetables.

This is no big deal, because in the broadest terms, fruits and vegetables are the same. They are collections of cellulose-walled cells that are cemented together by sticky substances known as pectins. The cellulose walls themselves are not digestible; we eat them for what they contain, which, as with most everything else we eat, is primarily water. While fruits have one biological function — reproduction — very generally speaking, the parts of plants we call vegetables work in one of three ways. They convert light to energy through photosynthesis. They store the energy thus created. Or they transport fluids and nutrients from one part of the plant to the other.

As all cooks know, some of these vegetable parts come wrapped in a troublesome peel — a tough layer of cells around the outside of the plant that exists primarily to keep the moisture and nutrients inside. The older the plant gets, the tougher this exterior becomes. One of the joys of the first vegetables of the season is their particular tenderness. Give them another month and they'll become toughened too. Particularly in very mature vegetables, the transport structures are tough as well, the most obvious example being the core of a carrot. And as the cellulose walls throughout the rest of the plant continue to thicken as the vegetable grows, they become tougher too, eventually turning into a woody substance called lignin (it's little crystals of lignin that give pears their distinctive grainy texture).

Even after being picked, plants continue to "respire," taking in and—more frequently—giving off oxygen and moisture. The pectic substances that cement the plants' cells together begin to weaken, dissolved by enzymes within the plants themselves. For a particularly dramatic example of what eventually happens to all plants' parts, consider leafy vegetables, which contain less cellulose than other plants and don't have peels to hold in moisture. The main thing that keeps them erect is the tension created by the water they contain. When they lose that moisture, they collapse. And because of the lack of a peel, they lose moisture quite rapidly. We call that wilting, and though it is most readily observable in lettuces and herbs, you can even see it in something as tough as a carrot if you leave it in the refrigerator for too long.

Knowing how these structures break down is invaluable when it comes to picking out the best vegetables. Remember: moisture is the key. You want vegetables that are heavy for their size (meaning they contain a lot of water), and you want them to be smooth and firm (meaning the cellulose breakdown has not progressed very far). When you get the vegetables home, store them in a way that will preserve their moisture. Cold is one key—it slows down respiration. (It also has other effects that make it undesirable for some things, most notably tomatoes and other fruits, but more about that later.) Most refrigerators are built with special vegetable drawers. These contain no magic properties for preservation; they are simply small and relatively tightly sealed, which prevents moisture from evaporating too quickly.

Within fruits and vegetables, dissolved in all of that water inside those tough cells, is a fascinating assortment of compounds.

Among the most interesting — both for the cook and the scientist — are the ones that give vegetables their color. By far the most common is chlorophyll, the stuff that makes plants green. In a curious extension of our life metaphor, the chemical structure of chlorophyll is similar to that of hemoglobin, a component of human blood. Actually, there are two kinds of chlorophyll that differ mainly in terms of one chemical group. Chlorophyll-a is the most common type, and the presence of one chemical group gives it a vibrant blue-green color. Think of kale. Chlorophyll-b, which contains a small amount of another chemical group, is a pale yellowish green. Think of cabbage. Sometimes both chlorophylls exist in the same vegetable. Broccoli florets are high in chlorophyll-a, while the paler stalks contain predominantly chlorophyll-b. Both chlorophylls are water-soluble, meaning that when you boil green vegetables, the water may turn green.

All vegetables are not green, of course, not even, for example, all cabbages. You can thank anthocyanin for that. It gives fruits and vegetables (including red cabbage) colors in the red-purple-blue range. You could think of anthocyanin as the chlorophyll coloring of fruits. There's not just one; there are several types of anthocyanin. They range from the blackish blue of the Concord grape (from the beautifully named delphinidin) through the purple ranging to deep red of blueberries and cherries (cyanidin) and on to the paler red of strawberries and raspberries (pelargonidin). And there's anthoxanthin too, which ranges from very pale, almost colorless, to yellow. Think of a parsnip or of the white spongy part of a citrus peel. Carotenoids are an especially prevalent group of pigments in the yellow-orange-red range. Considering the name, it's not surprising to learn that one carotenoid is the color of carrots. It is also the distinctive orange of oranges. Finally, there's betalain, which is relatively uncommon. It is the dark red color of beets. Unlike most of the other bright vegetable pigments, it is water-soluble and will spread and stain easily. Some of these pigments come with readily identifiable flavors; others do not. Chlorophyll-a, for example, we know as the grassy green taste of parsley. Pelargonidin has the bright red berry taste that is found not only in raspberries and strawberries but also in blood oranges (it's the pigment that makes them "bloody").

Fruits and vegetables are not all of one or the other pigment. In fact, they frequently start out predominantly one color and then change to another. This is especially true for vegetables colored by chlorophyll, which is very high in young plants but decreases as plants age. As plants mature, the chlorophyll green fades to reveal the underlying colors. This is why so many things change from green to red and other colors as they ripen (it is also the reason tree leaves turn colors in the fall). However, it's easy to be confused by a pretty blush — especially with fruit. Some fruit — peaches and nectarines primarily — is bred to show an early red color. This should not be mistaken for a sign of ripeness. Instead, look at the background color, the color of the fruit as a whole. It should not show any green. Colors also change after picking, as these pigments oxidize and lose their potency. Dull-colored vegetables are bound to be older and less flavorful.

In an odd way, all we're doing when we cook fruits and vegetables is exactly what would happen were we merely to leave them in the refrigerator too long. The result is delicious only because all the flavoring compounds haven't dulled as well. Fruits and vegetables soften during cooking because the pectins and the cellulose dissolve, at least partially (the more liquid present, the more they'll dissolve). At the same time, the heat causes the liquid inside the cells to expand, bursting the walls. Any starches that are present begin to soften, just as with flour in a sauce. Colors change too. At first, particularly with vegetables, they may become brighter and more intense as the heat drives off any oxygen in the cells, making the color appear more vibrant. Since leafy vegetables like spinach and chard have many more air pockets than other vegetables have, you'll notice they shrink dramatically when they are heated (or refrigerated for too long).

Eventually—perhaps after only seven or eight minutes of cooking—the bright colors begin to fade as the pigments break down because of the heat. To get really bright colors, cooks frequently blanch vegetables in boiling water. Usually a cold plunge in an ice-water bath follows. Chefs say this "sets" the color; what it really does is stop the cooking before the colors can fade. This is primarily done for green vegetables, because chlorophyll is the most sensitive of the pigments—it dulls with heat and leaches into cooking water. Blanching is also used for vegetables that tend to the sulfurous, such as broccoli, cauliflower and cabbage. Blanching removes enough of the chemical "precursors" so that those vegetables can then be cooked for a longer period of time without stinking up the house.

Perhaps more than any other food, though, vegetables are very sensitive to their cooking environment. Cook meat with an acid, like wine, lemon juice or vinegar, and there will be some small changes. But cook a vegetable with an acid and it may even change color. Chlorophyll, for example, will turn from a vibrant leafy green to a dull olive drab. The effect of acid on the red pigment, anthocyanin, on the other hand, is the opposite. Acid preserves the crimson in vegetables colored with it, such as red cabbage. Cook them with something as mildly alkaline as some tap waters (in reality, there aren't many other bases that are used in cooking), and those beautiful reds turn blue. Other changes aren't quite so noticeable. Vegetables that are a pale cream color (colored with anthoxanthin), such as cauliflower, will turn a very pale yellow if cooked with an acid. Vegetables that are yellow to orange (colored with carotenoids), such as carrots, are largely unaffected by the relative acidity or alkalinity of their surroundings (one exception is the rutabaga, which turns from a pale cream color to a golden orange when cooked—but that's another set of tints entirely).

Exposure to air will change the colors of vegetables too, once they've been cut. This is because cell walls that have been destroyed release enzymes that combine with oxygen to cause browning. The result is particularly noticeable in potatoes, artichokes and mushrooms, but the effect occurs in other foods as well. Part of the curing process for tea leaves involves this enzymatic browning. To avoid such browning, chop mushrooms just before using them. Potatoes can be covered in water to prevent contact with oxygen, and artichokes can be put in acidulated water.

Changes in color are not necessarily related to changes in flavor or texture, but they can be. Adding an alkaline, such as baking soda, as some cooks used to do to preserve color in peas or beans, has a dramatic effect on texture even when added in tiny amounts. It dissolves those cellulose structures so quickly, the vegetables become slimy and turn to mush in a matter of minutes. Acids, on the other hand, will delay that softening. So add that squeeze of lemon juice or shot of wine or vinegar only at the end of cooking, both to preserve color and to ensure that the vegetables soften as much as you want. And beware — as vegetables cook, they give off their own acids. Particularly with chlorophyll-colored vegetables, merely cooking them under a lid for too long will turn them drab as the released acids vaporize, condense on the underside of the lid and rain back down on the vegetables. (This isn't a problem as long as the vegetables are cooked without a cover or quickly.)

Flavors change in many ways during cooking. Even the presence of an entirely neutral liquid such as distilled water makes a difference, especially in texture. Water is vital to the dissolving of the pectins and cellulose and softens the cell walls. When sautéing vegetables, add a couple of tablespoons of water, and you'll find that the vegetables cook much more thoroughly. The water will then evaporate, leaving behind a nice syrup of vegetable juices. Cell walls burst as heated water expands, mingling their contents. And those contents change as they are heated. If they get hot enough, browning begins — mostly true caramelization of sugar, since vegetables lack the concentration of proteins that makes the Maillard reaction possible in meat (see page 229). But probably the most interesting to scientists and cooks alike are the changes in the sulfur chemicals. Ever wonder why cabbage gives off that awful reek when it's been cooked for too long? The culprit is the same thing that makes you cry when you chop an onion — sulfur. In the latter case, it's released by the mechanical action of chopping. In the former example, it's the cooking that does it. A sugar in the cabbage reacts with the hot water to form another sulfurous compound.

We cook vegetables in many different ways, but we can divide them by two important factors: whether the heat is moist or dry and whether there is an exchange of flavor involved. Moist cooking methods, such as boiling or steaming, will prevent any of the browning process from happening. It's that old boiling-point thing again — as long as there is moisture present, the temperature won't get hot enough to begin to cook the sugars in the food. Beyond that, there is a difference between boiling and steaming. That is because of the exchange — or lack of exchange — of flavors. When you boil a vegetable, some of the flavoring compounds leak into the surrounding water as the cell walls collapse. At the same time, the vegetable absorbs flavors from the liquid it is cooked in. In steaming, there is no contact with the liquid, so very little flavor is lost or gained. Steamed vegetables taste much more of themselves (whether this is a good thing or a bad thing depends on the vegetable and how you want to use it). But not all vegetable cookery involves added moisture. It is popular these days to roast or grill vegetables — cooking them with dry heat. Because there is no additional moisture, once the vegetable's internal moisture has evaporated, it can be heated past 212 degrees. That allows the caramelization of its sugars, adding a depth of flavor that you can't achieve with moist heat. With any dry-heat cooking, there will be very little exchange of flavors (smoke is really the only thing that can be added). That's why roasted or grilled vegetables are often bathed either before or after with a flavored oil or a seasoning mix.

Though fruits and vegetables may be similar at the most basic structural level, they're very different in other ways. While many fruits are used as vegetables, only a few vegetables are used as fruits (rhubarb, a stem, is one of them). The biggest difference between fruits and vegetables is that with vegetables, ripeness is usually considered automatic (one reason that it's important to remember that tomatoes are actually fruits). With fruits, ripeness is highly variable and critical. It is also vague. What does *ripeness* really mean?

Ripeness is not a fixed point, but a process. It begins with pollinated flowers forming fruit and ends with rot. As anyone who has eaten a dripping peach will tell you, when caught at the right point, that's not nearly so disagreeable as it sounds. Here's the process — call it "A Fruit's Progress." Within several days of being pollinated, a fruit has created all the cells it ever will. It will get larger, certainly, but that's because the cells expand, not because the plant is making more of them. The cells expand because they are filling up with water. Dissolved in that water is a rich variety of compounds, but of primary interest to us are the starches, acids and sugars. Technically, at that point a fruit has only matured. It doesn't begin to ripen until it reaches its maximum size. Ripeness is signaled by a series of changes. Frequently the skin turns color as the green chlorophyll fades, revealing the underlying pigments. The fruit softens too, as enzymes from within the fruit begin to dissolve the cell walls and even the pectin that holds them together.

Pectin is the reason immature fruit is so hard. It is also the reason why fruit cooked into jams and jellies can thicken without the addition of a starch. As fruit matures, the pectins turn into pectic acid, which has much less ability to form a gel. Consequently, very ripe fruit does not make good jam.

As the cell walls of the fruit dissolve, moisture is released, making the fruit juicy. At the same time, its chemical compounds intermingle, combining and forming new ones. Of special interest are the compounds that convert the complex carbohydrate starch to the simple carbohydrate sugar. Simple sugars like glucose are converted to complex sugars like fructose and sucrose. Fragrances and flavors develop. Left to itself, the fruit will eventually ripen to the point that it falls to the ground, where it then will either be eaten by animals or finish rotting. Either way, the seeds will be scattered to germinate, sprout and grow into a new plant.

But ripeness is not a single standard: in different types of fruit, it means different things. As the eminent food writer Jeffrey Steingarten has pointed out, there are five classes of fruit, each ripening in a different way. Some fruits do not ripen after being picked (berries, cherries, grapes, citrus fruits, watermelon and olives—yes, they're a fruit). One fruit, the avocado, ripens only after it's picked. Some fruits change color and texture and develop more complex flavor after being picked but won't develop any more sweetness (apricots, melons, figs, peaches, nectarines, plums and persimmons). Some fruits get sweeter but don't change color or texture (apples, kiwis, mangoes, papayas and pears). And then there's the banana, which will ripen on the tree or off (though there is little to compare with the flavor and aroma of a banana that's been allowed to hang to full ripeness).

Neither is ripeness an unmixed blessing—especially to the people who sell fruit for a living. Obviously, as the fruit softens with ripeness, it can become damaged more easily. This is true not only for accidents that occur during shipping but also for hazards in the field—anything from a poorly timed rain to a hailstorm, even a gust of wind that rubs branches against the fruit.

That is why farmers view the picking of fruit as a race against time. The sooner they can get it out of harm's way, the better. And because of the ability of many fruits to continue improving in quality after they are off the tree, farmers can pick them even when they appear to be dead green. This is especially true of stone fruits (apricots, peaches, plums and nectarines). Unfortunately, however, though that fruit might have already converted its starch to an acceptable level of sugar, it probably won't be as sweet as it would be if it were left to hang longer. And, almost as important, it won't have had time to develop many of those volatile chemicals that help define flavor.

There is also research that argues that ripeness is not the sole determiner of fruit quality. Though stone fruit left on the tree longer is inarguably superior in flavor up to a point, recent studies indicate that how the fruit is treated in its last days on the tree can be just as important. Fruit that is deprived of water in the last week or two before harvest has superior flavor to fruit that is irrigated right up to harvest. Put simply, adding water during the days leading to picking seems to dilute the fruit's flavor.

In addition to the more obvious rules for picking fruits — choose those that are heavy for their size; look for firm, smooth flesh — let's add one more: the closer to you the fruit is grown, the better it is liable to be. The implication for cooks is to buy fruit that is local. Peaches not grown with the expectation of having to be shipped 2,000 miles to market are more likely to be picked later and to be varieties in which flavor is more important than the ability to withstand truck transportation. The equally obvious corollary to this rule is that in much of the country, people will be able to eat these peaches for only one month a year, while in other parts they'll never see them at all.

One way growers get around the problems with ripeness is by tricking the fruit, particularly bananas, tomatoes and oranges. At a certain point in the maturation of the fruit, for reasons as yet not understood, it begins to produce ethylene gas, which acts as a trigger, telling the fruit it is time to ripen. Since ethylene gas is easily handled, growers and grocers ship fruit that has been picked hard and gas it with ethylene in special rooms. This softens the fruit and even encourages some color changes, but it does not add sugar or any of the other chemicals that create complexity of flavor.

There is another way to promote flavor, at least with some fruits. The first step is taking care of them once you get them home. Cold deadens the flavor in fruits such as strawberries and stone fruits, so you should be wary of sticking them in the refrigerator. Leave them at room temperature for as long as you can without courting spoilage (this will vary depending on the state of the fruit when you buy it and the temperature of your room). This presumes daily fruit shopping, which is not always practical, to put it mildly. Another solution is to go with what the supermarkets sell you, and then try to trick the fruit yourself. Stone fruit, for example, will soften and develop more complex flavors even if it is picked at a less-than-ideal state: stick a couple of hard but ripe peaches in a paper bag and leave them at room temperature; in a day or two they will be ready to eat.

As with vegetables, fruit gets softer and juicier when it is cooked. Because of the heat, its aromas and flavors become more pronounced. Because of the exchange of liquids, fruit that is poached or cooked with other fruits develops more complexity. And, as with vegetables, there are potential problems too. For one, color pigments change. While only a few vegetables are bright red, the troublesome anthocyanin pigment is common with fruits. Strawberries and cherries are two favorite fruits that contain it, and they will turn a bruised blue if they're not cooked carefully. Adding acidity is the key again: orange or lemon juice is good. In the case of strawberries, they can be cooked with rhubarb, which is highly acidic. Some fruits are also prone to enzymatic browning, just like some vegetables — apples and pears will turn dingy tan after being sliced. They can be kept bright white by covering them with slightly acidic water.

Sugar has a marked effect on fruit as well; it can actually "cook" it without heat. Because sugar draws water from whatever it touches, it will suck the moisture out of delicate fruit, collapsing the cell walls and drawing out all its juices. For that reason, it's best to delay sweetening fruit until just before you're ready to cook it. One exception is when making jam — then the fruit and sugar frequently are combined a day in advance to allow the fruit to give up its moisture, which mixes with the sugar to make a syrup that is reabsorbed by the fruit. Another exception is when making fruit-flavored ice creams. If the fruit isn't sugared well beforehand to draw off water, the ice cream will be littered with little fruit-flavored ice cubes.

Because many fruits are still in the process of ripening even after harvest, storage is trickier than it is for vegetables. Any fruit — including the tomato — that is still ripening should be stored at room temperature until it has softened and sweetened as much as it can. Moreover, chilling inevitably damages the enzymes that help create the flavors in fruits like tomatoes, peaches, plums, nectarines and apricots. It is far better to use such fruits as soon as they are ripe and avoid refrigerating them altogether. Other fruits, such as melons, apples, pears and mangoes, are safe to refrigerate after they're fully ripe and sweet. Again, with these fruits, the same rules apply as for vegetables: they should be kept in a space that is as humid as possible; the vegetable crisper is ideal. But while humidity is good — preserving the moisture within the fruit — moisture on the surface of the fruit is bad. Because the skins of so many fruits are delicate, moisture invites mold, which causes rapid spoilage. Don't wash fruit until you're ready to use it.

These changes are not limited to fruits, of course — botanical or not. Vegetables can be tricky too, especially potatoes. Chill a potato, for example, and it begins to create enzymes that convert starch to sugar. If you've ever had a sweet baked potato (as opposed to a baked sweet potato), it was probably stored too long in the refrigerator before it was cooked. And if your potatoes turn green when left out on the countertop, that's a natural reaction too. Potatoes grow in the dark, remember. When stressed (by being exposed to too much light), they begin to produce both chlorophyll and a toxic substance that is designed to protect them from predators. Even after being dug, a potato lives on, still trying to avoid being eaten.

- **Buying the best ingredients** is the real key to vegetable cookery. Pick those that are heaviest for their size and have the firmest texture. Bright colors are another good indicator of freshness.

- **Once you get vegetables home,** they should go straight into the refrigerator. The only exception is the tomato, which is a fruit, not a vegetable. Never refrigerate tomatoes. Their flavors will be irreparably damaged.

- **To peel or not to peel?** Some vegetables definitely need to be peeled — beets, for example. But most of the time the decision to peel is an aesthetic one. The peel is a tough, corky layer and is usually fairly dull in color, particularly once cooked. If none of this bothers you, there is some minor nutritional gain to be made by cooking vegetables with the skins on.

- **Some vegetables,** such as potatoes and artichokes, begin to brown from exposure to the air. After they've been peeled or cut, cover them with water (artichokes in water with vinegar or lemon juice added to it).

- **If not cooking vegetables whole,** make sure to cut them into similar shapes and sizes. Otherwise, a thin slice will turn to mush before a thick slice is even soft.

- **Cook green vegetables** either uncovered or for fewer than 7 minutes. Much longer than that, and the acids freed by cooking will begin to condense on the lid and rain back down on the vegetables, spoiling their color.

- **Don't be afraid** to cook vegetables until they've completely softened. Though "tender-crisp" or "al dente" vegetables are sometimes in fashion, you will get a much more developed, complex flavor by cooking them all the way through.

+ **Vegetables can be braised** just like meat. But rather than browning the vegetable and then adding the liquid, as you would with meat, reverse the process. Put the vegetable, some liquid and some oil in a cold pan. (Harder vegetables like carrots will take more water than leafy ones like spinach.) Cover and place over heat. Let cook, shaking occasionally, until the vegetable has begun to soften. Remove the lid from the pan and raise the heat to high to allow the liquid to evaporate. This gives you both a well-cooked vegetable and a delicious glaze made from the flavored cooking oil.

+ **Hold off adding an acidic ingredient** to any dish of green vegetables until just before you're ready to serve, so they retain their color. Vegetables that have been blanched (cooked in plenty of boiling water until just softened) can be dressed in a vinaigrette immediately, because hot vegetables will absorb it better.

roasted tomatoes with goat cheese

Roasting tomatoes concentrates their flavor wonderfully. This method is so much better than sun-drying, which seems to turn them to leather. Serve this dish as an appetizer (along with, say, a bowl of green olives and another of toasted almonds) or as a light dinner when paired with a salad.

---

10 plum tomatoes (about 1¾ pounds)

4 garlic cloves, minced

2 tablespoons olive oil

1½ teaspoons salt

Freshly ground black pepper

1 small bunch fresh basil

20 slices sourdough bread, toasted

⅔ cup fresh goat cheese (about 3 ounces)

Preheat the oven to 275 degrees.

Slice the tomatoes lengthwise in half, keeping as much of the seeds and pulp intact as possible. In a large mixing bowl, combine the tomatoes, garlic, oil, salt and pepper to taste and toss to mix well.

Arrange the tomatoes cut side up in a single layer in a jelly-roll pan. Reserve enough basil leaves to make 2 tablespoons (about 6 leaves); cover and refrigerate. Distribute the remainder of the basil, including the stems, over the tomatoes.

Bake until the tomatoes begin to brown on top and are soft but still moist, about 1 hour. Remove from the oven and turn the oven to broil. (The recipe can be prepared to this point several days in advance and stored, tightly covered, in the refrigerator.)

Thinly slice the reserved basil leaves. Using a fork, mash 1 tomato half on each slice of toasted bread and top it with a generous teaspoon of goat cheese. Broil just until the cheese begins to melt. Sprinkle with the sliced basil and serve.

20 croutons; 6 to 8 appetizer servings;
4 to 6 light lunch servings

butter-braised spinach

There is a famous spinach recipe from Brillat-Savarin that calls for spinach to be cooked for several days with a pound of butter added every day. It might have tasted good (as long as you liked butter), but can you imagine how brown the spinach would have been by the end of all that cooking? By cooking spinach briefly, you can retain more of the green color and still end up with something that tastes pretty damned luxurious.

3 pounds spinach (about 3 bunches)

4 garlic cloves, minced

4 tablespoons (½ stick) butter,
   cut into pieces

Salt

Rinse the loose spinach in a sink full of cold water, draining the water and repeating the process as often as necessary until the water runs clear. Remove the spinach, shake it dry and remove the leaves from the stems, either by tearing or cutting. (It is not necessary for the leaves to be completely dry.)

Heat a wok or large skillet over medium-high heat. Add the spinach and garlic. The wok will be very full of spinach, but it will cook down in about 5 minutes, as you stir and turn the spinach to prevent burning and sticking. Add 2 tablespoons of the butter, reduce the heat to low and continue cooking, stirring, for about 10 minutes, until the spinach absorbs all the butter. Add the remaining 2 tablespoons butter and continue cooking slowly until all the butter is absorbed. Season with salt. Serve hot.

4 servings

belgian endive braised with cream

Belgian endive is an exception to the rule about not cooking greens for more than about 7 minutes in order to preserve their color. Since endive is grown deprived of sunlight, it never develops chlorophyll and so can't turn brown.

Cutting an X in the bottom of each head allows the heat to penetrate to the center of the densely wrapped leaves, while keeping them together so they don't fall apart. The boiling, sautéing and final braising produce a rich, creamy texture that contrasts pleasantly with the endive's natural bitterness. This is based on a recipe from *The Epicurean*, by Charles Ranhofer, an American cookbook published in the 1880s.

- 8 heads Belgian endive
- 6 tablespoons (¾ stick) butter
- 1 tablespoon all-purpose flour
- 1 teaspoon salt
- ½ teaspoon sugar
- Freshly grated nutmeg
- ½ cup heavy (whipping) cream

Trim any green or wilted outer leaves from the endive. Trim the bottoms and cut an X through the base of each. Cook the endive in plenty of rapidly boiling water until tender, 15 to 20 minutes. Drain, rinse with cold water and pat dry. Press out any remaining moisture, then finely chop.

Melt 2 tablespoons of the butter in a medium skillet. Add the endive and cook over medium-high heat until very tender, about 10 minutes. Sprinkle the flour over the endive and stir to mix well. Season with the salt, sugar and nutmeg to taste, then add the cream and cook over medium-low heat until slightly thickened, about 5 minutes. Add the remaining 4 tablespoons (½ stick) butter, stir to mix well and serve.

8 to 10 servings

radicchio al forno

Just as with onions, roasting drives off much of the bitterness in radicchio, leaving a sweet vegetable with an intriguing edge. For this dish, I prefer to use the long-headed Treviso radicchio (it looks something like a red-blushed Belgian endive) because, when cooked, it seems to be creamier and sweeter than the more familiar red round-headed Chioggia radicchio, though that could certainly be used.

- 2 tablespoons olive oil
- 2 strips lean bacon, chopped
- 2 garlic cloves, sliced
- 2 pounds radicchio, preferably Treviso (see above)
- ¼ pound mozzarella, cubed
- ¼ cup freshly grated pecorino Romano cheese

Preheat the oven to 450 degrees.

Combine the oil, bacon and garlic in a small saucepan and cook over low heat, stirring occasionally, until the garlic softens, about 5 minutes. Do not let the garlic color.

While the garlic cooks, rinse the radicchio well in cold water and pat dry. Cut the radicchio with long heads lengthwise in half, the radicchio with round heads into quarters. Arrange the radicchio in a baking pan. (You can stack the heads in more than one layer; they will cook down.)

Pour the garlic-bacon mixture over the radicchio, turning the radicchio to coat evenly. Bake the radicchio until it is soft, about 40 minutes, turning occasionally to keep it coated with oil. (If the garlic slices begin to blacken, remove them from the pan.) Keep pushing the radicchio together in the center of the pan as it cooks down.

When the radicchio is soft, push it into the center of the pan and distribute the mozzarella over the top. Sprinkle with the grated pecorino cheese and return the pan to the oven. Bake until the mozzarella melts and begins to brown, about 15 minutes. Serve hot.

6 side-dish servings; or 4 light main-dish servings

glazed zucchini

Glazing is a technique that can be used for many different vegetables. First a little bit of water is added to the oil in the pan, which helps to break down the cellulose, softening the vegetable and cooking it through. Then the water evaporates, leaving behind the vegetable's flavors mingled with the oil in a light, tasty glaze. Beware of undercooking: it's important that the vegetable cooks completely to develop the full flavor. Soaking zucchini in water before cooking firms it, because it absorbs some of the water.

2 pounds medium zucchini
   ($1/2$–$3/4$ inch thick and 5–6 inches long)

2 tablespoons olive oil

2 garlic cloves

Salt

About $1/4$ cup water

1 tablespoon thinly sliced fresh basil

Trim the ends of the zucchini. Soak it in a large bowl of cold water for 30 minutes to freshen.

Drain the zucchini and pat dry. Cut it lengthwise in half, then crosswise into quarters.

In a large skillet, combine the zucchini, oil, garlic, 1 teaspoon salt and just enough water to cover the bottom of the pan. Cover and cook over medium heat until the zucchini begins to soften, 5 to 7 minutes. Remove the lid, raise the heat to high and cook, stirring, until the liquid evaporates and the zucchini is glazed with the oil and beginning to brown lightly.

Remove the garlic cloves. Carefully stir in the basil and more salt to taste (the zucchini will be somewhat fragile), and serve.

4 servings

california succotash
of squash, lima beans and corn

This is a dish for September and October, when we're getting the very last of the summer's produce. Adding a little water and covering the pot results in a moist cooking environment that will soften the beans and squash more readily than just sautéing them. Fresh limas will take more water than frozen ones; part of the freezing process involves blanching, so frozen beans are already partially cooked. Though the beans and squash are cooked covered for what seems like a long time, don't worry — neither of them is so high in chlorophyll that the color will dull. If you want to substitute zucchini for the yellow squash, though, you'll have to limit the cooking time. Zucchini is green, so it does have chlorophyll that will turn drab.

3 tablespoons butter

1 bunch green onions,
 white parts only, chopped

1 pound yellow summer squash, sliced

Salt

1 sprig fresh thyme

¾ pound shelled fresh lima beans or
 1 (10-ounce) package frozen
 baby lima beans, thawed

1½ cups water if using fresh beans,
 ½ cup if using frozen

2 ears corn, husked

½ pound cherry tomatoes

¼ cup torn fresh basil leaves

Combine the butter and green onions in a large skillet over medium heat and cook, stirring occasionally, until the onions begin to soften, about 5 minutes. Add the squash, 1 teaspoon salt, the thyme, fresh lima beans, if using, and the water (add frozen beans and water later). Cover the skillet, increase the heat to medium-high and cook, stirring occasionally, until the squash and beans have softened, about 15 minutes.

While the squash is cooking, cut the kernels from the ears of corn. Set the cobs aside.

When the squash has softened, add the frozen beans, if using, and the water along with the tomatoes and the corn kernels. Scrape the cobs with the back of a knife, adding the corn "milk" to the skillet. There should be just enough liquid in the pan to coat the vegetables when stirred. Cook for 5 minutes, until corn is tender.

Season to taste with salt, add the basil and serve.

6 light main-dish servings

creamed onions with shiitake mushrooms

Peeling the onions for this recipe takes a bit of handwork. You can find frozen peeled pearl onions in the grocery store, but they tend to be already overcooked and mushy. The texture is much better if you do the peeling yourself. Covering the onions with boiling water makes it easy to do—the quick heating releases the skins but doesn't overcook the onions. They retain just enough of their bite to counterpoint the richness of the cream and mushrooms.

----

2 pints pearl onions

1½–2 ounces shiitake mushrooms

2 tablespoons butter

1 shallot, minced

1½ cups heavy (whipping) cream

Salt

2 tablespoons minced fresh herbs
(mainly chives, with parsley,
rosemary and/or thyme)

Barely trim both ends of the pearl onions (leave some of the root and stem to keep the onions from falling apart). Cut a deep X in the root end of each, about one-quarter of the length of the onion, to allow the heat to penetrate. Place the onions in a large bowl and cover them with boiling water. Let stand until they have cooled to room temperature.

When the onions are cool enough to handle, squeeze them between your thumb and forefinger to pop them from their skins. Pat thoroughly dry. Set aside.

Remove the stems from the shiitake mushrooms, rinse the caps briefly under running water and pat dry. Chop them fine. Combine the butter and shallot in a medium heavy saucepan and cook over medium heat until the shallot is soft and translucent, about 2 minutes; do not let the shallot scorch or color. Add the mushrooms and cook until they are dry, about 3 minutes. Add the cream, raise the heat to medium-high and cook, stirring, until the cream reduces by half, about 5 minutes.

Add the onions and cook briefly, just enough to heat the onions through and reduce the cream again, if necessary — it may become thinner from the onion juices. (The onions can be prepared up to 1 day ahead, cooked and refrigerated. Reheat gently just before serving.) Season to taste with salt, stir in the herbs and serve.

6 to 8 servings

market mix

Root vegetables such as boiling potatoes, turnips and parsnips take well to roasting. Because they are so dense and take so long to cook, their natural sugars have a chance to caramelize. And because there is no moisture added, their flavors are not diluted. The key to good crusty browning is not to move the vegetables during the first half hour, so they get a chance to sear against the hot pan. Don't use baking potatoes, as they tend to fall apart when stirred.

2 pounds baby red potatoes, halved

1 bulb fennel, trimmed and
   cut into thick wedges

½ pound brown mushrooms, such as cremini
   or portobello, cleaned and quartered
   or cut into smaller wedges if large

6 garlic cloves, peeled

1 red bell pepper, cored, seeded and
   cut into thick wedges

¼ cup olive oil

Salt and freshly ground black pepper

Preheat the oven to 450 degrees.

Combine the potatoes, fennel, mushrooms, garlic and red pepper in a large shallow roasting pan. Pour the oil over and season to taste with salt and pepper. Toss well to coat all the vegetables.

Roast for 30 minutes without stirring.

Shake the vegetables to loosen them from the bottom of the pan and roast for another 20 minutes or so, stirring once or twice during the last 10 minutes. The potatoes should be browned and crusty.
Serve hot.

6 servings

baked tomatoes stuffed with mozzarella

Baking tomatoes briefly brings out all their flavor while allowing them to keep their shape. A few drops of balsamic vinegar provide that full-summer tanginess. Serve these as a side dish or a light main course.

- - - - - - - - - - - - - - - - - - -

6   medium-to-large tomatoes

Balsamic vinegar

Salt and freshly ground black pepper

6   anchovy fillets, preferably salt-packed,
rinsed well and cut in half (about 2 ounces)

6   small fresh mozzarella balls (about 7¾ ounces)

½   cup fresh bread crumbs

2   garlic cloves, minced

2   tablespoons thinly sliced fresh basil leaves

Extra-virgin olive oil for drizzling

Preheat the oven to 350 degrees.

Slice one-quarter off the top of each tomato (reserve for another use, if desired). Using a melon baller, remove most of the seeds and pulp, being careful not to damage the walls of the tomatoes. Sprinkle the inside of each tomato with a few drops of balsamic vinegar, a dash of salt and a grinding of pepper. Do not oversalt, as the anchovies are naturally salty. Cross the 2 halves of an anchovy fillet in the bottom of each tomato. Place a ball of mozzarella in each one. Place the tomatoes on a baking sheet and bake until the mozzarella softens, about 20 minutes (do not let the tomatoes collapse).

While the tomatoes are baking, combine the bread crumbs, garlic and basil in a small bowl.

When the mozzarella has begun to melt, turn the oven to broil. Spoon the bread-crumb mixture over the tops of the tomatoes. Drizzle with oil and broil until the topping is browned. Serve hot.

6 servings

rajas (grilled peppers and cream)

Rajas — strips of grilled peppers with their thin, papery peel removed — can be eaten either as a taco filling or as a vegetable side dish with a fairly bland main course. I like them with sausages. Queso ranchero is a tangy Mexican cheese that is mildly salty and melts easily. Like many other Mexican dairy products, including the slightly sour Mexican cream, it is available in supermarkets in some parts of the country and in Latino grocery stores. If you can't find either or both, you can substitute shredded Monterey Jack for the queso ranchero and sour cream or crème fraîche for the Mexican cream.

- 6 poblano chiles
- 4 yellow onions
- 2 tablespoons vegetable oil
- 4 garlic cloves, minced
- 1–2 tablespoons chopped fresh cilantro
- 2 tablespoons Mexican cream (see above)
- 1 teaspoon salt, or more to taste
- ¼ cup crumbled queso ranchero (see above)

Preheat the broiler or grill.

Roast the chile peppers under the broiler or on the grill (or over a gas burner), turning frequently, until the skins blacken, about 10 minutes. Place in a bowl and cover with a damp towel to steam and cool.

When the peppers are cool, peel off the blackened skin and discard. Remove the stems and seeds and tear the flesh into coarse strips. Set aside.

Cut the onions lengthwise in half, then into half-moons less than ¼ inch thick. Combine in a skillet with the oil and cook, covered, over low heat until the onions have thoroughly wilted and are beginning to brown, 15 to 20 minutes.

Remove the cover and raise the heat to medium. Add the garlic and 1 tablespoon of the cilantro and cook until the garlic is soft, about 3 minutes. Add the peppers and heat through, about 5 more minutes.

Stir in the cream and cook just long enough to thicken, 1 to 2 minutes. Add the salt (do not oversalt; the cheese is somewhat salty). Remove from the heat. (The recipe can be prepared to this point up to 1 day ahead and refrigerated, tightly covered). Add the crumbled cheese and the remaining 1 tablespoon cilantro and serve.

4 side-dish servings;
6 servings as taco filling

ratatouille

Ratatouille is always delicious but sometimes has a muddled flavor. That's because by the time all the vegetables have cooked together, they have lost their individual identities. This ratatouille is a bit of a production, because the vegetables are cooked singly before being reheated together, but the technique concentrates and defines the individual flavors.

1½ pounds eggplant (Asian or Italian)

3 red bell peppers

3 small zucchini (1 pound), ends trimmed, soaked in cold water for 30 minutes, drained and patted dry

4–6 tablespoons olive oil

1 yellow onion, coarsely chopped

3 garlic cloves, minced

Salt and freshly ground black pepper

6 plum tomatoes, peeled, seeded and chopped

1 tablespoon balsamic vinegar

3 tablespoons chopped mixed fresh herbs (parsley, thyme, basil, marjoram and/or oregano)

If using slender Asian eggplant, cut lengthwise into quarters and then into 1-inch sections (without peeling). If using round Italian eggplant, trim the ends, peel and cut into 1-inch dice. Set aside.

Cut the tops and bottoms off the red peppers, cut them lengthwise in half and remove the seeds and veins. Cut the peppers into 1-inch squares. Set aside.

Cut the zucchini lengthwise into quarters and then into 1-inch sections. Set aside.

Heat 1 tablespoon of the oil in a large nonstick sauté pan over medium-high heat. When hot, add the onion and cook, stirring, until translucent but not browned, 3 to 5 minutes. Add the garlic and cook, stirring constantly, just until the onion begins to brown; do not let the garlic brown. Season to taste with salt and pepper and transfer to a mixing bowl.

Add another tablespoon of oil to the pan and heat until hot. Add the eggplant and cook, stirring constantly, until it begins to brown, about 5 minutes. (If necessary, cook the eggplant in 2 batches, adding more oil if needed.) Reduce the heat to medium and continue cooking until the eggplant is rather soft, about 10 minutes more. Season to taste with salt and pepper and add to the onion mixture.

Add another tablespoon of oil to the pan and heat over medium-high heat. When hot, add the peppers and cook, stirring, until they become tender, 5 to 10 minutes. Season to taste with salt and pepper and add to the eggplant and onion.

Heat the remaining 1 tablespoon oil over medium-high heat. Add the zucchini and cook, stirring constantly, until it just begins to brown. Reduce the heat to medium and cook until it is tender-crisp. Season to taste with salt and pepper and add to the vegetables in the mixing bowl.

Increase the heat to high and add the tomatoes to the pan. Stir, then add the vinegar. Cook briefly, scraping the bottom of the pan to loosen any brown bits. Pour the tomatoes over the vegetables and stir to combine.

Transfer the vegetable mixture to a large sauté pan and cook, stirring, over medium-low heat until all the vegetables are cooked through, about 5 minutes. The onion, eggplant and peppers should be very soft, but the zucchini should still have some bite. During the last 5 minutes, add the herbs and stir well. Taste again and adjust the seasonings, if necessary. Serve hot or at room temperature.

6 servings

roasted beet and orange salad

Roasting beets concentrates their flavor and sweetens them nicely. Be careful when you unwrap them, as the red anthocyanin pigment will leak from the cut surfaces — and it will definitely stain. You can toast the nuts in the oven if you wish, in a single layer on a cookie sheet for about 10 minutes, or you can do it on top of the stove in a dry skillet for about 15 minutes.

- - - - - - - - - -

6 medium beets with tops

3 navel oranges

4 teaspoons prepared horseradish, or more to taste

¼ teaspoon minced garlic

2 tablespoons red wine vinegar

6 tablespoons olive oil, or more to taste

Salt and freshly ground black pepper

About 1 tablespoon fresh lemon juice (optional)

2 tablespoons chopped toasted pecans (see above)

Preheat the oven to 350 degrees.

Trim the beet tops to 1 inch and set the tops aside. Wrap the beets in foil and bake, turning once, until a small knife slips in easily, about 1 hour. Set aside to cool.

Peel the oranges, removing all the white pith. Working over a bowl to catch the juices, carefully remove the orange sections by cutting down both sides of each section between the flesh and the membrane and gently scooping the segment into the bowl. When you are finished, squeeze the juice from the membranes into the bowl and discard the membranes. Remove the orange sections with a slotted spoon and set aside.

Blanch the reserved beet tops in a large pot of boiling water just until their color brightens and their stems become tender, about 1 minute. Immediately transfer them to a bowl of cold water to stop the cooking. Drain well and pat dry with a kitchen towel. Set aside.

When the beets are cool enough to handle, slide the peels off with your fingers. Remove any remaining tops and trim the roots. Slice the beets into ¼-inch-thick rounds and set aside.

Whisk together the horseradish, garlic, vinegar and the juice from the orange sections in a mixing bowl. Whisking constantly, slowly add the oil, beginning with just a thread. Season to taste with salt and plenty of pepper. If necessary, add a little more horseradish, oil or the lemon juice (if desired) to correct the acidity. (Test by dipping an orange section and a piece of beet into the dressing. The flavor should be bright but well balanced.)

Add the beets to the dressing, toss well, remove with a slotted spoon and arrange in a low mound in the center of a serving platter. Add the orange slices to the dressing and toss well. Remove with a slotted spoon and arrange them over the beets. Add the beet tops to the dressing and toss well. Remove with a slotted spoon and arrange them around the beets, sprinkle with the pecans and serve.

6 servings

spring vegetable stew of snap peas, lettuce, new potatoes and artichokes

In this country we rarely cook lettuces, but when they're treated gently, they add a wonderful spring-green flavor to stews. Serve with crusty bread.

Juice of 1 lemon

4 artichokes

1 pound sugar snap peas

1½ pounds small white potatoes, cut into walnut-sized pieces

Salt

2 tablespoons butter

2 shiitake mushrooms, stems discarded, coarsely chopped

1 bunch green onions, white parts only, cut into 1-inch lengths

1 head romaine lettuce, interior leaves only (reserve outer leaves for another use), coarsely chopped

1 teaspoon chopped fresh mint

2 tablespoons chopped fresh oregano or marjoram

¼ cup chopped fresh parsley

Fill a large bowl with cold water and add half the lemon juice and set aside.

Trim the artichokes by pulling off any leaves clinging to the stem and the two outer rows of leaves around the base. Holding 1 artichoke in one hand and a sharp paring knife in the other, keeping the knife parallel to the stem, turn the artichoke against the knife, trimming away the outer leaves until only the pale green to yellow base remains. Lay the artichoke on its side and cut away the tops of the remaining leaves, roughly where the leaves swell out. With the paring knife, peel off the dark green skin of the artichoke heart from the base toward the stem, exposing the light green flesh underneath. Set the artichoke heart upside down on the work surface and cut it into quarters. Trim away the hairy chokes. Cut off the stems and cut them into ¼-inch pieces. Cut each artichoke quarter into 4 or 5 pieces. Add the artichoke, including the stems, to the lemon water and repeat the procedure with the remaining artichokes.

Cook the peas in a large pot of rapidly boiling lightly salted water just until they are bright green but still crisp, 30 to 45 seconds. With a slotted spoon, transfer the peas to a bowl of ice water to stop the cooking.

Cook the potatoes in the boiling water until they are barely tender, about 15 minutes. Remove them from the pan with a slotted spoon, and drain on a kitchen towel; salt lightly.

Drain the artichokes, add to the boiling water and cook until they are just tender, about 15 minutes. (The dish can be prepared to this point up to 4 hours in advance and the vegetables refrigerated until almost ready to serve.)

Melt the butter in a large skillet or Dutch oven over medium-low heat. Add the mushrooms and green onions and cook until the onions soften, 15 to 20 minutes.

Add the potatoes and artichokes and cook just until they are heated through. (Do not cook for too long, or the potatoes will begin to break down.) Drain the peas and add them with the lettuce and cook just until the lettuce wilts, about 5 minutes. Add the mint, oregano or marjoram and parsley and stir to mix well. Add the remaining lemon juice. Season to taste with salt. Serve in deep bowls.

6 servings

stew of charred tomatoes, pasta and cranberry beans

Charring the tomatoes in a dry skillet is a technique borrowed from Mexican cooking that concentrates the tomato flavor and adds a subtle smokiness. Don't overdo the roasting: you want the tomatoes to be just slightly blackened. Fresh cranberry beans are not as plentiful as fresh favas, but you can often find them at farmers' markets in the late summer and early fall. If you can't get them, use another fresh bean, such as favas or limas.

- - - - - - -

3 plum tomatoes

2 ounces prosciutto, minced

1 tablespoon olive oil

1 carrot, diced

½ yellow onion, diced

1 garlic clove, minced

1 small sprig fresh sage

1 pound fresh cranberry beans, shelled,
   or 1½ cups dried

1½ cups water

   Salt

½ pound dried pasta shapes, such as
   orecchiette or medium shells

2 tablespoons torn fresh basil leaves

Slice the tomatoes lengthwise in half. Heat a stovetop griddle until hot. Place the tomatoes cut side down on the griddle and cook until they begin to blacken and char, about 5 minutes. Turn the tomatoes over and char the opposite side, about 3 minutes. Cool, then gently squeeze out the seeds and chop. Set aside.

In a large sauté pan over medium heat, cook the prosciutto in the oil until lightly browned, about 5 minutes. Add the carrot, onion and garlic, reduce the heat and cook, covered, until the vegetables soften, about 10 minutes.

Add the sage, cranberry beans, tomatoes, water and 1 teaspoon salt. Bring to a boil, reduce the heat to a simmer and cook, covered, until the beans are soft, about 30 minutes if fresh, 1 hour and 15 minutes if dried.

Shortly before the beans are done, cook the pasta in plenty of rapidly boiling salted water until just al dente. Drain well. Add the pasta to the beans, raise the heat to high and cook, stirring, for 2 to 3 minutes to meld the flavors. Divide among 4 pasta bowls, garnish with the basil and serve.

4 servings

ragout of shrimp and fava beans

Though all dried beans begin fresh, today only fava beans are commonly consumed in that form. That's a shame, because all the so-called shelly beans are delicious. Fresh favas take a bunch of work to get ready — their bitter inner peels must be removed one at a time — but their delicate, sweet green flavor makes it worth it.

----

2   pounds shrimp with heads or
    1 pound shrimp without heads,
    peeled (shells and heads reserved)

3   garlic cloves, minced

1   teaspoon salt, or more to taste

2   tablespoons olive oil

1   cup dry white wine

1   small carrot, finely chopped

1   medium tomato, peeled,
    seeded and chopped

3   pounds fresh fava beans (in the pods)

1   teaspoon fresh thyme leaves

Combine the shrimp, one-third of the garlic, the salt and oil in a bowl. Stir well to coat. Seal tightly in a zipper-lock plastic bag and refrigerate for at least 1 hour, up to 4 hours.

Rinse the shrimp shells (and heads) well under running water. Combine them with the wine, the remaining garlic, the carrot and tomato in a large saucepan, add water just to cover, and simmer over medium heat for 45 minutes to 1 hour.

Remove the fava beans from their pods, then place the beans in a bowl, cover with boiling water and let stand for 5 minutes.

Dump the beans into a colander and cool with cold running water. Use your thumbnail to cut a slit in one end of each bean, then, with the thumb and forefinger of your other hand, squeeze the bean out into a bowl.

Strain the shrimp stock into a medium saucepan. You should have 2½ to 3 cups. Add the beans and bring to a simmer over low heat, cooking the beans just until tender, 5 minutes. (The dish can be made to this point up to 8 hours ahead and refrigerated, tightly covered.)

When ready to serve, bring the beans to a rapid boil and add the marinated shrimp and thyme. Cook the shrimp through, 3 to 5 minutes. Taste for salt and serve in bowls.

6 servings

grilled vegetable sandwich

Be generous with the oil in this recipe — it's necessary to re-place the moisture that evaporates from the cut surfaces of the vegetables during the intense dry heat of grilling. The vegeta-bles can also be broiled, but the heat won't be as intense, so the flavors won't be as concentrated and the vegetables will lack the smokiness that comes from grilling. The best loaf for this sandwich is a ciabatta, a long, flat rectangle that can be split neatly into sandwich-sized lengths. You can also use any long rustic loaf — preferably the larger bâtard, though a thin-ner baguette will do in a pinch. If using either of these, re-move some of the soft inner bread after splitting.

- -

2 long Asian eggplants

Olive oil for brushing, plus 2 tablespoons

Salt

2 red bell peppers

1 medium yellow onion

1 loaf rustic bread, preferably a ciabatta
   (see above)

1 medium tomato, sliced

6 ounces fresh goat cheese

¼ cup finely sliced fresh basil leaves

2 teaspoons red wine vinegar

Freshly ground black pepper

Preheat the grill.

Cut the stems off the eggplants and slice them lengthwise into quarters. Brush the quarters with oil and grill over medium-high heat, turning occasionally, until softened and darkened, about 10 minutes. Remove from the heat and salt lightly.

While the eggplants are cooking, grill the red peppers, turning, until they are blackened on all sides, about 10 minutes. Remove the peppers and place them in a zipper-lock plastic bag to cool.

Peel the onion, being careful to leave the root end intact, and cut it into 6 wedges. Grill the onion until soft, about 7 minutes, turning once.

Peel the peppers and remove the stems, seeds and veins.

Split the bread lengthwise in half. Arrange the grilled eggplant, peppers, onion and tomato slices in layers on the bottom half. Crumble the cheese over the top. Sprinkle with the basil.

Whisk together the 2 tablespoons oil, the vinegar and salt and pepper to taste and drizzle over the vegetables.

Place the top half of the loaf on the sandwich and press down lightly. Cut into 8 pieces and serve.

8 servings

stuffed zucchini

There is quite a cult of vegetable stuffing among European cooks. It's a great way to use up oversized vegetables and stretch a little bit of meat a long way. Best of all, stuffed vegetables taste good.

- - - - - - - - - - - - - - - - -

3 large zucchini (about 8 inches long
   and 3–3½ inches thick)

1½ pounds plum tomatoes

2 tablespoons olive oil, plus more if needed

1 pound ground pork

2 sprigs fresh thyme

1 teaspoon fennel seeds

¼ teaspoon crushed red pepper

Freshly ground black pepper

1 medium yellow onion, chopped

2 garlic cloves, minced

1 cup cubed stale bread, soaked in ½ cup milk

Salt

1 large egg, beaten

2 tablespoons tomato paste

½ cup freshly grated pecorino Romano cheese

Trim and discard the ends of the zucchini and cut them into sections roughly 2½ inches long. Soak them in lightly salted cold water for 30 minutes to refresh.

Cut a shallow X in the bottom of each tomato. Dip the tomatoes into rapidly boiling water just until the skins begin to come free, about 30 seconds. Drain and rinse briefly under cold running water. Set aside to cool, then peel.

Heat the 2 tablespoons oil in a large skillet or Dutch oven over medium heat. When hot, add the pork and stir to break it up. Cook, stirring occasionally, until the pork is lightly browned, about 10 minutes.

While the pork is cooking, use a small sharp knife or melon baller to make zucchini "cups": Remove the center of each zucchini section, leaving only about a ¼-inch shell of the vegetable around the sides and at the bottom; reserve the flesh. Salt the zucchini "cups" and stand them upside down on a platter to drain. Chop and reserve enough of the flesh to make 1 cup.

Preheat the oven to 350 degrees.

Add the thyme, fennel seeds, crushed red pepper and black pepper to taste to the pork and transfer the mixture to a bowl to cool. Drain most of the fat from the pan, but leave any browned bits that have stuck to the bottom. Add half the chopped onion to the pan and cook until translucent, about 5 minutes. Add half the garlic and cook until fragrant, about 1 minute. Add the reserved chopped zucchini and cook until light golden, about 5 minutes. Add to the cooked pork.

Squeeze the bread dry and add it to the pork mixture, along with ¾ teaspoon salt. Mix thoroughly, squeezing the mixture between your fingers to break up the bread and bind the mixture. Taste and correct the seasonings, then beat in the egg.

Spoon the pork mixture into the zucchini cups, packing it as tightly as possible and mounding it a little on top. Smooth the tops with the back of a spoon.

In the pan you used to cook the meat, cook the remaining onion over medium heat until translucent, about 5 minutes, adding a bit of oil only if necessary. Add the remaining garlic and cook until it is fragrant, about 1 minute.

Meanwhile, cut the tomatoes in half and squeeze out the seeds. Coarsely chop the tomatoes and add to the onion and garlic, along with the tomato paste. Increase the heat to high and cook, stirring and scraping the browned bits from the bottom and sides of the pan, until the tomatoes begin to soften and bubble, about 3 minutes. Season to taste with salt and pepper.

Pour the tomato sauce into a roasting pan. Arrange the zucchini cups (meat side up) in the pan. Cover tightly and bake until the zucchini can be pierced easily with a toothpick, about 45 minutes.

Remove the cover and sprinkle the cheese over the zucchini. Increase the heat to 450 degrees and bake until the cheese melts and begins to brown, about 10 minutes. Remove from the oven.

Transfer the zucchini cups to a warm platter. If the tomato sauce is too liquid, reduce it over high heat until it thickens, about 5 minutes (at most). Spoon the sauce around the stuffed zucchini and serve.

6 servings

eggplant and goat cheese casserole

Some cooks swear that eggplant has to be salted before cooking. They say it removes bitter juices. In fact, whether to salt or not depends on how the eggplant is to be cooked. Adding salt to eggplant that is going to be fried results in a softer, plusher texture, but it has little or no effect on eggplant that will be grilled.

- - - - - - - - - -

3 (1–to-1¼-pound) eggplants
   Salt
1 medium yellow onion, finely chopped
   About 1/2 cup olive oil
4 garlic cloves, minced
2 (28-ounce) cans crushed tomatoes
½ teaspoon crushed red pepper
   Freshly ground black pepper
2 tablespoons chopped fresh basil
1 (11-ounce) log fresh goat cheese
1 (8-ounce) ball mozzarella, grated

Peel the eggplants and cut lengthwise into slices ¼ to ½ inch thick. Salt liberally on both sides and arrange in overlapping layers on a jelly-roll pan. Prop upright over the sink and let drain for at least 1½ hours.

Preheat the oven to 400 degrees.

Sauté the onion in 2 tablespoons of the oil in a large saucepan or skillet over medium-high heat until it begins to soften and turn translucent, about 5 minutes. Add the garlic and cook until highly fragrant, about 2 minutes. Add the tomatoes and crushed red pepper and cook until the sauce is slightly thickened, about 20 minutes. Season to taste with salt and pepper, add the basil and keep warm.

Rinse the eggplant slices under cold running water and pat dry with paper towels. Heat 2 tablespoons of the oil in a large nonstick skillet over medium-high heat. Add 4 slices of the eggplant and cook until lightly browned on one side, about 10 minutes. Flip and cook, without adding oil, until the second side is lightly browned, about 10 more minutes. (This can be done in two skillets to speed the process.) Repeat until all the eggplant is fried, using more oil as needed.

Spread about 1½ cups tomato sauce over the bottom of a large gratin or baking dish. Arrange half of the eggplant in 1 layer, overlapping the slices on top of the sauce. Dot each slice with a walnut-sized knob of goat cheese and ladle over enough tomato sauce to barely cover.

Repeat, using the remaining eggplant slices. Dot the slices with the remaining goat cheese, and ladle on the remaining tomato sauce. Distribute the mozzarella evenly across the top.

Bake until the mozzarella melts and browns, about 30 minutes. Remove from the oven and let cool for 10 minutes before serving.

8 to 10 servings

+ **Buy the following fruits fully ripe:** berries, cherries, grapes, watermelon and citrus. All except berries can be refrigerated without losing flavor.

+ **These fruits will soften** and develop more complex flavors (though not more sweetness) after picking: apricots, melons, figs, peaches, nectarines, plums and persimmons. Store them at room temperature until they are as ripe as you want them. After that, refrigeration will extend the life of the fruit, though it will mute the flavor.

+ **You can refrigerate fruits** such as apples, ripe pears and ripe mangoes as soon as you buy them with no ill effects.

+ **If you buy stone fruit** and pears that are hard, you can ripen them by storing them at room temperature in a closed paper bag. Adding an apple will speed the process.

+ **Fruits such as apples and pears** will brown when cut and exposed to oxygen. They should be covered with acidulated water (water with lemon juice) if they are going to be held for very long.

+ **Fruit can be "cooked" without heat.** Sugar draws the water out of the cells, collapsing them and softening the fruit. For this reason, whenever you use sugared fruit in a recipe, either use it immediately after sugaring or be careful to drain off the liquid before adding it.

+ **You can produce complex flavors** by combining fruits and poaching them very gently in a simple sugar syrup (water and sugar brought just to a boil, then cooled). For a fruit compote, use equal measures of sugar and water; for a lighter syrup, use half as much sugar as water.

✦ **Some fruits**—most notably peaches—need to be peeled before cooking. Cut a shallow X in the bottom of the peach and drop it into boiling water for a few seconds. Remove and immediately plunge the peach into ice water to stop the cooking; the peel should slide right off. If it doesn't, return the peach to the boiling water for a little longer.

✦ **Most fruits that are cooked** need a little acidity such as citrus juice, not only to brighten their flavors but to maintain their color.

---

strawberry soup

This is a wonderful way to punch up berries that are a little too firm or not quite sweet enough. The combination of red wine and vanilla effectively makes up for any lack of flavor, and the sugar both sweetens and slightly softens the fruit.

----

  1 (750-milliliter) bottle light dry red or rosé wine
  1 cup sugar
  1 (3-inch) piece vanilla bean
  2 pints strawberries, washed and hulled
1½ cups vanilla ice cream
  6 almond or sugar wafer cookies

Combine the wine and sugar in a large bowl and whisk well to dissolve. Split the vanilla bean in half and scrape the seeds into the wine mixture. Add the bean.

Leave small strawberries whole; cut larger berries into pieces of similar size. Add to the wine combination and let macerate in the refrigerator for at least 2 hours, or overnight.

To serve, ladle the berries and wine into bowls. Top each with a ¼-cup scoop of ice cream and a cookie.

6 servings

sliced melons in lime-mint syrup

By adding lime and mint, you can heighten the flavor of melons that might be less than perfect. But these complementary flavors will improve even great melons. This recipe is adapted from a dish served at Echo, a small treasure of a restaurant in Fresno, California. Partners Tim Woods and Adams Holland treat local produce simply and with respect. Their version of this dessert uses only mint in the syrup, but I've found that grated lime zest adds another dimension. Mix two or three melon varieties for an assortment of colors, flavors and textures.

The peeling method detailed here works well for firm melons. With riper, softer melons, it's better to cut them into thin slices with the rinds attached, then stack several slices and remove the rinds. If your melons are very sweet, decrease the sugar to ½ cup; if they're on the bland side, increase the sugar to ¾ cup.

- - - - - - - - - -

    2 cups water
    ⅔ cup sugar
    2–3 sprigs fresh mint
         Grated zest of 1 lime
    2½ pounds assorted melons

Combine the water and sugar in a small saucepan and bring to a boil, whisking until the sugar is completely dissolved. Remove from the heat. Add the mint and lime zest and let stand until cool.

Strain the syrup into a lidded jar, cover and chill.

Cut the melons in half and remove the seeds. Place each half cut side down on a cutting board and slice off the top ½ inch. Cut away the peel with a sharp knife, working down the melon in 2-to-3-inch strips. Cut each half lengthwise into quarters, then into ¼-inch slices. (The melons can be tightly covered and refrigerated for about 2 hours.)

Arrange the melon slices on a large, deep platter, pour the syrup over and serve.

8 to 10 servings

fall fruit compote

You can use this as a model for other compotes. Add the fruit that takes the longest to cook to the syrup first and proceed, adding other fruits in order of their cooking times. Here, the quinces take a long time, while the dried fruits merely need to plump up a bit. Instead of quinces, you could use apples, which need to poach for about 10 minutes, or pears, which need only 5 to 7 minutes, depending on ripeness. Serve with plain butter cookies or pound cake.

- -

1½ pounds quinces (see above)
 1 cup water
⅓ cup sugar
½ cup Muscat or other raisins
⅓ cup dried apricots
⅓ cup dried sour cherries

Peel the quinces, cut them into quarters and remove the cores. Cut each quarter lengthwise in half and then in half across, making roughly walnut-sized pieces.

Combine the quinces, water and sugar in a medium saucepan and bring to a simmer over medium-low heat, stirring to dissolve the sugar. Cover tightly and continue cooking until the fruit is rosy and tender, 45 to 60 minutes.

Add the raisins, apricots and cherries, cover and cook for 10 minutes. Remove from the heat and let stand until the dried fruits have plumped and softened, about 10 more minutes.

Serve warm or at room temperature.

4 servings

quince applesauce

Quinces are delicious in applesauce, adding a musky spiciness and a delicate pink color. They do take much longer to cook than apples, though, so be sure to slice them very thin and to cut the apples into large chunks to ensure that the two are done at the same time. If you're one of those people who habitually douse applesauce with ground cinnamon or cloves, taste this one first — seasoning probably won't be necessary. Every apple variety has its own flavor and texture when cooked. Almost any of them will work well in this recipe, with the exception of Red Delicious, which usually tastes like wet cardboard when cooked. This applesauce is not too sweet and is wonderful with roast pork or duck.

----

6 apples (not Red Delicious), peeled,
  cored and quartered

1 quince, peeled, cored and thinly sliced

¼ cup water

6 tablespoons sugar

Combine the apples, quince and water in a medium saucepan. Cover tightly and cook over medium heat, stirring occasionally to prevent sticking, until the quince is tender, about 20 minutes.

Add the sugar and cook, stirring, until the apples begin to fall apart, about 5 minutes. Finish the puree with a handheld immersion blender or a potato masher. Serve warm or cold, according to your taste.

6 servings

dreamsicle oranges

Sliced oranges with vanilla-scented sugar syrup are a grown-up version of a favorite little-kid taste. Serve this incredibly easy dessert with good sugar cookies.

6 navel oranges
2 cups water
2 cups sugar
1 vanilla bean, split lengthwise

With a thin, sharp knife, slice off the tops and bottoms of the oranges so that the flesh shows. Stand an orange on the cutting board. Starting with the knife at the point where the white of the peel meets the orange flesh and following the curve of the orange, use a gentle downward sawing motion to slice a 1½-to-2-inch-wide strip of peel from the orange, cutting away all the white but leaving as much flesh as possible. Repeat until all the peel is removed. Repeat with the remaining oranges, reserving the peel of 2 oranges.

Combine the water and sugar in a saucepan, bring to a boil over medium heat and cook for 5 minutes. Scrape the seeds from the vanilla bean into the pan and then add the bean halves. Add the reserved orange peels and boil for 2 to 3 minutes, then remove from the heat and let steep for 30 to 60 minutes.

While the syrup is cooling, carefully slice the oranges horizontally into ½-inch slices. Carefully remove any seeds.

Layer the orange slices in a large, shallow serving bowl. Pour the syrup through a strainer over the slices. Arrange the vanilla bean strips in an X on top. Cover tightly with plastic wrap and chill for at least 1 hour before serving.

6 servings

candied citrus peel

Citrus peel is impossibly bitter when raw, but repeated blanchings and a good soaking in sugar syrup tame the pucker to a pleasant tingle. This is a wonderful treat to keep on hand during the holidays.

- - - - - - - - - - - - - - - - -

5 cups sugar

2½ cups water

5 pounds citrus fruit
    (grapefruit, orange or lemon)

Combine 4 cups of the sugar and the water in a large saucepan. Bring to a boil, stirring to combine. (You will have about 2½ cups syrup.) Remove from the heat.

Meanwhile, score the peel of the citrus fruit into 2-inch-wide sections, cutting through the peel but not into the fruit. Using your fingers, pull off the peel, carefully running your thumb between the peel and the fruit to separate the two. Reserve the fruit for another use.

Put the peel in a saucepan, cover with water and bring to a boil; drain and rinse briefly under cold water. Blanch in the same manner two more times; drain. Using a thin, sharp knife, remove as much of the soft pith as possible. You should be able to see some color through any remaining pith, but the peel will be much thicker than plain zest. Cut into shreds ⅛ to ¼ inch wide.

Return the peel to the saucepan, cover with cold water and bring to a simmer. Cook until the peel begins to lose its raw look, 5 to 10 minutes. Drain and immediately, without rinsing the peel, transfer it to a large mixing bowl. Cover with the hot sugar syrup and set aside for 1 hour to candy.

Preheat the oven to 250 degrees.

Place the remaining 1 cup sugar in another large mixing bowl. Add the peel and toss to coat well. Shaking to remove the excess sugar, transfer the peel to a cooling rack set over a jelly-roll pan to catch the dripping syrup, arranging it in a single layer as much as possible. Place in the oven for 30 minutes to dry.

Remove the peel from the oven and let stand at room temperature to finish drying. The peel will continue to become firmer and chewier over several days. When the peel reaches the desired texture, store it in an airtight container until ready to use. The candied peel will keep for about 2 months.

About 40 dozen pieces

ultimate strawberry shortcake

The great American shortcake is really a slightly sweetened cream biscuit. It should be light and flaky — nothing like those rubbery shock absorbers you find in the grocery store.

STRAWBERRIES

4 pints strawberries, rinsed and hulled

¼ cup sugar

SHORTCAKES

2 cups all-purpose flour

1 tablespoon baking powder

3 tablespoons sugar

Dash of salt

8 tablespoons (1 stick) unsalted butter, chilled and cut into 8 pieces

¾ cup heavy (whipping) cream

2 cups heavy (whipping) cream, whipped to soft peaks

Prepare the strawberries: Cut the strawberries in half. Put them in a large bowl and toss them with the sugar. Set aside for 30 minutes to macerate.

Make the shortcakes: Preheat the oven to 350 degrees.

Sift the flour, baking powder, sugar and salt into a mixing bowl. Scatter the butter over top and rub the butter and flour between your fingers or cut the butter in with a pair of knives or a pastry cutter, until the mixture resembles coarse cornmeal, with a few larger lumps of butter left intact. Add half the cream and stir it in with a fork. Add the remainder of the ¾ cup cream bit by bit, until a mass forms that pulls cleanly away from the bottom and sides of the bowl; you may not need all the cream.

On a lightly floured work surface, quickly and lightly knead the dough until it is smooth and cohesive. Gently roll it out ½ inch thick. Cut out the shortcakes with a 3-inch biscuit cutter or a lightly floured juice glass. Gather the leftover dough together, knead it again briefly and roll it out again. Cut out more shortcakes. You should have 10 shortcakes.

Place the shortcakes 1 inch apart on an unbuttered baking sheet and bake until lightly browned and slightly crusty, 10 to 15 minutes. Remove from the oven and cool slightly.

Assemble the shortcakes: Split each shortcake while it is still warm and place the bottom halves on dessert plates. Spoon plenty of strawberries over the bottom halves, add a generous spoonful of whipped cream, top with the remaining halves of the shortcakes and serve.

10 servings

perfumed strawberries
in meringue baskets

Strawberries are from the same botanical family as roses, and if you sniff hard enough, you can detect a trace of the flower's perfume. For that reason, the addition of rose geranium to the fruit is not as whimsical as it may seem. If you'd rather not make your own, ready-made meringue baskets or shells can be bought at many bakeries.

MERINGUE BASKETS

4 large egg whites

⅛ teaspoon cream of tartar

½ cup sugar, preferably superfine

1 teaspoon vanilla extract

STRAWBERRIES

2 pints strawberries, washed and hulled

2 tablespoons sugar

1 tablespoon snipped (unsprayed)
    rose geranium leaves (optional)

Make the meringue baskets: Preheat the oven to 250 degrees. Line a baking sheet with parchment.

Beat the egg whites in a large bowl until foamy. Add the cream of tartar, then add the sugar 1 tablespoon at a time, beating well after each addition, until the whites are stiff and glossy and the sugar is completely dissolved. Fold in the vanilla extract.

Spoon the meringue into a pastry bag with a medium star tip. Pipe six 3-inch disks of meringue onto the parchment-lined baking sheet; smooth each disk with the back of a spoon. Pipe a ring of meringue around the edge of each disk. Repeat twice to form three-tiered baskets.

Bake the meringues for 1 hour. Turn off the oven and leave the meringues in it for 6 more hours to dry. The baskets can be stored in an airtight container for 1 week.

Prepare the strawberries: Put one-quarter of the berries in a large bowl and crush them with a fork. Add the sugar and geranium leaves, if using, and stir to combine well.

Cut the remaining berries into bite-sized pieces. Combine them with the crushed berries and spoon them into the meringue baskets. Serve immediately.

6 servings

mango crepes with mexican cream

This all-purpose crepe batter can be used for savory dishes if you simply leave out the sugar and cinnamon. Mexican cream is available in the cheese section of many supermarkets or in Latino grocery stores. If you can't find it, use crème fraîche or sour cream thinned with a little heavy cream.

CREPES

3/4–1 cup milk

½ cup water

3 large eggs

1 cup all-purpose flour

1 tablespoon sugar

½ teaspoon salt

¼ teaspoon ground cinnamon

4 tablespoons (½ stick) unsalted butter, melted, plus more for cooking

FRUIT

4 mangoes

1 (½-pound) piece seeded papaya

1 tablespoon sugar

2 tablespoons orange liqueur, such as Grand Marnier or Cointreau

Juice of 2 limes

1 cup Mexican cream (see above)

1 tablespoon sugar

1 tablespoon orange liqueur, such as Grand Marnier or Cointreau

Make the crepes: Combine ¾ cup of the milk, the water, eggs, flour, sugar, salt and cinnamon in a blender and pulse until smooth. With the blender running, add the butter. The batter should be the thickness of heavy cream. If necessary, add up to ¼ cup more milk. Strain into a bowl, cover and refrigerate for 1 hour.

Remove the batter from the refrigerator and stir with a whisk. Heat a 9-inch nonstick skillet over medium-high heat. Rub it lightly with butter. Pour about ¼ cup of the batter into the center of the pan, tilting the pan to spread the batter evenly over the entire bottom. Return the pan to the heat and cook until the top of the crepe appears dry, about 1 minute. Turn the crepe and cook it briefly on the other side until it is speckled. Remove it to a plate and repeat until all the batter is used, adding a little more butter if the crepes begin to stick. (You will need 12 crepes. Any leftover crepes can be stored in the refrigerator wrapped in plastic wrap, with sheets of waxed paper between them, for 1 week.)

Prepare the fruit: Remove the flesh from each mango by making a slightly concave downward cut with a sharp knife parallel to the pit and slicing off the flesh; turn the mango around and repeat on the other side. Make diamond-shaped cuts through the flesh on each mango half down to, but not through, the skin. Invert each mango half so it turns inside out and the diamonds pop up, then cut the diamonds free into a bowl. Remove the skin from the flesh remaining around each mango pit and cut the flesh into the bowl.

Grate the papaya, using the big holes on a box grater, directly into the bowl with the mangoes. Add the sugar, liqueur and lime juice and toss to coat well.

Whisk the cream in a small bowl until it is slightly thickened. Whisk in the sugar and liqueur.

Assemble the crepes: Lay a crepe on a dessert plate, browned side down. Spread it lightly with the whipped cream and top with about ¼ cup of the fruit. Fold the crepe into quarters. Repeat with a second crepe on the same plate. Repeat using the remaining crepes. Garnish with the remaining fruit and serve.

6 servings

cornmeal crepes
with spiced plum compote

The cornmeal adds a slight crunch and a little nutty taste to the crepes. Because of that, you don't need to add melted butter to this batter — it has enough flavor of its own.

- -

CREPES

 2 large eggs

 2 large egg yolks

 2 cups milk

 1 cup all-purpose flour

 ½ cup fine cornmeal

 1 teaspoon sugar

 Dash of salt

COMPOTE

 4 cups coarsely chopped pitted plums
   (about 1½ pounds)

 1½ cups sugar

 2 cinnamon sticks

 4 whole cloves

 Powdered sugar

Make the crepes: Combine the eggs, egg yolks, milk, flour, cornmeal, sugar and salt in a blender and pulse until smooth. The batter should be the consistency of whipping cream. If it's not, adjust the thickness by adding a little more flour or milk as necessary. Refrigerate, covered, for at least 1 hour so the gluten strands relax.

Remove the batter from the refrigerator and stir with a whisk. Heat a 9-inch nonstick skillet over medium-high heat. Rub it lightly with butter. Pour about ¼ cup of the batter into the center of the pan, tilting the pan to spread the batter evenly over the entire bottom. Return the pan to the heat and cook until the top of the crepe appears dry, about 1 minute. Turn the crepe and cook it briefly on the other side until it is speckled. Remove it to a plate and repeat until all the batter is used. (You will need 12 crepes. Any leftover crepes can be stored in the refrigerator wrapped in plastic wrap, with sheets of waxed paper between them, for 1 week.)

Make the compote: Combine the plums, sugar, cinnamon sticks and cloves in a small saucepan and cook over medium heat until the plums are soft and the juices have thickened, 20 to 30 minutes, depending on the ripeness of the plums. Remove from the heat and let cool. Remove and discard the cinnamon sticks and cloves.

Assemble the crepes: Preheat the broiler. Spread about 1/4 cup of the compote over 1 crepe, then fold the crepe into quarters. Sprinkle it lightly with powdered sugar. Place the crepe on a baking sheet and repeat with the remaining crepes and compote. Glaze the crepes under the broiler for 2 to 3 minutes; be careful not to burn. Serve immediately.

4 servings

cornmeal waffles
with winter fruit compote

These waffles are delicate and airy, with a nice crunch and a slightly bitter edge from the cornmeal. They're wonderful by themselves, and they make a truly elegant brunch dish or dessert when served with the compote. The compote is also good on its own or served with butter cookies or a slice of pound cake.

- - - - - - - - - -

COMPOTE

1 cup pitted prunes, quartered

1 cup dried apricots, quartered

1 cup dried apple slices, cut into ½-inch pieces

4 large ripe pears, such as Bartlett or Comice, peeled, cored and cut into ½-inch dice

2 teaspoons grated orange zest

1½ cups fresh orange juice

½ cup sugar

½ cup water

WAFFLES

¾ cup cake flour

¼ cup cornmeal

4 teaspoons sugar

2 teaspoons baking powder

½ teaspoon baking soda

¼ teaspoon salt

1 cup buttermilk

½ cup sour cream

2 large eggs, separated

Make the compote: In a large nonreactive saucepan, combine the prunes, apricots, apples, pears, orange zest, orange juice, water and sugar. Bring to a boil over high heat. Reduce the heat to low, cover and simmer until the fruit is tender, 7 to 8 minutes. Keep warm over low heat while you make the waffles.

Make the waffles: Preheat the waffle iron. Sift together the flour, cornmeal, sugar, baking powder, baking soda and salt in a large bowl.

In a large measuring cup or a small bowl, stir together the buttermilk, sour cream and egg yolks. In a medium bowl, beat the egg whites until stiff peaks form. Add the sour cream mixture to the dry ingredients, stir briefly just until the batter takes on a pebbly texture. Fold in the egg whites.

Pour the batter into the waffle iron and bake according to the manufacturer's instructions. Serve the waffles immediately, each one topped with ¼ cup of the compote. (Store any leftover compote tightly sealed in the refrigerator for up to 1 week.)

6 servings

vanilla-baked apples
with bourbon sauce

There's nothing simpler than a baked apple. There are a couple of things to be careful about, though. First, be sure to cut off a strip of peel from around the top of each apple. If you don't, the skin will crack and slip down as the flesh begins to swell from the heat. Serve the apples with crème fraîche or vanilla ice cream.

- - - - - - - - - - - - - -

2 tablespoons chopped pecans

6 large baking apples (preferably
   Pink Lady or Golden Delicious)

¼ cup sugar

¼ cup packed light brown sugar

1 vanilla bean

¾ cup bourbon

   Slivered zest of ½ lemon

2 tablespoons butter

Preheat the oven to 350 degrees.

Toast the pecans in a small dry skillet over medium heat, stirring occasionally, until fragrant, about 5 minutes. Do not scorch. Transfer to a small mixing bowl.

While the pecans are toasting, core the apples to within ½ inch of the bottom, leaving the bottom intact to act as a cup. Trim a thin band of peel from around the top of each apple and place the apples in a large baking pan.

Add both sugars to the bowl with the pecans and stir to combine well. Cut the vanilla bean into 6 segments and place 1 segment in the center of each apple. Spoon a liberal amount of the sugared pecans into the center of each apple, but do not pack. Sprinkle the remaining pecan mixture over top of the apples.

Heat the bourbon in a small pan until it is almost boiling. Remove from the heat and, being careful to protect your hands and face, ignite with a match. Allow the flame to die out.

Scatter the lemon zest around the apples and pour the bourbon into the pan. Cover with aluminum foil and bake, checking occasionally and adding water if necessary to keep the bottom of the pan moist, until the apples are almost done, about 45 minutes. Remove the foil, increase the heat to 450 degrees and bake until a sharp knife can be inserted easily into the apples, 10 to 15 minutes more.

Remove from the oven and place the apples on 6 dessert plates. With a slotted spoon, remove the lemon zest. Stir the butter into the hot reduced bourbon in the pan until a sauce forms. Spoon the sauce and any bits of nuts remaining in the pan over the apples and serve.

6 servings

apricot-almond clafoutis

A clafoutis batter is closely related to a pancake batter. You can substitute cherries or any other fruit (halved or cut up, as appropriate) for the apricots. Letting the batter stand relaxes any gluten strands that develop during the brief mixing, so the texture of the clafoutis will be delicate.

- ¼ cup sugar, plus more for sprinkling
- 3 large eggs
- ¾ cup heavy (whipping) cream
- ¾ cup milk
- ½ teaspoon almond extract
- ½ cup all-purpose flour
- 8 apricots, cut in half and pitted
- ⅓ cup slivered almonds

Preheat the oven to 400 degrees. Heavily butter a 9-inch pie plate and sprinkle with sugar.

Combine the ¼ cup sugar, eggs, cream, milk and almond extract in a blender or a food processor and blend until smooth. Sift the flour over the mixture and pulse just to mix. Let the batter stand for 10 minutes.

Arrange the apricots cut side down in the prepared pie plate. Pour the batter over the apricots. Sprinkle the top with the almonds and 1 to 2 tablespoons sugar.

Bake until puffed and brown, about 45 minutes. Serve immediately.

6 to 8 servings

berry ice cream

This mix of milk, half-and-half and cream yields a total fat percentage of about 18 percent, the right amount for a texture that is rich but not so fatty that it coats the palate. The generous half cup of sugar is just enough to sweeten the ice cream lightly. The berries need to be sugared beforehand to draw off some of their liquid. Otherwise, they'll turn into ice cubes when you freeze the ice cream.

1½ cups whole raspberries or blackberries or
    quartered strawberries, or a combination

½ cup plus 3 tablespoons sugar

1 cup milk

1 cup half-and-half

2 cups heavy (whipping) cream

Dash of salt

In a medium bowl, combine ½ cup of the berries and 2 tablespoons of the sugar. Mash well. Add the remaining 1 cup berries and stir. Let the mixture stand for at least 30 minutes.

In a separate bowl, combine the milk, half-and-half, cream, the remaining ½ cup plus 1 tablespoon sugar and the salt. Stir well to dissolve the sugar.

Freeze the mixture according to the instructions provided with your ice-cream maker. When it is almost frozen, drain the berries and stir into the ice cream.

Pack into a glass or metal dish, cover tightly and harden in the freezer for at least 1 hour before serving.

1 quart (8 servings)

stone fruit ice cream

Peach ice cream should be really peachy. I've doubled the usual proportion of peaches here. Sugar the fruit beforehand to prevent it from freezing into rock-hard slices.

2½ cups sliced, peeled peaches, plums
or nectarines, or a combination
½ cup plus 1 tablespoon sugar
1 cup heavy (whipping) cream
½ cup milk
½ cup half-and-half
¼ teaspoon almond extract
Dash of salt

Combine the fruit and ¼ cup of the sugar in a bowl and toss well to mix. Let stand for at least 1 hour at room temperature.

In a separate bowl, combine the remaining ¼ cup plus 1 tablespoon sugar, the cream, milk, half-and-half, almond extract and salt.

Freeze the mixture according to the instructions provided with your ice-cream maker. When it is almost frozen, drain the sugared fruit, stir it into the mixture and finish freezing. Pack into a glass or metal dish and harden in the freezer for at least 1 hour before serving.

1 quart (8 servings)

white peach and fig ice cream

Papain, an enzyme in ripe figs, will curdle milk (it's sometimes used in cheese making). For that reason, this ice cream must be eaten within a day of being made. As delicious as it is, that shouldn't be a problem.

----

2 white peaches

4 fresh figs, preferably Kadota (light green)

1 cup plus 1 tablespoon sugar

1 tablespoon amaretto or
    other almond-flavored liqueur

2 cups heavy (whipping) cream

1 cup milk

1 cup half-and-half

   Dash of salt

Peel, halve and pit the peaches. Cut the flesh into 1/4-to-1/2-inch cubes, taking care not to bruise it, and place in a mixing bowl. Remove the stems from the figs and coarsely chop them. Add to the bowl with the peaches and gently stir in 1/2 cup plus 1 tablespoon of the sugar and the amaretto. Cover tightly with plastic wrap and chill for at least 1 hour and up to 4 hours.

In a separate mixing bowl, combine the cream, milk, half-and-half, the remaining 1/2 cup sugar and the salt. Stir to combine well.

Freeze the cream mixture according to the instructions provided with your ice-cream maker until it is almost solid, then add the fruit mixture and finish freezing. Pack the ice cream into a glass or metal dish, cover tightly and freeze for 1 hour before serving.

1 quart (8 servings)

+ **You don't need** a lot of special equipment to make jam, but cleanliness is all-important. You will need a big pot with a liner, such as one used to cook pasta, and a heavy saucepan or skillet. A special wide-mouthed funnel for transferring the jam to the jar is handy.

+ **You can reuse jam jars,** but you'll need to buy new lids each time. Jars, lids, ladle, funnel and any other equipment should be boiled for 2 to 3 minutes to sterilize them.

+ **Do not use old fruit** for jam making. As fruit ages, its pectins break down. The best fruit for jam and jellies is slightly underripe.

+ **For most jams and jellies,** use slightly less sugar by weight than the amount of prepared fruit.

+ **Cook jams and jellies** in small batches so you can heat the mixture to a uniform temperature without scorching it on the bottom.

+ **There are many ways** to tell when a jelly has set. None of them seem to work for everyone all the time. Here are the two that seem to be best: First, scoop up some of the liquid part of the jelly in a metal spoon; when it has properly set, the mixture will drip off the spoon at different points rather than in one smooth stream. The other method is to spoon a small amount of jelly onto a chilled saucer. If it sits upright rather than immediately spreading out, it is set.

+ **Fill the sterilized jars** to within 1/4 inch of the top, place the sterilized lids on top and then tighten the bands. Arrange the jars in the liner of the pot and submerge in boiling water for 10 minutes. Remove the jars from the water and set them aside. As they cool, you'll hear a pinging sound — that's the lids sealing tight.

+ **When the jars are completely cool,** press the center of each lid; there should be no springiness. If there is, repeat the canning procedure or store the jars in the refrigerator.

strawberry preserves

The best way to tell when a mixture has reached the jellying point is by feel: the syrup will thicken into a jam. This recipe is a variation on one by Sylvia Thompson, author of *The Kitchen Garden Cookbook*.

- - - - - - - - - - - - - - - -

2 pounds strawberries,
    washed and hulled

2½ cups sugar

¼ cup fresh lemon juice
    (or a combination of
    lemon and orange juices)

Set aside half the berries, choosing the largest and firmest ones. Place the remaining berries in a large bowl, add 1¼ cups of the sugar and the juice and crush with a fork. Add the remaining sugar and stir well, then add the reserved whole berries.

Place the berries in a wide heavy pot over high heat. Cook, stirring, until the mixture comes to a full rolling boil. Skim off the foam, transfer to a mixing bowl and set aside, uncovered, for at least 6 hours or overnight to let the syrup penetrate the fruit.

The next day, ladle 1½ cups of the berry mixture into a heavy saucepan or skillet. Bring to a boil over high heat and cook, stirring, until the mixture jells, as described on page 118. Ladle into sterilized jars. Repeat with the remaining fruit and process as described on page 118.

4 (½-pint) jars

nectarine and rose geranium jam

This, if I do say so myself, is a great jam. The sprigs of leaf add just a hint of flowery rose flavor to the nectarines.

- -

  2 pounds sliced nectarines

1¾ cups sugar

  ½ teaspoon fresh lemon juice

  3 sprigs (unsprayed) rose geranium

Bring the nectarines and sugar to a boil in a large skillet, stirring constantly. Cook over medium-high heat until the juices are translucent and the fruit is softened. Add the lemon juice and stir well. Pour into a large, shallow dish, skim off the foam and set aside, uncovered, for at least 6 hours or overnight to let the syrup penetrate the fruit.

The next day, ladle 1½ cups of the fruit mixture into a heavy saucepan or skillet. Bring to a boil over high heat, stirring, until the mixture jells as described on page 118. Place a sprig of rose geranium in the bottom of each sterilized jar. Ladle into the jars and repeat with the remaining fruit. Process as described on page 118.

3 (½-pint) jars

meyer lemon marmalade

Meyer lemons are a particularly fragrant, sweet variety that are found in backyards and farmers' markets on the West Coast. If you can't find them, use regular lemons but substitute grapefruit or tangerines for half of the weight of lemons.

1¼   pounds Meyer lemons
       (4 or 5 lemons)
      About 3 cups water
      About 3⅓ cups sugar

Slice the lemons thin and discard the ends and seeds. Place the lemon slices in a large bowl and cover with water. Let stand overnight.

Measure the lemons and the soaking water into a large nonreactive pot. Add ⅔ cup sugar for every 1 cup of lemons-and-water. Bring to a boil and cook, stirring, until the sugar dissolves. Remove from the heat.

Ladle 1½ cups of the lemon mixture into a heavy saucepan or skillet. Bring to a boil over high heat and cook, stirring, until the mixture jells, as described on page 118. Ladle into sterilized jars and repeat with the remaining fruit. Process as described on page 118.

3 (½-pint) jars

miracle in a shell

It's sometimes fun to speculate about how the world would be different given a slightly altered set of ingredients. For example, if onions were scarce and truffles were plentiful, is there any doubt which would be selling for hundreds of dollars a pound? And what about the egg? How many lab-coated food scientists would have to labor for how long before they could invent something so versatile and so useful? If the way most foods work is fascinating, the egg is nothing short of a miracle. Eggs can be used as a protein glue to bind ingredients together, as in batters for frying. They can be used as emulsifiers, performing the seemingly impossible feat of holding water and oil in a permanent solution. And they can be used as thickeners, turning water into sauce.

Essentially, there are three parts to the egg: the shell, the white and the yolk. The shell is made of calcium. It is rigid and resistant to water yet porous to air. Leave a whole egg next to something with a strong odor (say, onions or truffles), and after it has been cooked, you will find it has absorbed some of those flavors (bad in the case of onions, good in the case of truffles). The white is almost pure protein suspended in water—in fact, nearly 90 percent of the egg white is water. The yolk is more complicated, but it is roughly half water, mixed with protein and fat (35 percent fat). These differences are anything but minor, as we will discuss more fully later on.

For right now, let's take something a little more basic. It is a demonstration of the egg's complexity that even the processes that seem the simplest are fraught with mystery. Take a hard-boiled egg, for instance. On the surface, what could be simpler: you cover the egg with water and boil it. Ah, but how long? Connoisseurs of hard-boiled eggs (admittedly, less than legion) check the surface of the yolk after shelling to see whether it has been properly cooked. In an overcooked hard-boiled egg, the yolk will have turned a gray-green color. That's caused by a chemical reaction between the traces of iron in the yolk and the traces of sulfur in the white. The longer they're heated together, the greener the yolk will get.

But, you ask, since the egg is encased in a shell, how do you know when it has cooked enough? That's the $64,000 question. In fact, you can't know. But what you can do is use science and a touch of ingenuity. Cover the egg with cold water and bring it to a boil. Immediately turn off the heat and leave the egg until the water has cooled enough to retrieve it. What you're doing is using a temperature curve. Picture a graph of the temperature of the water. It will be a bell curve — first it heats up, then it cools down. By cooking the egg this way, you're minimizing the time it spends at the extreme temperature that produces the iron/sulfur reaction while maximizing the amount of time it spends at the temperature that will firm the proteins in the white and yolk (above 160 degrees).

There's an added benefit as well. You know how when you add an egg to boiling water, the shell cracks? It won't happen if you heat the eggs this way. All eggs contain an air pocket. When the air is heated quickly, as happens when you thoughtlessly dump an egg into boiling water, the air expands rapidly because of the heat and fractures the shell. But remember that an eggshell is a miraculous thing. It's hard yet porous. Heat the egg slowly and that air pocket will slowly leak out through the shell, relieving the pressure without cracking.

Amazing? That's kid stuff. Let's talk about how eggs work in sauces. If you've ever tried to make mayonnaise by hand, you don't need to be told that eggs are a miracle. You start with egg yolks, vinegar and oil, and after some concentrated whipping, you wind up with a creamy white sauce that bears little or no resemblance to any of its ingredients. That's the ideal, anyway. If you don't know what you're doing, you're more likely to wind up with a mess. That's because mayonnaise is based on an emulsion, and there is little in cooking that is trickier or more temperamental. By definition, an emulsion is a paradox — a smooth combination of two usually antagonistic substances (kind of like a friendly, functioning Congress). Oil and water is the most common emulsion in cooking, and you don't get more antagonistic than that. In science, when two things refuse to combine, they are said to be immiscible. This description does not mean that it is impossible to combine them, but it's very difficult. And once they are combined, they will try to separate again.

For two immiscible ingredients to be able to get along, something has to happen. That something can be either chemical or physical. For example, you can make a simple emulsion just with a thorough shaking. That's how you might make a vinaigrette — oil plus water (well, vinegar, which is roughly 98 percent water). Combine oil and vinegar in a glass jar, seal the lid tight and then shake for all you're worth. If you watch carefully while you're shaking, you'll notice that the oil, which begins as one single cohesive mass, gradually breaks up into smaller and smaller drops. Pretty soon, the drops are barely visible to the eye. Indeed, if you shake long and hard enough, you will no longer be able to see them at all. The only way you'll know they're there is that the mixture no longer resembles either vinegar or oil but instead is a rather creamy combination. One of the side effects of these tiny little oil droplets being coated with vinegar is that light no longer readily passes through the mixture. That's what makes it creamy-looking.

This vinaigrette is a very basic emulsion, and it probably won't last much longer than the time it takes you to pour it over lettuce. Emulsions that are formed by this kind of mechanical action are very unstable. A vinaigrette prepared in a blender will be creamier and longer-lasting, thanks both to the extremely fine droplets formed by the ferocious mixing and to the air that has been beaten into the mixture. But it, too, will eventually break down. Even though you've stopped shaking or blending the dressing, momentum will keep the droplets of oil moving. And as they move, they inevitably bump into each other, and when they bump into each other, they stick together. Sooner or later, the dressing will return to its original state — like a junior high prom after a fast dance, the boys on one side and the girls on the other. Still, this kind of physically induced emulsion is more common and more durable than you might realize. For example, milk and cream are both emulsions, and so is butter. Homogenization is nothing more than breaking the fat in the milk into very fine particles that are dispersed in the water part. If you let unhomogenized milk sit for a while, the fat will collect at the top of the jar. Similarly, once the fat in butter melts, the water quickly separates out. The churning process emulsified it. Gently pour off the clear fat, leaving the milky solids behind, and you have clarified butter — an incomparably luxurious frying fat.

To get back to our salad dressing, though, you may have noticed that if you add certain other ingredients to the oil and vinegar, the mixture comes together more easily and also lasts longer. These ingredients are called emulsifiers. Probably the simplest one — culinarily at least — is prepared mustard. Add a tablespoon of mustard to that vinaigrette, and you'll notice a couple of things. First, the dressing will come out creamier and smoother than a simple vinaigrette. Second, it will last longer. Rather than having those droplets of oil simply dispersed in the water and gradually coming back together, the mustard surrounds the oil droplets with a very thin film. The dispersed oil drops may collide, but their mustard jackets keep them from hooking back up so readily. Rather than emulsifiers bringing differing things together, which would seem to be the obvious thing they do, they are actually separators, keeping similar things apart.

Probably the most useful emulsifier culinarily is the egg yolk. It is also one of the most interesting. Most substances on this planet can be characterized as being either attracted to water (hydrophilic) or repelled by it (hydrophobic). Things that are attracted to water are repelled by oil and vice versa. But there is also a strange third class of substances that are attracted to both oil and water. With these emulsifiers, one end of the molecule actually likes water, while the other end hates it. So when you beat together oil, water and one of these emulsifiers, something very interesting happens: you get an emulsion that will be very difficult to separate. Not only does the emulsifier coat the droplets, it locks them into a kind of network. In the case of egg yolks, the primary emulsifier is lecithin, which is one of the fats in the yolk. There are also other emulsifying fats (including cholesterol) — and some minor constituents as well.

While the discussion of just how an egg yolk emulsifies is fascinating to scientists, the only important thing to cooks is that it does. Of that, there is no question — though it may hardly seem that way when you try it yourself. In fact, we know quite a bit about egg yolks and emulsions, and while that knowledge may never make the process of whipping up a mayonnaise easy, it can help you along. For example, we know that it is important to start with all the ingredients at room temperature — this lessens the surface tension of the yolks and the oil and makes it easier to mix the ingredients together thoroughly. Oddly, egg yolks that have been frozen and defrosted are actually better for making mayonnaise than fresh — in the freezing and defrosting, they lose some water. Measure all the ingredients and set them aside. The ideal proportion of oil to yolk is between 65 and 75 percent. That works out to roughly ¾ to 1 cup oil per egg yolk. Use less oil than that, and you'll have a very stable emulsion, but it will flow more like a liquid than a sauce. Use too much more than that, and you will have a very thick sauce, but it will be highly unstable — look at it wrong, and it will separate back into oil and yolk. There's too little emulsifier to hold that amount of oil (though in a laboratory setting, it is possible to make mayonnaise that is 93 percent oil). On the other hand, a greater proportion of egg yolks does not necessarily mean a mayonnaise that is either easier to form or more stable. You need only enough to form a thin layer around each droplet of oil. Beyond that, there is no gain. Make sure you are working with the right size bowl too. If you try to make mayonnaise in too big a bowl, the egg yolk will be spread too thin to begin the emulsion.

Before you begin adding the oil, beat the egg yolks, a little bit of the vinegar and any dry ingredients (such as prepared mustard) to a smooth, heavy paste. Then begin adding the oil in a very thin stream. The stability of the mayonnaise is affected by the size of the droplets of oil that are added to it. Wait until you've already formed an emulsion before adding most of the vinegar and any other flavorings. If you add too much vinegar before you add the oil, the oil will be suspended in bigger droplets. The mayonnaise may come together a little more easily, but it won't be as stable. It's better to start out with finer droplets. Salt and seasonings increase the stability of the mayonnaise, and for reasons both culinary and chemical, you're better off dissolving the salt in the vinegar before adding it (it disperses better throughout the mayonnaise that way, and it also increases the stability).

To make mayonnaise most easily, cheat. Start with a little bit of prepared mayonnaise, and the emulsion will form like a snap. For a little closer to "scratch" method, use a blender or food processor. As long as the oil is added slowly, the violent beating of these machines is almost guaranteed to turn out a mayonnaise that is thick and stable and, even better, is accomplished without the necessity of slowly adding oil with one hand while whisking madly with the other. This was one of the big original selling points of the food processor — the feed-tube plunger has that tiny hole in the bottom to allow oil to be added in a very thin thread.

Once you've mastered mayonnaise, you're ready for something more complicated. Hot emulsified sauces such as hollandaise are made just like cold emulsifications except that both the egg yolks and the fat (butter, usually) are heated before being combined. This is no small change. While mayonnaise is based on the egg yolk's ability to emulsify, warm sauces use that plus another twist, one scientists call denaturing. Egg yolks are high in protein. These proteins come in little balls of tightly wound strands. Beating the egg yolks as you do in mayonnaise partially relaxes these strands, but when you heat them while you're beating them, they really unfold. When all of these little strings of protein are fully extended, they begin to bump into each other and link up. When they link up, they form a kind of soft network that is roughly similar to what the starch linkages form in a white sauce. The network traps the moisture and the fat, while the emulsifying properties of the yolk help to hold everything in place.

Hollandaise is among the most feared of all sauces. That's because there is a very narrow range of temperature between a successful sauce and a complete flop. To get the egg proteins to the point that they have completely unfolded, they must be heated to a temperature of 160 to 165 degrees. But cook them much further — only to 180 degrees, in fact — and those linkages become too pronounced. That's a polite way of saying the eggs have curdled into clumps and you've got scrambled eggs.

But, though it sounds difficult, once you understand the temperatures, hollandaise isn't really all that hard. To make it, beat the egg yolks to break them up. Beat in the vinegar and then warm everything in a heavy saucepan over medium-low heat, whisking constantly. (Some recipes recommend doing this in a double boiler, but that can actually increase the chances of curdling—because the heat is so low, it will take the yolks a long time to thicken, and inattention is almost inevitable.) Gradually you will see the yolks thicken and change color to a kind of creamy yellow as they incorporate more and more air. When the yolks have thickened to the point that you can just catch a glimpse of the bottom of the pan after a whisk stroke, they are at the right temperature. (The Italian dessert sauce zabaglione is made by heating and beating yolks, sugar and wine to just beyond this point, when the yolks are a little more puffed and a little lighter in color.) When the yolks have reached the right temperature, it's time to start adding butter. Professionals use melted butter, adding it a drop at a time at first and then gradually escalating to a thin stream (some chefs also prefer clarified butter, which they say produces a thicker sauce). But for beginners, it's easiest to start by adding the butter cold, in teaspoon-sized bits. This moderates the heat of the egg yolks and reduces the chances of their curdling (you can make super-creamy scrambled eggs by using the same technique—just use more eggs than butter, rather than the other way around, and deliberately overcook them). Add roughly a quarter of the butter this way, and you will have a stable emulsion. Then you can add the melted butter in a stream with some assurance that it will not break. In a hollandaise, allow between ¼ and ½ cup melted butter for every egg yolk.

As you've seen, it is but a short skip from hollandaise to scrambled eggs. And it is only a hop from there to puddings. The principles are nearly the same. The major difference is that puddings (and their cousins, sweet or savory mousses) are not stirred while they are being cooked. This allows the protein strands to hook up more tightly and results in a firmer emulsion. The most important things are the same: the eggs must be heated slowly and gently, and they cannot be allowed to overcook. In fact, you can think of custards as extremely thick egg-based sauces — as close kin to hollandaise and even mayonnaise. In the case of custards, the egg proteins are denatured by heat. As the tightly coiled strands relax, they link up. As they link up, they form a network that traps any liquid present and holds it in place.

Just any liquid won't do, though. If you try to make a custard with water instead of milk, no matter what you do to it, you'll end up with floating scrambled eggs. It's the chemical salts in the milk that allow the custard to firm up. Other ingredients influence what kind of custard you wind up with too. By themselves, egg proteins cook at between 140 and 160 degrees. (Because they contain different proteins, whites are cooked firm at lower temperatures than yolks, a fact easily demonstrated by sunny-side-up eggs.) Adding sugar to the custard raises the temperature at which the egg proteins coagulate. On the other hand, if you add an acid to the custard — lemon juice, for example — that temperature is lowered.

How you reach the appropriate cooking temperature makes a big difference. Slow heating allows egg proteins to relax slowly and completely. If they are cooked too quickly or if the temperature of the egg proteins gets above 180 degrees, they link up so tightly that they gather in clumps — what we call curdling. For this reason, baked custards are usually cooked in water baths — the temperature of the water (at the most, 212 degrees) is much more moderate than an oven temperature would ever be. The difference made by temperature can be quite astonishing. At 185 degrees, egg proteins coagulate 600 times faster than they do at just 10 degrees cooler. At the same time, cooking the custard at a lower temperature for a longer time makes it easier to avoid curdling. Another factor that affects the temperature at which the custard sets is the amount of egg present. The higher the percentage of protein, the lower the temperature at which the custard firms. Because of the danger of curdling, custards are usually removed from the oven before the centers are completely set; the heat retained in the cooking dish and in the custard itself is sufficient to finish the job.

How the custard is treated while it is cooking makes a difference too. Custards that are baked set more firmly than custards that are stirred and cooked on the stove. Stirring disrupts the formation of the protein network, making a much softer, even flowing texture. In general, custards are baked; custard sauces are stirred.

Sometimes starches such as flour or cornstarch are added to custards to give a firmer, more stable set. This is most commonly done in puddings and pie fillings. The starch is usually cooked with the liquid (cream or milk or a combination of the two) to soften it completely, and then that combination is beaten into the egg yolks—a bit at a time to discourage curdling. The whole is then finished, either on the stove or in the oven. It is essential that the custard be cooked thoroughly when this is done. The egg yolk contains an enzyme that can dissolve some of the starch, weakening the custard and making it runny; eggs must be cooked to at least 185 degrees to kill the enzyme. For that reason, custards fortified with starch usually contain more sugar as well, to raise the temperature at which the eggs curdle. After all, sometimes even miracles need a little help.

+ **The simplest emulsion sauce** is a vinaigrette. Combine ¼ cup olive oil and a bit more than a tablespoon of lemon juice in a jar. Add a bit of salt and maybe some minced garlic. Put a lid on the jar and shake it as hard as you can.

+ **If you want your vinaigrette** to last longer, add some prepared mustard before you shake it. The mustard will help prevent the oil and lemon juice from separating.

+ **To make a permanent emulsion,** work in an egg yolk. This is called mayonnaise.

+ **When making mayonnaise,** be sure all of the ingredients are at room temperature.

+ **Any oil will work** in a mayonnaise, but be aware that its flavor will be very noticeable. If using one with a strong flavor, such as olive oil, it's best to mix it with some plain vegetable oil.

+ **A 2-egg mayonnaise** is about the smallest batch that is practical to make by hand. That will take about 1¼ to 1½ cups oil and 2 to 3 tablespoons of either vinegar or lemon juice. You can also add mustard and salt to taste.

+ **If you're making a mayonnaise** that will be eaten soon, you can make the process easier by adding as much as half of the acid to the beaten egg yolks before you begin adding the oil, then add the remainder when the sauce is finished. This will form an emulsion more easily, but it won't last as long.

+ **Adding a bit** of prepared mustard to the egg yolks for mayonnaise will help the emulsion form more easily.

+ **To make beating the oil** into a mayonnaise easier, form a damp tea towel into a ring or collar and rest the mixing bowl in the center. That way, the bowl will remain steady while you're whisking with one hand and adding oil with the other.

✦ **If your mayonnaise separates,** make a new emulsion by beating a fresh egg yolk in a clean bowl, and then gradually add the broken mayonnaise to that.

✦ **Mayonnaise is very easy to make** with a food processor or a blender, but its texture will be fluffier than one made by hand because of all the air that is beaten into it.

✦ **Never heat mayonnaise,** or it will separate.

celery salad with walnuts and blue cheese

This dressing is a good example of a simple vinaigrette. I've experimented with different sizes of celery slices and found interesting results. The thicker the slice, the more dominant the celery is. The thinner the slice, the more it blends into the background. Serve this either as an appetizer salad or as a cheese course in a big meal.

- ¾ teaspoon minced shallots
- 1 tablespoon sherry vinegar
- ¾ cup walnuts
- 1 bunch celery, bottoms and leafy tops trimmed
- ¼ cup olive oil
- 1 cup crumbled blue cheese (about 2 ounces)
- Salt and freshly ground black pepper

Combine the shallots and vinegar in a small lidded jar and set aside.

Toast the walnuts on a baking sheet in a 350-degree oven or in a small skillet over medium heat, stirring once or twice, until fragrant. Be careful not to scorch them. Remove them from the heat and set aside.

Slice the celery on a bias, making exaggerated V-shaped pieces. Place the celery in a large serving bowl.

Add the oil to the shallots and vinegar and shake well until thoroughly mixed. (Do not add salt and pepper yet; many blue cheeses are very salty.)

Coarsely chop the walnuts and add them to the celery. Pour one-half to two-thirds of the dressing over the salad and toss to coat well. Add more dressing as needed; the salad should be moistened, but there shouldn't be any extra dressing in the bottom of the bowl. Add the cheese and toss lightly to combine. Taste and add salt, if needed, and pepper to taste. Serve at room temperature.

6 servings

green goddess salad

To my mind, this is the queen of mayonnaise-based dressings. Developed by Victor Hirtzler at San Francisco's Palace Hotel in the 1920s, it makes an elegant first course.

- 1½ cups mayonnaise
- 4 anchovy fillets
- 2 green onions, green parts only
- 1½ tablespoons chopped fresh parsley
- 2 tablespoons chopped fresh tarragon
- 2 tablespoons minced fresh chives
- 2 tablespoons tarragon vinegar
- 2 avocados
- 1 pound peeled, deveined shrimp (about 1¼ pounds in shell)
- Salt
- ¾ pound asparagus
- 1 cup water

Combine the mayonnaise, anchovies, green onions, parsley, tarragon, chives and vinegar in a food processor or a blender and process to a rough puree. Or grind with a mortar and pestle. Set aside.

Cut the avocados away from the pit in thick lengthwise wedges. Peel them and cut them into large cubes.

Cook the shrimp in boiling salted water just until firm, 3 to 4 minutes. Drain. Trim the woody bases of the asparagus. If they are bigger around than a pencil, peel the ends of the stalks. Lay the spears in a broad pan, add the 1 cup water, cover and bring rapidly to a boil. Cook over high heat, shaking the pan occasionally to turn the asparagus, until the spears are bright green and beginning to soften, about 4 minutes. Drain and cut into 2-inch sections.

Combine the avocados, shrimp and asparagus in a large bowl. Add half of the mayonnaise and toss gently to coat. Add just enough of the remaining mayonnaise to loosely bind the ingredients.

Mound lightly on 6 chilled plates and serve.

6 servings

smoked tuna salad in tomatoes

Here's another composed salad, this one for summer. Salting the inside of the tomatoes not only seasons them but draws out moisture, concentrating the flavor. If you can't find smoked tuna, substitute hot-smoked salmon — the kind that cuts into chunks rather than thin slices.

---

4 large tomatoes

Salt

1 pound thin green beans,
    stem ends trimmed

1 tablespoon extra-virgin olive oil

1 teaspoon thinly sliced fresh basil leaves

1 pound smoked tuna, in 1 or 2 thick slices
    (see above)

5 tablespoons mayonnaise

2 tablespoons capers, plus
    some juice (to taste)

1 tablespoon fresh lemon juice

3 tablespoons diced celery

Freshly ground black pepper

4 anchovy fillets

Slice off the top quarter of each tomato and, using a melon baller, remove as much of the insides as possible without breaking the skin. (Reserve the tops and insides for another use, if desired.) Salt the inside of the tomatoes lightly and turn them upside down on a platter to drain.

In a large pot of rapidly boiling salted water, cook the beans until they are bright green, 5 to 7 minutes, depending on the freshness. Drain and chill in an ice-water bath to stop the cooking and set the color. Drain again and pat dry with paper towels. Toss lightly with the oil and basil in a medium bowl; set aside.

Cut the tuna lengthwise into ¼-inch-thick strips, then crosswise into ¼-inch strips.

Combine the mayonnaise, capers and juice, lemon juice and celery in a bowl. Stir to mix well. Fold the tuna gently into the mayonnaise. Be careful not to break up the fish. Season to taste with salt and pepper.

Lightly season the insides of the tomatoes with salt and pepper. Spoon one-quarter of the tuna filling into each tomato. Place 1 anchovy fillet on top of each tomato. Put the tomatoes in the center of individual salad plates or arrange on a platter.

Lightly season the beans with salt, tossing well. (Salting them earlier would change the color.) Arrange the beans around the tomatoes and serve.

4 servings

+ **Begin to make a hot emulsion sauce,** such as hollandaise, by beating the yolks and the acid over low heat until the yolks start to foam and swell. You should be able to see the bottom of the pan between strokes.

+ **To make the sauce the easiest way,** start by adding pats of cold butter, whisking them into the eggs to temper the heat and to form the emulsion. Then, if you wish, you can finish the sauce with melted butter, adding it in a thin stream and whisking constantly. Allow about 3 tablespoons butter per egg yolk.

+ **There is no fixing** a broken hot emulsion sauce. Keep a constant eye on the temperature of the pan. If there's one thing that will kill your sauce, it's overcooking the eggs.

+ **You can hold a hot hollandaise** or other emulsion sauce for 30 to 45 minutes before serving, but you've got to be careful. Place the saucepan in a bain-marie, or water bath — a roasting pan or other large pan that is filled with hot, but not boiling, water.

+ **If a hot emulsion sauce is kept warm** for too long before being used, little pools of butter appear on the surface. What has probably happened is that too much of the liquid has evaporated from the emulsion. Beating in a couple of tablespoons of hot water should fix this.

+ **Once you've mastered** a basic hollandaise, you can vary the flavor dramatically by using an "infusion" of wine or vinegar reduced with other flavorings, such as fresh or dried herbs, for the acid portion. A béarnaise is a hollandaise flavored with tarragon.

+ **Eggs must be cooked gently.** When baking custards or similar egg-based dishes, always use a water bath. Place the custard cups in a baking pan, place the baking pan in the preheated oven and then add boiling water to come halfway up the sides of the custard cups. This moderates the temperature of the custard and keeps the eggs from cooking too quickly.

✦ **When eggs are overcooked,** they begin to squeeze out any moisture they hold. This is why you sometimes find drops of liquid on top of custards.

✦ **To make the best scrambled eggs,** heat the eggs with some of the butter over low heat. When the eggs start to thicken, beat in more cold butter. Scrambled eggs should be soft but firm — not runny, but certainly not dry.

✦ **Even fried eggs** should be cooked gently. Use medium heat rather than high to keep them from forming that tough, brown, frizzled bottom.

---

scrambled eggs with morels and asparagus

The combination of morels and asparagus is quintessentially spring-like. It's especially nice that they taste so good together. This is one of my favorite ways of combining them. Squeeze all of the excess moisture out of the morels after soaking, or they may turn the eggs an unappetizing shade of brown.

- ¾ ounce dried morels
- 1 pound asparagus
- 12 large eggs
- 4 tablespoons (½ stick) butter, cut into 3 or 4 cubes
- 1 tablespoon minced fresh chives
  Salt and freshly ground black pepper

Cover the morels with hot water and set them aside until softened, about 10 minutes.

Meanwhile, trim the woody bases from the asparagus. Cut off the tips and reserve. Slice the asparagus stalks crosswise very thin.

When the morels have softened, drain them thoroughly. Slice the caps lengthwise and squeeze out any excess moisture.

Stir together the eggs, morels and asparagus tips and slices in a large mixing bowl.

Pour the egg mixture and 1 tablespoon of the butter into a large skillet and place over medium heat. Cook, stirring continuously, until the eggs just begin to set on the bottom. Add the remaining 3 tablespoons butter, reduce the heat to medium-low and cook, stirring constantly and scraping up any set egg from the bottom of the pan, until the eggs have formed wet, shiny, fairly loose curds and you can see the pan bottom when you stir. Remove the pan from the heat, add the chives and season to taste with salt and pepper. Continue stirring until the eggs are completely set. Caution: the eggs go from too wet to too dry extremely quickly; it is important that they are firmly set but remain creamy. Serve immediately.

4 to 6 servings

MIRACLE IN A SHELL

trout mousse

Custards and mousses aren't always sweet — this one is savory — but the process is much the same. The eggs and trout form an emulsion when pureed with the half-and-half, which sets to a firm, creamy consistency when the custard is baked. This is based on a technique I learned from cooking teacher Madeleine Kamman. Serve warm or cold, as an appetizer or light lunch, along with a frisée salad.

- 1 pound boned, skinned trout fillets
- 1 large egg, separated
- 1 large egg white
- ⅓ cup half-and-half
- 8 tablespoons (1 stick) unsalted butter, at room temperature, plus more for greasing the ramekins
- 1½ teaspoons salt
- Freshly ground black pepper
- ¼ teaspoon freshly grated nutmeg
- 2 cups heavy (whipping) cream, well chilled

In a food processor, puree the fish, egg and egg white with the half-and-half until smooth. For a perfectly smooth mousse, push the puree through a fine strainer. Cover the puree tightly and refrigerate for at least 2 hours, until thoroughly chilled.

Combine the butter, salt, pepper to taste and nutmeg in the food processor and puree for 15 seconds. Gradually add the fish puree, processing to a homogeneous consistency. With the machine running, add 1½ cups of the cream through the feed tube. As soon as all the cream has been absorbed, stop the processor.

Transfer the mixture to a bowl placed in a larger bowl of ice. With a large rubber spatula, fold in the remaining ½ cup cream. Cover tightly and refrigerate for at least 1 hour or until ready to use. (The mousse can be refrigerated for as long as 24 hours.)

Preheat the oven to 325 degrees. Heavily butter 8 glass or ceramic ½-cup ramekins.

Pack the mousse into the ramekins and place in a large baking pan.

Place the baking pan on a lower oven shelf and add enough very hot water to the dish to come halfway up the sides of the ramekins. Lay a sheet of parchment paper or foil over the top and bake until a skewer inserted in the center of the mousse comes out clean and feels hot when touched to your bottom lip, 15 to 17 minutes. Let cool slightly and serve warm, or let cool to room temperature.

To serve, carefully run the blade of a thin knife around the outside of each mousse, place a plate over the top and invert with a quick, forceful thrust to unmold the mousse. Serve.

8 servings

chocolate pots de crème

When the eggs are cooked with the milk and cream in this recipe, they form a protein matrix that holds everything in place. In cooking terminology, that's known as a pudding, and this one is the most elegant chocolate pudding you can imagine. Although there are many different ways to make pots de crème, some of them incredibly complex, I found that this technique, adapted from Richard Sax's *Classic Home Desserts*, is the easiest and — most happily — gives the best results.

4 ounces bittersweet or semisweet chocolate, finely chopped

1 cup heavy (whipping) cream

1 cup milk

2 large eggs

2 large egg yolks

⅓ cup sugar

Lightly sweetened whipped cream for serving (optional)

Preheat the oven to 300 degrees.

Combine the chocolate, cream and milk in a small saucepan over low heat and bring to just below the boiling point, stirring occasionally. When steam appears at the edges of the pan, remove it from the heat and whisk until smooth.

While the chocolate mixture is heating, lightly beat the eggs, egg yolks and sugar in a medium mixing bowl. Do not let the mixture get foamy.

Whisking gently, dribble ¼ cup of the hot milk mixture into the eggs. Whisk until smooth. Gradually add the remaining hot milk, whisking constantly. Pour the mixture through a strainer into a pitcher or 1-quart measuring cup.

Divide the mixture equally among 8 (½-cup) ramekins; it should fill them only two-thirds to three-quarters full. Place the ramekins in a baking pan and place the pan on the middle rack of the oven. Fill the pan with enough very hot water to come halfway up the sides of the ramekins. Cover loosely with a sheet of foil or a baking sheet and bake until the edges of the custard are set but the center still trembles when shaken, 30 to 35 minutes. Remove the ramekins from the baking pan and set aside to cool.

Cover the ramekins tightly with plastic wrap and refrigerate until chilled. Serve, passing whipped cream, if desired.

8 servings

lemon sponge pudding

This is an old-fashioned dessert that is made in a way that's really quite odd. You mix a very liquid batter, then during baking, a kind of light cake floats to the top and a custard forms below. No matter how tempted you might be, don't try this without the water bath. Direct heat would scramble the eggs.

- 3 tablespoons all-purpose flour
- ¾ cup sugar
- ¼ teaspoon salt
- 1 cup milk
- 3 large eggs, separated
- 2 tablespoons grated lemon zest
- 6 tablespoons fresh lemon juice
- 1 tablespoon butter, melted
- 1 large egg white

Preheat the oven to 350 degrees. Butter 1 (3-cup) mold or 6 (½-cup) ramekins.

Stir together the flour, sugar and salt in a small bowl.

Stir together the milk, egg yolks, lemon zest and lemon juice in a large bowl. Add the dry ingredients to the wet ingredients and stir together to form a smooth, liquid batter. Stir in the melted butter.

In a medium bowl, beat the egg whites until stiff but not dry. Gently but thoroughly fold the egg whites into the batter.

Pour the batter into the buttered mold or ramekins. Place in a large baking pan, place in the oven and add 1 inch of hot water to the baking pan. Bake until the top is set and well browned, about 40 minutes for the mold or 20 minutes for the ramekins. Serve hot or at room temperature.

6 servings

lemon curd tart

This is the ideal winter filling for a tart. It's rich, buttery and quite tart, so you don't want to use too much — the recipe makes just enough to spread a thin layer across the bottom of the pastry. The sugar and the lemon juice allow the eggs to cook at a higher temperature than normal without forming curds. You can also serve the lemon curd with fresh hot biscuits for breakfast.

- 2 large eggs
- 2 large egg yolks
- ½ cup sugar
- ¼ teaspoon salt
- Grated zest of 1 lemon
- ½ cup fresh lemon juice
- 6 tablespoons (¾ stick) unsalted butter, chilled and cut into pieces
- Short Pastry Crust (page 296), baked and cooled

Beat the eggs, yolks, sugar and salt in a small saucepan until smooth and light-colored. Add the lemon zest, lemon juice and butter and cook over medium heat, stirring constantly, until the butter melts, about 5 minutes. Reduce the heat to medium-low and continue cooking, stirring, for about 5 minutes, until the curd is smooth and thick enough to coat the back of a spoon; there should be a definite track when you drag your finger across the spoon.

Pour the curd through a fine strainer into a chilled bowl. (You will have about 1¼ cups curd.) Cover tightly with plastic wrap, pressing it flat against the surface of the curd to prevent the formation of a skin, and refrigerate until chilled.

Spoon the lemon curd into the crust and spread it in a thin, smooth layer. Cut into wedges and serve.

6 servings

from a pebble to a pillow

It's one of the mysteries of cooking: how some of the softest, most luxurious foods we eat actually start out as tiny little seeds, hard as rocks. Whether it's the smooth richness of a white sauce made with flour and milk, the creamy miracle of risotto, the voluptuousness of cooked beans or the silken springiness of fresh pasta, no alien, freshly landed on earth and tasting these foods for the first time, would ever guess that the rough materials they come from — wheat kernels and dried beans — could easily break a tooth. This is the magic of starch: the tough little granules turn soft with the addition of a bit of water or other liquid and a lot of heat. Whether you're talking about the finest flour or the fattest dried fava bean, that's exactly what happens.

Starches, substances that are found in certain types of plants — mostly in the seeds and roots — are the plant's energy stores. The starch itself is formed in tiny granules. Whatever the source of the starch, each granule consists of concentric layers of two substances, amylose and amylopectin, that are held together by chemical bonds (this is an oversimplification, but it is close enough to illustrate the point). Amylose is soluble; it will absorb and be absorbed by water. Amylopectin is more resistant. As starch granules are heated in liquid, parts of the amylose layer

149

break off and go into solution in the liquid. The liquid then enters the gaps left behind, penetrating farther into the starch granule, swelling and softening it. As the amylose swells and softens, some of the amylopectin breaks away too, allowing the water to penetrate even farther. As the granule progressively absorbs more liquid, more amylose is freed to absorb liquid and more amylopectin breaks away. This process is called gelatinization, and it occurs every time water and starch are heated together. Though the cooking of starch embraces a staggering variety of forms, gelatinization is the core principle at work.

It's in sauce making, though, that the process is most obvious. Take something as commonplace as turkey gravy. The first step in making a flour-thickened gravy is to heat the starch with some fat, either butter or turkey drippings — scientifically, at least, it makes no difference. This step breaks up any clumps of flour and incorporates it into a smooth paste. Then the stock is slowly added. At first, you can still see the individual flour granules in the liquid. Gradually, as the sauce is heated, the granules become fuzzier. Pretty soon, you can't make them out at all. At this point, the starch is gelatinized. Yet you didn't add nearly enough flour to account for the way the liquid is thickening. With sauce making, there's a little something extra going on as well. As the starch granules absorb liquid, swell and soften, the ratio of liquid to solid is reduced. In addition, all of those amylose and amylopectin bits that are now floating loose begin to bump into each other. When they bump, they bond, forming new connections, and when this happens, they make a soft network that traps liquid inside. So not only does the starch thicken by reducing the amount of "free" liquid, it also fixes in place the liquid that is still free, forming a gel.

You can see this process happening. First, and most obviously, you'll see the liquid thicken and flow more slowly. You'll also see the color — or, more accurately, the quality of the color — change. Light shines very clearly through water and not at all through solids. As the solid disperses in the liquid, the sauce will become cloudier, to the point that you will no longer be able to see through it at all. But then, when it is finished, there will be a remarkable change—the sauce will have turned shiny and in some cases even translucent, since the starch has softened to the point that it is no longer blocking light. The color of our turkey gravy is a cloudy beige because it was thickened with flour, which, in addition to starch, contains proteins that block the light. Careful cooks always skim the dry film that appears on the surface of flour-thickened sauces; other impurities collect on top. Starches that don't contain as much protein—cornstarch, potato starch and arrowroot—are called "pure" and make almost clear sauces or gravies. They don't need skimming.

This is the rough outline of what happens during the making of a starch-based sauce. But it is with the variations that things get really interesting. Different starches thicken in different ways and at different temperatures, depending on the ratio of amylose to amylopectin, what other substances they contain and how they are cooked. Starches come from all sorts of things and cook in different ways. Generally, in cooking, we think of cornstarch and flour (wheat starch). They both come from seeds. But starches can be found in many other kinds of seeds and in many roots as well. Remember, starch is a plant's energy savings account—eventually it will be converted to sugar to be used for growth. Root starches, such as arrowroot, tapioca and potato, dissolve and thicken more quickly and thoroughly than cereal starches because they are higher in amylopectin. On the other hand, they are weaker. If you use a root starch, you will need less starch and less time to thicken your turkey gravy (root starches cook at a much lower temperature—they are fully softened well below the boiling point of water). But the gravy will never be as thick as one made from a cereal starch—flour or cornstarch. More problematically, if a root starch is overcooked, it turns stringy. Cornstarch and flour make the thickest sauces, and because they don't fully soften until just below the boiling point, they are harder to over-cook (though certainly not impossible — cornstarch in particular loses its thickening ability if boiled too long).

Whatever the kind of starch and whatever the final temperature at which it gelatinizes, the softening of the granules happens gradually. For most starches, it starts at between 135 and 150 degrees. The resultant swelling and thickening occurs shortly after, at about 160 degrees. These soft granules are delicate. When starches are overcooked, they will explode, releasing all the water they hold. Excessive stirring similarly can rupture the granules once they've softened. That is why it is important not only to monitor the temperature of the sauce once it's made but to handle it gently as well.

The basic starch-thickened sauce is remarkably flexible. According to the French classification of sauces, our turkey gravy is technically a velouté, since it is made with stock. Any stock can be used in a velouté, depending on what the dish is going to be. Or you can use milk, and then you'll have sauce béchamel, or good old American white sauce. Vary the amount of flour, and you will get different thicknesses, from light and flowing, like a cream soup, to thick and pasty, like the base for soufflés or croquettes.

Sometimes we add other things to starch-thickened sauces, and these too can have an effect. Sugar is a common addition, not for turkey gravy, certainly, but for pastry creams (used to fill cream puffs and éclairs) and fruit pies. Sugar is hydrolytic, meaning it absorbs water quite readily. If all the liquid has been absorbed by the sugar, it can't be absorbed by the starch. Sugar also delays the start of the softening of the starch granules, raises the final temperature for gelatinization and decreases the thickening strength of the starch — that's why you use a comparably high amount of flour for such a soft set in pastry cream.

Acid — such as wine, lemon juice or vinegar — weakens a starch-based sauce too, but in a different way. It breaks down the starch molecules, resulting in a thinner sauce, though this effect can be minimized by carefully controlling the temperature. Rapid heating without overcooking is the key—the less time the acid has to break down the starch before the sauce is thickened, the better.

Finally, browning a starch before adding liquid breaks it down and weakens its thickening ability. This explains why Cajun roux, which is browned to a deep coffee color before being added to gumbos, contains so much flour to so little thickening effect.

So important is the thickening ability of starch that the food industry has developed special varieties that have been refined to create properties not found in nature. Instant puddings, for example, contain special quick-thickening starches. Other packaged foods contain starches that have been treated to make them easier to dissolve and to discourage clumping. At home, of course, you don't have those specialized starches available, so how do you make the best use of the ones you do have? Careful handling is the key, from start to finish. First, it is important to make sure that the starch granules — flour, cornstarch, arrowroot or whatever — are well dispersed in the liquid before you begin heating them. This will defeat their natural tendency to clump together and form lumps. It's like one of those icebreaker games people used to play at parties: get everybody mixed together initially, and they'll stay that way all night. You can do this by combining starch and liquid in a cold-water slurry or by making a paste with a fat, such as butter or oil. Once you've added the liquid, stir frequently during the cooking to make sure the starch granules are both heated and exposed to the liquid evenly. When thickening has started, reduce both the heat and the stirring. You don't want to break the starch cells by either overcooking or bruising. And, above all, never boil a starch-thickened sauce once it is made.

All starch-thickened sauces are basically colloidal systems— like mud. When they are hot, they are what scientists call a sol —a liquid that contains solids. But remember that heat is motion. As the mixture cools, it loses energy and the solids slow down.

Gradually, the network formed by the bits of amylose and amylopectin becomes more and more solid. To a scientist, that is called a phase-shift, meaning that the sol has turned into a gel. In lay terms, it has become more solid than liquid. While this is fascinating to scientists, the practical point to cooks is that sauces which have cooled are much thicker than when they were hot. Before adjusting the consistency of a starch-thickened sauce by adding more liquid, be sure it is at the temperature at which you intend to serve it.

Though most cooks rarely use anything other than flour or cornstarch to thicken a sauce, they will use other starches to thicken the fillings for fruit pies—it's not exactly a sauce, but without some kind of starch thickener, that cherry pie filling would be cherry soup. In general, the starches used for pie fillings can be divided between cereal starches (wheat and rice flour, cornstarch) and root starches (potato, arrowroot, tapioca). Cereal starches set more firmly, meaning that the cooled pie slices more cleanly. But because of the stray bits of protein they contain, they are opaque and make the fruits' juices cloudy. Root starches give a softer set—the filling may flow when cut—but they are crystal clear, giving the fruit a jewel-like appearance. Root starches also cook at lower temperatures than cereal starches. How much starch you use will depend on the kind of fruit you use and how juicy it is. It will also depend on the amount of sugar you use for sweetening. Remember that sugar attracts water. The more you add, the more water will be drawn out from the fruit and the more starch you will need to absorb it. Furthermore, sugar raises the temperature at which the starches are completely cooked, which can give you an even softer set. Whatever starch you use, be sure the pie has a top crust with this sort of filling. Without it, the steam created by the cooking will escape, the moisture won't be absorbed evenly and you'll wind up with bits and clots of uncooked starch in the pie. Open-topped pies are usually made with raw fruit and are just painted with jam to make them look as if they've been cooked.

Fascinating, you may say, but what in the world does this have to do with rice or beans or even pasta, for that matter? They're all made primarily of starch. Of course, there's much more to it than that, but in its simplest outline, the cooking of all of these foods comes down to softening starch granules — much like the making of a turkey gravy. And while you may not immediately see the connection between dried pasta and turkey gravy, both are made from flour and water. Take a closer look at dried pasta while it's cooking. If you pull out a piece from time to time and cut it in half, you can see the gradual softening of the starch granules. As they soften, they become translucent, while the uncooked part remains hard and white. But if flour and water can be made into a sauce, how can the same combination make pasta? In a word, gluten. When flour is moistened and then subjected to mechanical action (Mom called it kneading), proteins in the flour combine to form long, stringy sheets of gluten that hold the flour and water together. While we tend to think of pastas as being made from wheat flour (because of wheat flour's high protein content, these doughs are the easiest to form), they can also be made from a wide variety of other starches — rice flour, lentil flour, even mung bean flour. Gnocchi is a type of pasta that is made from potatoes and flour — the moisture from the cooked potato kneaded with the flour develops the gluten.

In general, most pastas that we buy are made simply with starch and water — no fat. They are dried rock-hard before being sold. Fresh pastas are made with some kind of added fat, usually eggs or egg yolks. Even when dried, they retain a certain amount of flexibility because the fat prevents the gluten structures from forming hard linkages (this is the same thing that happens in a piecrust, and we'll talk more about it later). The difference is evident in the cooked noodles. Commercially made dried pastas take as long as 10 to 12 minutes to soften, while even the driest fresh pastas usually cook in much less than 5. Because the gluten is better developed, dried pastas have a firmer bite after cooking, while fresh pastas are silky. Since the starches in pasta are not tightly bound, careless cooking can be a disaster. Noodles will simply fall apart if overcooked. Cooking noodles in too little water can result in a sticky mess because of the amount of amylopectins that leach from the pasta during cooking.

Rice and, yes, beans are nothing more than very big, very complicated collections of starch granules trapped in a protein matrix and wrapped in a water-permeable cellulose skin. In fact, with rice, our old friends amylose and amylopectin are at center stage again. While the assortment of rices can be bewildering, particularly if you've started shopping for it in ethnic markets, most of them fall into two main families: long-grain rices and short- and medium-grain rices (so-called wild rices aren't rices at all; they are grasses, and they contain little starch). The difference between the two families is vital. Short- and medium-grain rices have a higher percentage of amylopectin than long-grain rices, so they tend to be sticky, while the grains of long-grain rice tend to remain separate and distinct after cooking. Short- and medium-grain rices are perfect for things like puddings, risottos and sushi. Long-grain rices are better for pilaf and its relatives. Because short-grain rices finish cooking at a lower temperature, they are very sensitive to overcooking. If you overcook them, the swelling starches will burst through the outer layer, emptying into the cooking liquid and thickening it.

In fact, some types of cooking seem to have been developed specifically to take advantage of that difference. Risotto, for example, is made from medium-grain rices, so it is bound to be somewhat sticky and creamy in the first place. But beyond that, the liquid is added in increments and the rice is stirred constantly, crushing the kernels and releasing as much amylopectin as possible into the cooking liquid, thereby thickening it and contributing to the luscious creamy texture. (Thus, as food writer Matt Kramer has pointed out, risotto is rice that comes with its own sauce.) The opposite extreme would be an authentic pilaf, where the long-grain rice is rinsed and soaked beforehand and is cooked without stirring to make sure as little starch escapes as possible. In this dish, separate and fluffy kernels are the goal.

Rice is served cold as well as hot, which can cause some problems. When starches are cooled after they've been cooked and softened, they sometimes become hard again. This is called retrogradation, and it is the same process that causes bread to go stale. Essentially, all of those starch components that were freed from their hard matrix during cooking begin to link up again. But it is a problem that is easily solved. Slowly rewarming the rice will resoften it (and, if the stale bread isn't too far gone, rewarming will freshen it too). Nor is this retrograde tendency all bad news. It can also be a big help to cooks. If you let long-grain rice cool even slightly before serving it or before stirring in other ingredients, you'll find that it stays light and separate far better than if it were mixed immediately (because the outer shell has set again and will better resist breaking). Chinese fried rice is an extreme example: the cooked rice is refrigerated overnight before being stir-fried so the kernels will remain intact and separate during the brief second cooking. The same thing is true of salads made with rice and beans — the grains remain separate because of the chilling. On the other hand, always be sure to add some of the seasoning to the rice or beans while they are still hot, which allows the dressing to penetrate farther into the center of the kernel before the starches on the outside harden.

The cooking of beans, in comparison, is straightforward. All beans have roughly similar chemical makeups and cook in much the same way. Cover them generously with water and cook them over low heat to provide a smooth, even softening of the starch granules. Despite this apparent simplicity, though, the cooking of beans is the subject of some controversy. Perhaps this is because of their unique impact on the human digestive system. The butt of many jokes, beans inevitably cause flatulence. Some people soak them in the belief that doing so will remove some of the gassy compounds. This is pointless. The compounds in beans that cause gas are complex sugars, for which the human body doesn't create digestive enzymes. Most seeds contain small amounts of these sugars, but legumes are extremely high in them. Because they pass through the stomach undigested, they create an uncomfortable surprise for the intestinal tract. It should be obvious, once you think about it, that soaking will have no effect, because these sugars are the seed's stores of energy for germination and growth. Since soaking is also the first step in germinating, it wouldn't make sense for the seed to give up these all-important sugars so easily. Moreover, these sugars are only part of the cause for beans' unfortunate side effects. Even if they were removed entirely, the fact remains that beans are extremely high in fiber — something for which the American diet is not known and something that also seems to catch our digestive tracts unaware. At the most, presoaking beans shortens their cooking time and provides for a more even softening of the starch granules (since beans are dried ingredients, part of the cooking process is simply adding the water that was lost in drying). On the other hand, soaking also removes a marginal amount of nutrients and, in the case of beans, a noticeable amount of flavor. In fact, in the cultures that best love beans, they are rarely soaked.

Perhaps because of their aftereffects, perhaps because they come from non-European sources, beans have been the subject of a seemingly endless assortment of old wives' tales (remember, tomatoes were once held to be poisonous). One common myth is that beans should never be salted before cooking because that toughens the skins. Not only is there no scientific evidence for this, but practical experience says otherwise as well. Actually, salting before cooking has no effect on cooking time or digestibility, and because the bean absorbs some of the salt during cooking, it is seasoned through, allowing you to use less salt than if it were added afterward. Furthermore, many of the same recipes that claim it's necessary to hold back on salt until the beans are soft call for cooking beans with salt pork or bacon: an obvious contradiction. In fact, commercially canned beans are usually cooked with salt and without soaking.

It is also said that cooking beans with certain herbs — epazote, fenugreek, asafetida or seaweed, depending on the culture — can help reduce gas. This, too, is false; while these additions may taste good, there is no demonstrated benefit to either cooking or digestion. Some claim that a pinch of baking soda will help beans cook more quickly. This is true, after a fashion. Because baking soda is an alkaline, it will break down the cellulose in the beans, making them softer more quickly, but it will do so unevenly; the outside will become slimy before the inside is finished cooking. Some people believe you should avoid adding acidic ingredients, such as tomatoes, until the beans are almost cooked. Again, this is true, but only when extreme amounts are involved. As with all vegetables, acid slows the softening of beans by delaying the breakdown of cellulose and starch — but it probably doesn't delay it enough to make much of a difference unless you're talking about adding a helluva lot of tomatoes. Perhaps surprisingly, the water you use is much more likely to make a difference. Starches soften much more slowly in the presence of certain chemical salts. If you live in an area where the water is very hard — meaning that it contains a lot of dissolved calcium and magnesium — you may find that beans take much longer to soften. It is the presence of these compounds in molasses that allows Boston baked beans to be cooked for an almost infinite amount of time before breaking down. (It is also the reason the molasses isn't added until the beans are thoroughly cooked.)

Probably the main predictor of how long beans will take to cook is not variety but vintage. The older beans are, the drier they will be and the longer they will take to cook. If you suspect your beans are more than a year or two old, you might do well to soak them —the time saved will be worth the bother and the loss in flavor. In general, buy beans at stores that cater to groups who eat them a lot—Latino and Indian markets, especially. Where there is a ready audience, the turnover in stock is more rapid, and you'll be assured of getting fresher dried beans.

Of the other legumes, lentils and split peas never require soaking. They are so small, they soften quickly, in as little as 30 minutes. Garbanzo beans (chickpeas), on the other hand, almost always seem to need to be soaked in order to shorten the cooking time to a matter of hours, rather than days.

Whether you've soaked them or not, always cook beans and other legumes starting with cool water so the starches will swell more gradually and thoroughly. It's also really best to cook them in the oven, rather than on top of the stove, since the heat is steadier and more easily controlled.

Though most starches come from seeds or roots, not all of them do. Potatoes and winter squashes are paradoxes, with one foot in the world of vegetables and the other in starch. When it comes to their actual cooking, however, it is the starch that again determines all. As with rice, there are many different varieties of potatoes, but they can all be divided into two easily identifiable families. Baking potatoes are usually long, with russeted, almost cork-like skin. They are high in starch, and their starch is high in amylose. When cooked—particularly with dry heat—they will turn light and fluffy. Boiling potatoes can be either long or round, but they all have thin, smooth skins. Boiling potatoes are higher in sugar and moisture and lower in starch than bakers. When they are cooked, the starch granules in baking potatoes swell and break apart, while the granules in boiling potatoes don't. The reasons for this are not well understood. One theory to explain why boiling potatoes hold together while baking potatoes fall apart is that boiling potatoes are higher in amylopectin, which forms linkages that hold the granules together. Another theory is that boiling potatoes are slightly higher in the pectin glues that stick the granules together. And a little bit of pectin can make a big difference. The difference between crisp and mealy apples, for example, comes down to a less than 2 percent difference in pectin content. Crisp apples are tightly glued, and when you bite into one, you have to fracture the cells; mealy apples are more weakly glued, and they fracture along the cell boundaries.

Whatever the reason, because of this difference in texture, baking potatoes are best used when you want a creamy result — as the starch cells soften and swell, they break apart and so are easily dispersed in the dish. Because the cells of boiling potatoes remain tightly connected even after cooking, use them when you want potatoes that hold together, as in soups or potato salads. If you use baking potatoes in a soup, they will eventually fall apart (again, this is a seeming disadvantage that sometimes can be turned to the cook's advantage, as when they are used as a thickener).

Depending on your preference, you can use either bakers or boilers for mashing. Boiling potatoes will give you a homey, lumpy mash. Baking potatoes will give you an ethereally light, creamy puree. If you're going to mash them, baking potatoes should be steamed or boiled — baking concentrates the potato's flavors in a way that can be distracting in the final dish. Actually, "boiling" is a misnomer. Because the starches in potatoes reach full gelatinization at 160 to 180 degrees, the potatoes should be cooked at a simmer rather than a rolling boil to avoid overcooking the starch granules and bursting them. Furthermore, when mashing potatoes, don't overbeat the puree. Never use a food processor or a mixer. Those starch granules are delicate, and when ruptured, they'll leak amylopectins, which will link up into a sticky, gluey mess no matter what kind of potato you use.

Baking potatoes are the ones to use for french fries. Because boiling potatoes contain more sugar, they will brown too quickly. Also, only a baking potato can give you the contrast of crisp skin and fluffy inside that is the secret to great fries. True connoisseurs of the french fry even insist that they should be made from old potatoes—the reduced moisture gives the lightest, fluffiest fry.

Sweet potatoes and hard-shelled, or winter, squashes can be used in much the same ways as potatoes. But because they are lower in starch, they will neither thicken as thoroughly (more on this to come) nor develop gluten when handled roughly.

The starchy nature of all of these ingredients also allows them to be used as thickeners, in place of, for example, butter or cream. You can make quite luxurious cream soups with a minimal amount of added fat by cooking and pureeing a baking potato or some cooked rice along with the other ingredients (silky bisque soups, in fact, are traditionally thickened with rice rather than cream). The softened starch granules will absorb some of the liquid from the soup, thickening it. Be careful when doing this, though, not to overpuree the soup. Remember that those swollen starch granules are delicate—they will bruise and lose their water-holding capability if worked too hard.

The famous dish potatoes gratin is yet another example of using the natural starches in the vegetable for thickening. In a gratin, the potatoes are cooked in milk or cream. The starch released in cooking thickens the liquid and binds the dish together. And beans can be used the same way, though their pronounced earthiness would not work with more delicately flavored dishes. When cooking beans without soaking them first, you'll notice the broth is much thicker than if they'd been soaked—that's starch that has been released by the beans during cooking. Those delicious refried beans are nothing more than cooked beans that have been mashed to release their starch. In other words, the beans have made their own sauce.

+ **Use flour for sauces** that you will cook for a long time or that you will reheat. Flour-based sauces take longer to make than other starch-based sauces — they must be thoroughly cooked to remove the raw taste from the protein — but they are more stable and can be held longer.

+ **Use cornstarch** for last-minute sauces only. It cooks very quickly, but it breaks down when heated for very long.

+ **Make sure the starch** is well dispersed before adding the liquid. With flour, this usually means cooking it with fat (roux) or thoroughly kneading it with butter (beurre manié). With cornstarch or potato starch, just mix the starch with a little cold liquid. You can dissolve flour straight into liquid, but you'll need to use a blender. Save this method of thickening for emergencies, since the raw taste is then harder to cook away.

+ **When cooking flour with fat,** do not let the flour brown; that weakens the starch in the flour, which means you'll need more flour to thicken the sauce.

+ **When adding liquid to a roux,** it is better to have the liquid cold or at room temperature. Add the liquid a bit at a time, stirring well with each addition to make sure the starch is thoroughly dispersed.

+ **Be careful when adding** anything acidic, such as vinegar, lemon juice or even wine, to a starch-based sauce. The acid will reduce the thickening power of the starch.

+ **Once a sauce has thickened,** keep the stirring to a minimum to avoid breaking it down.

+ **Hold starch-thickened sauces** over low heat; never allow them to boil.

✦ **If you are going to be holding** a starch-based sauce for very long, rub the surface with a piece of butter to create a thin layer of fat to prevent the top from drying out and forming a skin.

✦ **Since raw foods contain so much water,** make sure that all the ingredients added after a sauce has thickened have already been cooked so they don't thin it.

✦ **To make a white sauce,** remember these ratios: 3 tablespoons each of fat and flour per cup of liquid makes a thick paste that can be used for croquettes and soufflés; 2 tablespoons each of fat and flour per cup of liquid produces a more saucelike texture; 1 tablespoon each of fat and flour per cup of liquid is thin enough for a cream soup.

----

smoky cream of corn soup

This recipe shows just how good a well-made flour-thickened cream soup can be. Its silkiness is nicely offset by the chewy bits of corn.

----

6 ears corn, shucked and silk removed

2 tablespoons butter

1 cup diced ham

1 dried (not canned) chipotle chile, split and seeded

½ cup chopped green onions, white parts only, plus ¾ cup minced green onions, green parts only

2 tablespoons all-purpose flour

4 cups milk

½ teaspoon salt

Grill the corn over medium heat until the kernels soften, about 10 minutes, turning several times.

Combine the butter, ham, chile and white parts of the green onions in a medium soup pot over medium heat and cook, stirring occasionally, until the ham renders its fat and softens, about 5 minutes.

Meanwhile, slice the kernels from the ears of corn into a large bowl. Using the back of a heavy knife, scrape the "milk" and any remaining kernels from the cobs into the bowl.

Add the corn to the soup pot and cook, stirring, until the corn begins to soften, about 5 minutes. Stir in the flour. Cook, stirring, until the flour is absorbed by the vegetables. Add the milk, raise the heat to medium-high and cook, stirring, until the soup thickens slightly, about 10 minutes. Reduce the heat to low and simmer until the corn is soft and its flavor permeates the soup, about 15 minutes. Stir from time to time and skim off any "scum" that floats to the top.

Just before serving, remove the chile. Add the salt, stir, taste and adjust the seasoning. Ladle into large bowls and garnish each with 2 tablespoons of minced green onions.

6 servings

+ **The cardinal rule** of cooking any pasta is to use plenty of water. This is especially true of dried pasta, which cooks for longer and throws off more starch than fresh. If cooked in too little water, all of that free starch will stick to the noodles and glue them into a large clump.

+ **Just as with rice,** heating cooked pasta along with the sauce, even if only very briefly, will allow the flavorings to penetrate the exterior surface of the noodles.

+ **Use the right pasta shape** for the sauce. Tubular pasta will catch bits of chunky sauces; thin noodles are better for smooth sauces.

+ **Take advantage of the starch** released by dried pasta by adding a ladleful of the cooking water to the sauce to thicken it.

+ **Let pasta dough rest** between rolling it out and cutting it to let the gluten strands formed by the intensive kneading relax.

+ **When making lasagna,** put the cooked noodles into a bowl of cold water to keep them from sticking together. Just be sure to pat them dry with a towel before layering them into the baking dish.

orecchiette with prosciutto and peas

If you can't get fresh peas, you can still make this dish. But remember that frozen peas have already been blanched, so when thawed, they'll need to cook for only a few seconds.

¾ pound orecchiette or
　 medium shell pasta

1 cup shelled fresh peas or
　 thawed frozen peas

2 tablespoons butter

1 garlic clove, minced

2 ounces thinly sliced prosciutto,
　 cut into thin strips

¼ cup half-and-half

2 fresh sage leaves, cut into thin strips

3 tablespoons freshly grated
　 Parmigiano-Reggiano cheese,
　 plus more for serving

In a large pot, cook the pasta in plenty of rapidly boiling salted water until tender, about 10 minutes. If using fresh peas, add to the boiling water after the pasta has cooked for 5 minutes. If using thawed frozen peas, add at the last minute.

While the pasta is cooking, combine the butter and garlic in a sauté pan over medium-low heat and cook until the garlic turns translucent, about 3 minutes. Add the prosciutto and half-and-half and cook until the sauce thickens slightly, 2 to 3 minutes. Move the sauté pan to the top of the pasta pot to keep warm.

Drain the pasta and peas, reserving a little of the pasta water, and add them to the sauté pan with the garlic cream. Add the sage and cheese and toss well to coat. If the sauce is too thick, add some of the reserved pasta water, no more than 1 tablespoon at a time. Sprinkle with more cheese and serve.

4 servings

pasta with broccoli rabe

The great thing about this recipe — aside from the way it tastes — is its convenience. Both the broccoli rabe and the pasta are cooked in the same pot of boiling water. The sauce is made simply by heating olive oil with some flavorings. Essentially, it's a kind of hot pasta salad. Broccoli rabe (you'll also see it sold as rapini or broccoli di rape) can be found in most produce markets. It's mainly skinny stalks with a lot of leaves and little tops, and it has a forceful bitterness that stands up to virtually any seasoning.

When you add the anchovies in a dish like this, do it over low heat, stirring them so they melt into the sauce. Cooking over heat that is too high can turn them tough and bitter.

- ⅓ cup olive oil
- 4 garlic cloves, minced
- ½ teaspoon crushed red pepper
- 2 tablespoons chopped fresh parsley
- 1 tablespoon grated lemon zest
- 6 anchovy fillets, chopped
- ¾ pound broccoli rabe
- 1 pound dried corkscrew pasta
- Juice of ½ lemon, or to taste
- Salt and freshly ground black pepper

Warm the oil, garlic and crushed red pepper in a large skillet over medium-low heat until the garlic turns pale brown, about 5 minutes. Do not let the garlic scorch. Remove the skillet from the heat and let cool slightly.

Add the parsley, lemon zest and anchovies and stir until the anchovies "melt" into the oil, about 2 minutes. Set the skillet aside.

Meanwhile, cook the broccoli rabe in a large pot of rapidly boiling salted water just until tender, 2 to 3 minutes. Remove from the pot, keeping the water boiling, and chop the broccoli rabe into roughly ½-inch pieces.

Add the pasta to the boiling water and cook until tender, about 10 minutes. Drain the pasta, reserving ½ cup of the water.

Place the skillet with the flavored oil over high heat and add the broccoli rabe, pasta and reserved pasta water. Cook, stirring frequently, until the water boils away, about 3 minutes. Season to taste with the lemon juice, salt and a good grinding of pepper and serve.

6 servings

macaroni and cheese
with green onions and ham

> You can make this dish fancy by using a combination of differ-
> ent cheeses in the cheesy white sauce that binds together all of
> the ingredients. I like Fontina with a little fresh goat cheese
> and some Parmigiano-Reggiano (they're not very strong, so
> add the mustard to the white sauce). But the classic is good old
> American Cheddar.

6 tablespoons (¾ stick) butter plus
   more for greasing the pan

¼ cup all-purpose flour

3 cups milk

1 pound elbow macaroni or
   other dried short noodles

1 tablespoon Dijon mustard (optional)

   Salt and white pepper

¾ pound cheese, grated
   (see headnote above)

½ pound ham, cubed

1 bunch green onions, sliced

1½ cups fresh bread crumbs

Preheat the oven to 350 degrees. Generously butter a 2-quart
gratin dish.

To make the white sauce, melt 4 tablespoons (½ stick) of the butter
in a medium saucepan over medium-low heat. Add the flour and
whisk until smooth. Cook for 5 minutes, stirring occasionally, to
remove the raw taste of the flour. Gradually add 1 cup of the milk
and whisk until smooth. Raise the heat to medium and add the
remaining 2 cups milk, whisking occasionally to prevent lumping.
Cook until the sauce has thickened, about 10 minutes.

Meanwhile, cook the macaroni in plenty of rapidly boiling lightly
salted water until barely tender, about 8 minutes. Drain, transfer
to a large mixing bowl and toss with 1 tablespoon of the butter to
prevent sticking.

Add the mustard to the white sauce, if using, and season to taste with salt and pepper. Add the cheese and stir to mix. Add the ham and green onions and mix again. Add the white sauce to the macaroni and combine thoroughly. Turn out into the buttered gratin dish.

In a small skillet, melt the remaining 1 tablespoon butter. Add the bread crumbs and fry, stirring constantly, until lightly toasted, about 5 minutes.

Scatter the bread crumbs over the top of the macaroni. Bake until the top is browned and bubbling, about 30 minutes. Serve immediately.

6 to 8 servings

broccoli lasagna

This is a hearty old-fashioned lasagna. If you don't have time to prepare fresh pasta, you can substitute dried without too much loss of texture. You'll need to cook the noodles for 10 to 12 minutes in that case.

PASTA DOUGH

- 1½ cups all-purpose flour
- ¼ teaspoon salt
- 1 tablespoon olive oil
- 2 large eggs
- Water (optional)

TOMATO SAUCE

- 2 tablespoons olive oil
- 1 medium yellow onion, minced
- 4 garlic cloves, minced
- 1 (28-ounce) can tomatoes
- 1 teaspoon crushed red pepper
- Salt and freshly ground black pepper

FILLING

- 1 pound broccoli
- ½ pound broccoli rabe
- 1 (15-ounce) container ricotta cheese
- ½ pound fresh goat cheese
- 1 tablespoon freshly grated pecorino Romano cheese
- Salt

- 1 tablespoon minced fresh parsley

Make the pasta dough: Combine the flour, salt and oil in a food processor and pulse to combine. Add the eggs and process until the dough forms a rough ball that holds together, about 20 seconds. If necessary, with the processor running, slowly add up to 1 tablespoon water. Continue processing for 10 to 15 seconds, until the dough forms a smooth ball that rides on top of the blade. Wrap the dough tightly in plastic wrap and set aside to rest for 30 minutes.

Cut the dough in half. Cover one half with a damp tea towel. Flatten the remaining dough slightly with your hand, then dust it lightly with flour and pass it through the widest setting on a pasta machine. Fold it in half, dust with flour and roll it through again, on the same setting. Repeat until the dough becomes silky to the touch, about 7 or 8 passes.

Adjust the pasta machine to the next setting and roll the dough through it again. Repeat until the dough is as thin as possible without tearing. Cut into 6-inch lengths and set aside.

Make the tomato sauce: In a medium saucepan, heat the oil. Add the onion and garlic and cook over medium-low heat until translucent, about 10 minutes. Add the tomatoes and crushed red pepper and cook until the tomatoes fall apart when chopped with a spoon, about 5 minutes.

Puree the sauce using a food mill or food processor and transfer to a clean saucepan. Cook the sauce over medium heat until it is smooth and combined, about 10 minutes. Season to taste with salt and pepper. Set aside.

Make the filling: Separate the florets from the broccoli stalks and reserve. Peel the stalks, trim the bottom ends and cut the stalks into small cubes. Separate the leaf tips from the broccoli rabe and reserve. Cut the stems into small cubes.

Cook the cubed stems in plenty of rapidly boiling salted water until tender-crisp, 5 to 7 minutes. Remove them from the water and drain. Add the florets and leaf tips to the boiling water and cook until tender, 2 to 3 minutes. Drain. Chop the leaves and florets into rough pieces.

In a bowl, combine the stems, leaves and florets with the cheese. Mix well and add salt to taste. (Romano is salty, so be cautious.)

Preheat the oven to 350 degrees.

Cook 4 or 5 sheets of pasta at a time in a large pot of boiling salted water until they float to the surface. (Do not overcrowd the noodles, or they will stick together.) With a skimmer, transfer to a large bowl filled with cold water.

Assemble the lasagna: Spread $\frac{1}{2}$ cup of the tomato sauce in the bottom of a lightly oiled 13-x-9-inch glass baking dish. Pat a couple of sheets of pasta dry with a towel and place them over the sauce. Spread one-quarter of the filling evenly over the noodles. Repeat, alternating the noodles and the filling, until all the filling is used, and end with a layer of noodles. Compress and smooth the filling by pressing lightly on the top layer with the palms of your hands. Spread the remaining tomato sauce over top of the lasagna.

Bake the lasagne until heated through, 20 to 30 minutes. Before serving, sprinkle the parsley over top and let stand for 5 minutes to set.

6 to 8 servings

free-form lasagna of roasted asparagus

This is an unusual lasagna—in fact, because it doesn't contain a gushy filling, you might not consider it a lasagna at all. It's definitely in the new-wave Italian style. This is one dish where fresh pasta is a must.

¾ cup all-purpose flour

   Salt

2 teaspoons olive oil,
   plus extra for roasting

1 large egg

1 pound fresh asparagus

   Juice of ½ lemon

8 tablespoons (1 stick) butter, melted

¼ cup freshly grated
   Parmigiano-Reggiano cheese

Combine the flour, a pinch of salt and the oil in a food processor and pulse to combine. Add the egg and pulse until the dough forms a ball that rides around on top of the blade. Remove from the food processor and wrap in plastic wrap and set aside for at least 30 minutes.

Preheat the oven to 500 degrees.

Flatten the dough slightly with your hand, then dust it lightly with flour. Pass it through the widest setting on a pasta machine. Fold it in half, dust with flour and roll it through again, on the same setting. Repeat until the dough becomes silky to the touch, about 7 or 8 passes. Lightly flour the dough between rollings if it begins to feel sticky.

Adjust the machine to the next setting and feed the dough through it again. Repeat until you are at the narrowest setting. Cut the pasta sheets into 6-inch lengths, dust with flour and set aside until ready to use.

Snap the bottoms off the asparagus spears and discard; do not peel. Place the spears in a jelly-roll pan and lightly coat with oil. Salt to taste. Roast the asparagus until cooked through, 7 to 10 minutes, shaking the pan occasionally to keep it from sticking. Remove from the oven, squeeze the lemon juice over and set aside to keep warm. Reduce the oven temperature to 350 degrees.

Cook 4 or 5 pasta sheets at a time in a large pot of rapidly boiling salted water. (Do not overcrowd the noodles, or they will stick together.) The pasta is done when the sheets float to the surface, 1 to 2 minutes. Remove from the boiling water and drain on a tea towel if using immediately, or transfer to a large bowl of cold water. (The dish can be prepared to this point at least 1 hour and up to 4 hours ahead of time. The asparagus should be cooled and refrigerated, tightly covered; the cooked pasta sheets should be left in the bowl of water.)

Drain the pasta and pat dry. Combine the pasta in a mixing bowl with the asparagus, butter and 2 tablespoons of the cheese and toss to mix well. Divide among 4 ovenproof plates and return to the oven to heat through, about 5 minutes.

Pour any butter remaining in the mixing bowl over the pasta and dust lightly with the remaining 2 tablespoons cheese. Serve immediately.

4 servings

wild mushroom lasagna

A white sauce, rather than the usual ricotta, acts as the binder in this lasagna. This sauce is actually very traditional in Italian cooking, though not necessarily in Italian-American cooking. You'll want to use fresh pasta in this recipe to get the full benefit of its texture. Mexican cream can be found in many supermarkets and in most Latino markets. If you can't find it, substitute crème fraîche or sour cream.

----

1 ounce dried morels, soaked in
    warm water to cover until soft

5 tablespoons butter

½ medium yellow onion, minced

3 tablespoons all-purpose flour

2 cups milk

1 bay leaf

2 sprigs fresh thyme

1 (15-ounce) jar Mexican cream (see above)

Salt

2 (8-ounce) packages mushrooms,
    trimmed and quartered

4 garlic cloves, minced

2 tablespoons Cognac

Pasta Dough (page 172), rolled out as directed
    on page 173 and cut into 6-inch sheets

1 cup tomato puree

½ pound mozzarella, shredded

2 ounces Parmigiano-Reggiano cheese, grated

Remove the morels from the soaking liquid, straining and reserving the liquid, and coarsely chop. Set aside.

Melt 3 tablespoons of the butter in a medium saucepan over medium-low heat. Add the onion and cook, stirring, until the onion becomes translucent, about 5 minutes. Add the flour and cook, stirring, until the flour turns light golden, about 3 minutes. Gradually add the milk and the bay leaf and cook stirring until the sauce thickens, about 5 minutes. Add ¼ cup of the reserved soaking liquid from the morels, the thyme and all but ¼ cup of the Mexican cream. Season to taste with salt. Reduce the heat to as low as possible and keep warm, stirring occasionally to keep the cream sauce from sticking.

Meanwhile, melt the remaining 2 tablespoons butter in a large sauté pan over high heat. Add the fresh mushrooms and cook, stirring, until the mushrooms release their moisture, then reabsorb it and gradually become golden, 7 to 10 minutes. When the mushrooms begin to brown, add the garlic and cook until it is fragrant. Add the morels, then pour in the Cognac and cook until the alcohol smell is gone. Add the reserved ¼ cup Mexican cream and ½ cup of the cream sauce and season to taste with salt. Stir well and reduce the heat to low.

Preheat the oven to 325 degrees.

Cook 4 or 5 sheets of pasta at a time in a large pot of boiling salted water until the noodles float to the surface. (Do not overcrowd the noodles, or they will stick together.) With a skimmer, transfer to a large bowl filled with cold water.

Remove the thyme and bay leaf from the cream sauce and discard. Coat the bottom of a lightly oiled 13-x-9-inch lasagna pan or glass baking dish with ½ cup of the tomato puree and top with ½ cup of the cream sauce. Lightly pat 2 noodles dry and lay them over the sauce. Repeat to make a solid layer. Distribute roughly one-third of the cooked mushrooms over the noodles, then scatter one-quarter of the mozzarella and one-quarter of the Parmigiano-Reggiano over the mushrooms. Add another layer of noodles and lightly press everything evenly into place. Repeat with 2 more layers of mushrooms, cheese and noodles. Spoon the remaining tomato puree around the edges of the pan and spoon the remaining cream sauce over the center. Scatter the remaining mozzarella and Parmigiano-Reggiano over top.

Bake until lightly browned on top, about 30 minutes. Remove from the oven and let cool for 5 minutes to firm up before serving.

6 to 8 servings

pasta with potatoes

Starch on starch may sound odd, but it is traditional in some parts of Italy — and, more important, it is delicious. Be sure to allow the potatoes to develop a good crust before you stir them.

- 1 pound large boiling potatoes, peeled
- 6 tablespoons olive oil
- 2 garlic cloves, minced
- 1½ teaspoons minced fresh rosemary
  Salt and freshly ground black pepper
- 1 pound short dried pasta shapes, such as fusilli
- 3 tablespoons snipped fresh chives

Cut the potatoes into an even ½-inch dice. Blanch them in rapidly boiling lightly salted water until they are barely tender, 7 to 10 minutes. A knife should just penetrate a cube when it is poked. Remove the potatoes from the water (keeping the water at a boil), spread them on a tea towel and gently but thoroughly pat them dry.

Heat the oil in a medium skillet over medium-high heat. When the oil is very hot but not smoking, add the potato cubes in a single layer and cook, without stirring, until they are slightly crusty and lightly browned on the bottom, about 5 minutes. Reduce the heat to medium, stir gently and cook for another 5 minutes. Add the garlic and rosemary, stir gently again and cook until all sides of the potatoes are crisp and lightly browned, about 5 more minutes. Season to taste with salt and pepper.

Meanwhile, after you turn the potatoes the first time, add the pasta to the boiling water. Cook until tender, 8 to 10 minutes, depending on the variety and shape.

Drain the pasta well and add it to the skillet with the potatoes. Add the chives and stir gently to mix well. Cook for 1 more minute to combine the flavors, and serve.

6 servings

soft polenta with ragù

In some parts of the world, cornmeal is the dominant starch. While it makes an imperfect pasta, can you imagine making polenta with wheat flour? I got this no-work method for cooking polenta from Paula Wolfert, who got it from the back of a bag of polenta. The dish is so good it could be served by itself, with only a little butter and grated Parmigiano-Reggiano beaten in at the last minute. But I find polenta is a wonderful sponge to serve under juicy stews, or ragùs, like this one I came up with using spareribs. If you're feeding a crowd, add some whole sausages for the last 20 minutes of cooking. This makes a lot of sauce, so you'll probably have some left over — serve it the next day with lightly buttered boiled noodles. Don't try to multiply the polenta, though, unless you want to bake it in two pans. Simply doubled in one pan, it takes forever to cook.

RAGÙ

- 2 tablespoons olive oil
- 6 country-style pork ribs
  Salt and freshly ground black pepper
- 3 Italian sausages, removed from casings
- 2 medium yellow onions, diced
- 2 medium carrots, diced
- 1 stalk celery, diced
- 4 garlic cloves, minced
- 2 teaspoons minced fresh rosemary
- 1 cup dry red wine
- 1 (28-ounce) can crushed tomatoes
- ¼ cup tomato paste

POLENTA

- 2 quarts water
- 2 teaspoons salt
- 2 cups coarse cornmeal
- 2 tablespoons butter
- 2 tablespoons minced fresh parsley

Make the ragù: Preheat the oven to 300 degrees.

Heat the oil in a Dutch oven over medium-high heat. Season the ribs with salt and pepper to taste. When the oil is very hot, almost smoking, add the ribs to the pot and brown them quickly on all sides, about 15 minutes.

Leave the ribs in the pan and crumble the sausages over top. Reduce the heat to medium, stir and cook until the sausage is no longer raw, about 5 minutes. Add the onions, carrots and celery and cook, stirring, until they are lightly browned, about 5 minutes. Add the garlic and rosemary and cook until fragrant, 2 to 3 minutes. Pour the wine over the top, increase the heat to high and cook until the wine reduces, about 5 minutes. Add the tomatoes and tomato paste and stir to combine well.

Cover and bake until the ribs are fork-tender, about 2 hours. (The ragù can be made to this point up to 2 days in advance, covered and refrigerated.)

Increase the oven temperature to 350 degrees.

Make the polenta: Combine the water, salt, cornmeal and butter in a 3-to-4-quart ovenproof saucepan. Bake, uncovered, for 1 hour 20 minutes. Stir the polenta and bake for 10 more minutes. Remove from the oven and set aside for 5 minutes to rest.

Meanwhile, if the ragù was refrigerated, remove it from the refrigerator and reheat it on top of stove.

To serve, spoon the polenta into 6 warmed shallow pasta bowls. Place 1 rib on each and spoon the ragù over top. Garnish with the parsley and serve immediately.

6 servings

✦ **Use the right rice** for the job. Long-grain rices, such as commercial white rice, will be light and separate when cooked. Short- and medium-grain rices, such as those used for risotto and paella, will be creamy and sticky.

✦ **When using long-grain rice,** always rinse it well under running water before cooking it. This does remove a very small amount of nutrients, but it also washes away a lot of excess surface starch that can make the rice clump.

✦ **When long-grain rice is cooked,** set it aside off the heat but still covered for 5 minutes. This will allow the surface of the grains to harden, making them even more separate.

✦ **Gently fluff** cooked long-grain rice with a fork, but avoid stirring it, which can bruise the grains and release the sticky starch.

✦ **If you are going to cook** the rice again (as for fried rice), boil it in advance and refrigerate it until cold so it will remain firm and separate after the second cooking.

✦ **To keep rice salads** from being sticky and starchy, cook the rice as you would dried pasta—in plenty of rapidly boiling salted water. When you drain it, any free starch will wash off with the water, rather than stick to the rice.

✦ **Dress rice salads** while they are still warm so that the rice will absorb some of the flavorings before the outer starch shells of the grains harden. Bring refrigerated rice salads to room temperature before serving to return some of the tenderness lost during chilling.

✦ **For risottos and pilafs,** sauté the rice in fat, with any flavorings, until the grains turn opalescent or pearly on the outside before adding liquid. This will set the exterior shell of the grains and help to keep them separate.

+ **For risottos,** add the liquid a little at a time, stirring constantly. This technique releases as much starch as possible into the liquid, resulting in creamy rice.

+ **When making risotto,** use a fairly weak broth in order to avoid covering up the flavor of the rice and the featured ingredient. Or, to emphasize the main flavor, strengthen the broth with peelings and trimmings from the featured ingredient.

+ **Finish risottos** by beating in some butter or grated cheese. Do so vigorously in order to release as much starch as possible and produce the creamiest risotto.

artichoke risotto

You can use this risotto technique with a wide variety of vegetables, from fennel to bitter greens. Storing the trimmed artichokes in acidulated water (water with lemon juice) keeps oxygen from darkening the cut surfaces. For risotto, use a light-flavored stock so the flavor of the rice and the main ingredient will predominate.

Juice of 1 lemon
4 medium artichokes
1 quart chicken stock
2 tablespoons olive oil
2 garlic cloves, minced
1½ cups Arborio rice
¼ cup freshly grated
    Parmigiano-Reggiano cheese
Salt and freshly ground
    black pepper

Fill a large bowl with cold water and add the lemon juice.

Trim the artichokes by pulling off any leaves clinging to the stem and the two outer rows of leaves around the base. Holding 1 artichoke in one hand and a sharp paring knife in the other, keeping the knife parallel to the stem, turn the artichoke against the knife, trimming away the outer leaves until only the pale green to yellow base remains. Lay the artichoke on its side and cut away the tops of the remaining leaves, roughly where the leaves swell out. With the paring knife, peel off the dark green skin of the artichoke heart from the base toward the stem, exposing the light green flesh underneath. Set the artichoke heart upside down on the work surface and cut it into quarters. Trim away the hairy chokes. Cut off the stems and cut them into ¼-inch pieces. Cut each artichoke quarter into 4 or 5 pieces. Add the artichoke, including the stems, to the lemon water and repeat the procedure with the remaining artichokes.

Bring the stock to a boil and maintain at a simmer.

Drain the artichokes thoroughly. Combine the oil, artichokes and garlic in a broad, deep, heavy nonreactive skillet (a classic sauté pan is best). Place the pan over medium heat and cook until the garlic is translucent. Do not let the garlic brown. Add the rice and stir with a wooden spoon until the outside of the grains becomes translucent and shiny and you hear a dry "singing" sound when you stir the rice against the side of the pan.

Add 1 cup of the simmering stock to the pan (there will be much bubbling and hissing) and cook, stirring constantly, until the rice is almost dry. You shouldn't see any liquid in the bottom of the pan when you stir. Add another cup of stock and repeat the procedure. Continue to add the stock and cook until the rice swells and softens. The risotto should be very creamy but just short of soupy, and the individual grains should be cooked through but still have a distinct bite at the center (the centers of the grains should not be chalky, though).

Remove the risotto from the heat and add the cheese. Stir briskly and forcefully to release more starch from the rice and increase the creaminess. Season to taste with salt and pepper and serve.

6 servings

zucchini and porcini risotto

This is based on a risotto I had at the superb Italian restaurant Dal Pescatore, midway between Cremona and Mantova, in Canneto sul'Oglio. Although that kind of three-star cooking is beyond home cooks, this is a nice late-summer/early-fall dinner dish that is good enough for us mortals. Using water instead of broth for some risottos is one trick I learned from the restaurant. Water lets the flavor of the other ingredients shine through. You will have to add a little extra salt to make up for what would be normally absorbed from the broth.

½ pound zucchini

2 ounces dried porcini mushrooms (about ¼ cup)

2 quarts water

¼ pound plum tomatoes

1 stalk celery, minced

1 garlic clove, peeled

1 tablespoon chopped fresh parsley

4 tablespoons (½ stick) butter

3 cups Vialone Nano or Arborio rice

1 cup dry white wine

2 tablespoons minced fresh chives

1 teaspoon torn fresh mint leaves

Salt

Trim off the ends of the zucchini and place it in a bowl of lightly salted cold water to cover. Soak for 30 minutes to firm.

Combine the mushrooms and just enough hot water to cover in a small bowl. Soak until the mushrooms soften (place another small bowl on top to weight the mushrooms until they've absorbed enough water to sink on their own), about 20 minutes.

Bring the 2 quarts of water to a boil in a large pot. Cut a shallow X in the bottom of each tomato and add them to the boiling water. Cook for 30 seconds, remove and rinse under cold water. (Keep the water near a boil.) Peel the tomatoes, cut them in half and squeeze out the seeds. Coarsely chop and set aside.

Shred the zucchini on a grater or in a food processor. Drain the mushrooms and squeeze dry, reserving the soaking water for making soup, if desired (don't add it to the risotto, or the mushroom flavor will be too strong). Finely chop the mushrooms and set aside.

Combine the celery, garlic, parsley and 2 tablespoons of the butter in a large skillet and cook over medium heat until the celery softens, about 5 minutes. Add the rice and cook, stirring with a wooden spoon, until the outside of the grains becomes translucent and shiny and the rice "sings" dryly when stirred across the bottom of the pan, about 3 minutes. Add the wine and cook, stirring, until it evaporates.

Add 1 cup of the simmering water to the skillet and cook, stirring, until it has been absorbed. Add 2 more cups of water, 1 cup at a time, in the same manner; then add the zucchini. Add 1 more cup of water and cook, stirring, until it has been absorbed. Add the mushrooms and tomatoes, and begin to add the water only ½ cup at a time, cooking and stirring, until the rice is creamy and slightly chewy but not at all chalky. The total amount of water added will be about 5 cups.

Remove the pan from the heat, add the remaining 2 tablespoons butter, the chives and mint and stir vigorously for 1 minute. Season to taste with salt—about 1 teaspoon—and serve immediately.

6 main-dish or 8 appetizer servings

seafood rice salad

Rice salads are a great way to use up bits and pieces of leftover ingredients. The important things are to cook the rice in lots of water, like pasta, so that it isn't starchy and sticky and to dress the rice while it is still warm.

- 2 cups long-grain white rice, rinsed well

    Juice of 2 lemons, plus more to taste, if needed

- 1½ teaspoons salt
- 1 teaspoon crushed red pepper
- ½ cup olive oil
- ½ pound small shrimp, peeled
- ½ pound cleaned calamari (squid),
    bodies sliced into rings, tentacles halved
- 1 pound mussels, scrubbed and debearded,
    or clams, scrubbed
- ¼ cup dry white wine
- ¼ pound sliced soppressata or other
    spicy salami, cut into thin strips
- 1 red onion, diced small

    Minced fresh herbs, such as basil,
    mint and parsley (optional)

Cook the rice in a large pot of rapidly boiling lightly salted water until it is tender, about 15 minutes. Do not overcook or undercook it: the rice should be soft all the way through but should not be beginning to "explode" at the ends. Drain, place in a large mixing bowl, cover with a towel and set aside for 5 minutes.

Add half of the lemon juice, the salt, crushed red pepper and oil to the rice and stir gently to mix well. Do not stir too rapidly, or you will crush the rice and it will become sticky. Cover and chill for 1 to 2 hours.

Cook the shrimp and calamari separately in rapidly boiling water just until firm (1 to 2 minutes for small shrimp; 30 to 45 seconds for calamari). Drain. Place in a small bowl, toss with half of the remaining lemon juice and chill for 30 minutes.

When you are almost ready to serve, combine the mussels or clams, the wine and the remaining lemon juice in a large saucepan and bring to a boil over high heat. Cover tightly and cook just until the mussels or clams open, about 5 minutes. Discard any that do not open.

Remove the rice from the refrigerator and strain the warm mussel cooking juice over the top. Add the shrimp and calamari, the salami and onion and gently toss to mix well. Adjust the seasonings to taste. The salad should be pleasantly tart with just a hint of olive oil flavor. If you like, add some minced herbs, but don't go overboard. Place the mussels or clams, in their shells, in the rice and serve.

8 to 10 servings

✦ **You don't need to soak** dried beans before cooking them. Soaking them will speed their cooking time, but it will diminish their flavor.

- -

✦ **Salt dried beans** when you start to cook them, to season them through. Allow about 1 teaspoon of salt per pound of beans. After cooking, you can add more salt if you want.

- -

✦ **Always begin cooking** beans, lentils and other legumes in cold water.

- -

✦ **Mineral salts** will slow the softening of dried beans. If you have repeated problems with legumes that don't soften, have your tap water checked.

- -

✦ **If you want** your beans to be separate and light — like rice — cook them in lots of water.

- -

✦ **Beans are done** when they are tender through — there should be no chalky center. Another way to test is by picking up a bean on a spoon and then blowing on it. If the skin wrinkles, the underlying starch has been cooked thoroughly.

- -

✦ **When serving** beans or lentils cold, as in a salad, follow the same guidelines as for rice: season them while they are still warm so that the flavors can penetrate, and allow the refrigerated beans to come to room temperature before serving.

- -

white bean crostini

Canned white beans are nobody's idea of a luxury ingredient, yet here their bland starchiness pairs perfectly with the final drizzle of white truffle oil. White truffle oil is one of those ingredients that should be used with a light hand. A hint of it will lend an aura of truffles without the expense. Too much, and it smells like hair tonic. You can find it in gourmet stores.

1 (18-inch) baguette

¾ cup canned white beans, rinsed and drained

½ cup walnut halves

2 tablespoons butter, at room temperature

Salt

2 tablespoons white truffle oil

Preheat the broiler. Slice the baguette into ½-inch-thick slices and toast on both sides under the broiler until golden brown, 7 to 10 minutes.

Puree the beans, walnuts and butter in a food processor. Taste and add salt as needed (some beans are saltier than others).

Just before serving, with the food processor running, add the oil in a thin stream. Spread a dollop of the puree on each piece of toast and serve immediately.

36 crostini, 8 to 10 servings

pinto bean puree

The starch from the smashed beans thickens into a thick, heavenly puree. Many foods are more complicated; few are as delicious. Cotija is a dry, crumbly cheese that can be found in many supermarkets and any Mexican market. If you can't find it, substitute Monterey Jack. It's important to use dried chipotle chiles for this recipe, not the canned ones that come in an adobo sauce. If you can't find them, substitute anchos or leave them out altogether. Epazote can be found in Mexican markets. Serve this as a side dish with grilled meats.

- 1 pound dried pinto beans, picked over and rinsed

  Salt

- 3 dried chipotle morita chiles or 2 dried chipotle meco chiles

- 2 medium yellow onions, chopped

- 2 garlic cloves

- 1 large sprig fresh epazote (optional)

- 5 cups water

- 2 tablespoons bacon fat

  Freshly ground black pepper

- 2 medium tomatoes, chopped, for garnish

- ¼ cup chopped red onion, for garnish

- ½ cup crumbled cotija cheese or shredded Monterey Jack cheese, for garnish

Preheat the oven to 350 degrees.

Combine the beans, 1 teaspoon salt, chiles, onions, garlic, epazote (if using) and water in a large Dutch oven. Bring to a simmer over medium-high heat. Cover the pot tightly and place in the oven. Cook until the beans are soft, 1½ to 2 hours. Check after about 45 minutes to make sure there is enough water, and add more if needed. The beans should not be soupy, but they should not dry out either. (The beans can be made to this point 2 to 3 days in advance; cover and refrigerate.)

Melt the bacon fat in a large skillet over medium-high heat. Ladle the beans and their liquid into the skillet, removing the chiles. Cook, stirring, until the beans begin to bubble, about 2 minutes. Continue cooking, smashing half of the beans with the back of the spoon, until the mixture thickens, about 5 minutes. Remove from the heat and season with additional salt, if needed, and pepper.

Divide among 6 bowls, garnish with the tomatoes, red onion and cheese and serve.

6 servings

white bean and swiss chard stew

This is one of those dishes that came together on a harried Sunday when home projects overlapped with friends coming to dinner. Every ingredient had been in my house at least a week, including the chard, which was left uncooked from the weekend before. The final blessing of olive oil is what makes the dish. Do not neglect it — and the fruitier and more peppery the oil, the better.

1 pound dried Great Northern beans,
   picked over and rinsed

Salt

2 tablespoons olive oil

2 strips bacon, cut into 1-inch squares

1 medium carrot, chopped

2 garlic cloves, minced

1 bunch Swiss chard

2 sprigs fresh thyme

Fruity olive oil for serving

Coarse salt

Preheat the oven to 300 degrees.

Combine the beans and 1 teaspoon salt in a large Dutch oven. Add enough water to cover the beans amply and bring to a boil over medium heat.

Cover the pot and place in the oven. Cook until the beans are just soft, about 1½ hours. From time to time, check the beans and add more water if necessary. (Older and drier beans will take much more water than fresh ones.)

When the beans are almost done, heat the oil in a large stew pot. Add the bacon and cook until it is lightly browned, about 5 minutes. Add the carrot and cook until soft, another 5 minutes. Add the garlic and cook until fragrant, about 2 minutes.

While the bacon mixture is cooking, cut up the chard. Separate the leaves from the stems and cut the stems into 1-inch pieces. Cut the leaves into thin strips.

Add the chard stems and thyme to the bacon mixture, then add the beans, plus enough water to make a light stew consistency. Cook, covered, over medium heat until the stems have softened, about 20 minutes, stirring from time to time. Stir in the chard leaves and cook just until soft, about 5 minutes.

Serve with the coarse salt and a good olive oil on the side.

6 servings

pinto bean and squash stew

Pinto beans, chiles and squash combine for a flavor that is earthy, spicy and sweet, just the thing for a fall or winter dinner.

- -

1 pound dried pinto beans,
   picked over and rinsed

1½ quarts water

Salt

¼ medium yellow onion, chopped

2 garlic cloves, minced

1 ¼-inch-thick slice salt pork

Freshly ground black pepper

4 slices bacon, diced

1 jalapeño chile, seeded and minced

2 green onions, minced

1 butternut squash, peeled, seeded
   and cut into 1-inch cubes

1 cup beef stock

½ red onion, finely diced, for garnish

¼ cup chopped fresh cilantro, for garnish

¾ cup sour cream, for garnish

Preheat the oven to 300 degrees.

Combine the beans, water, 1 teaspoon salt, the onion, garlic and salt pork in a large Dutch oven. Bring to a boil on top of the stove, then cover and bake until the beans are cooked, 1½ to 2 hours. Season to taste with salt, if necessary, and pepper. Check the water level to make sure the beans don't dry out.

About 45 minutes before the beans are cooked, cook the bacon with the jalapeño and green onions in a large sauté pan over low heat until the bacon is crisp.

Add the squash and stock, cover and cook until the squash is just tender, about 30 minutes.

Add the squash mixture to the beans and mix gently but well. Do not smash the beans or squash. Spoon the bean-and-squash stew into 6 serving bowls, garnish each with the red onion, cilantro and 2 tablespoons of the sour cream and serve.

6 servings

pork and beans . . . and endive

I find that the bitter green edge of endive (the curly kind, not Belgian) cuts through the richness of this dish nicely. Save the pale green inner leaves for a salad, dressed with a mustardy vinaigrette. Those who disdain the idea of matching food and wine should serve this dish with any red wine and then try it with a decent Chianti. The latter is an absolutely superb match.

2	tablespoons olive oil
1	pound Italian sausage
1½	pounds country-style pork ribs
	Salt and freshly ground black pepper
2	medium carrots, chopped
2	medium yellow onions, chopped
3	garlic cloves, sliced
1	pound dried white beans, picked over and rinsed
5	cups water
2	cups chopped curly endive (tough green leaves only)

Preheat the oven to 300 degrees.

Heat the oil in a large Dutch oven over medium-high heat. Cut the sausages in half. Sprinkle the ribs with salt and pepper to taste. Brown the sausages and the ribs in the hot oil, transferring them to a plate when they are done.

Pour off all but 2 tablespoons of the fat from the pot and add the carrots, onions and garlic. Reduce the heat to medium, cover and cook, stirring occasionally and scraping the bottom of the pot to free all the brown bits, until the vegetables soften, about 15 minutes.

Add the beans to the pot and stir to mix with the vegetables. Add the water and 2 teaspoons salt and return the meat to the pot. Place a sheet of aluminum foil over, but not touching, the surface of the meat so it is loosely covered, cover and bake until the beans are soft, 1½ to

2 hours. After the first hour, begin checking the beans every 20 minutes, stirring and adding more water if necessary. The dish should have a stew-like consistency when the beans are done.

Remove the pot from the oven and add the endive. Stir well to mix, cover and set aside until the endive has wilted, 5 to 10 minutes. Serve hot.

8 to 10 servings

braised duck and lentils

Lentils have the earthy flavor of dried beans, but they cook much more quickly. I find they are helped mightily by a shot of vinegar just before serving.

4 medium carrots

2 medium yellow onions

2 stalks celery

2 garlic cloves

1 (750-milliliter) bottle dry red wine

¼ cup red wine vinegar

2 whole cloves

¼ teaspoon black peppercorns

6 duck legs (about 3 pounds)

3 slices prosciutto

2 shallots

4 plum tomatoes

2 tablespoons butter

1 tablespoon oil

   Salt and freshly ground black pepper

1 pound lentils, picked over and rinsed

¼ cup minced fresh parsley

Chop 2 of the carrots, 1 onion, 1 stalk celery and the garlic.

In a medium saucepan, combine the wine, 2 tablespoons of the vinegar, the chopped carrots, chopped onion, chopped celery, garlic, cloves and peppercorns and bring to a boil over medium heat. Remove from the heat and let cool slightly.

Place the duck legs in a single layer in a large baking dish and pour the wine mixture over them. Cover tightly and marinate, refrigerated, for at least 8 hours, or overnight.

When you are ready to cook the duck legs, preheat the oven to 300 degrees.

Chop the remaining carrots, onion and celery. Mince the prosciutto and the shallots. Peel, seed and chop the tomatoes.

Melt 1 tablespoon of the butter in a heavy Dutch oven over medium-low heat with the prosciutto. When the prosciutto starts to sizzle, add the carrots, onion, celery, shallots and tomatoes and cook, covered, until the vegetables begin to soften, 10 to 15 minutes.

While the vegetables are cooking, combine the remaining 1 tablespoon butter and the oil in a large skillet over high heat. Remove the duck legs from the marinade, reserving the marinade, and pat dry with paper towels. Sprinkle the duck legs lightly with salt and pepper on both sides. When the fat is very hot, add the duck legs skin side down and brown well just on the skin side, 3 to 5 minutes. Remove the duck legs from the pan and set skin side up on top of the vegetables in the Dutch oven.

Pour off the fat from the skillet and return to high heat. Strain the marinade into the skillet and scrape the bottom to loosen any browned bits sticking to the pan. Pour the marinade over the duck legs and vegetables. Place a sheet of aluminum foil over, but not touching, the surface of the meat so it is loosely covered.

Cover the pot and bake until the duck legs are fork-tender, about 1½ hours. Remove the duck legs from the pot and set them aside, covered.

Skim off as much fat as possible from the vegetables. Add the lentils to the pot, cover, return to the oven and cook until the lentils are soft, about 40 minutes, adding ½ cup water if necessary to keep the lentils moist but not soupy.

When the lentils are soft, add the remaining 2 tablespoons vinegar and the duck legs to the pot, cover and cook just until heated through, 10 to 15 minutes. Sprinkle with the parsley and serve.

6 servings

sausages and ribs with red wine–braised lentils

This dish would be almost as good made with beans, but lentils have two advantages: they're faster and their flavor is brilliant with the tart sauce. Why does combining pork in different forms add up to so much more than the sum of the parts? I'm not sure, but I do know that the marriage of pork sausage and pork ribs here is absolutely heavenly.

- 2 tablespoons oil, plus more if needed
- 1 pound Italian sausage, cut into 2-inch sections
- 1½–2 pounds meaty country-style pork ribs
- 2 medium carrots, coarsely chopped
- 2 medium yellow onions, coarsely chopped
- 4 garlic cloves, minced
- 2 cups dry red wine
- 1 cup prepared tomato sauce or tomato puree
- 1 pound lentils, picked over and rinsed
- 1 bay leaf
- 2 tablespoons red wine vinegar

Preheat the oven to 350 degrees.

Heat the oil in a heavy Dutch oven over medium-high heat. When it is very hot, add the sausages and lightly brown them on all sides. Remove the sausages from the pot and set aside on a plate. Add more oil if necessary, add the ribs and turn to brown them on all sides. Transfer the ribs to the plate with the sausages and cover to keep warm.

Reduce the heat to medium, add the carrots and cook until they begin to brown, about 5 minutes. Add the onions and garlic and cook until the onions are tender. Turn the heat to high, add the wine and cook, stirring, until it is reduced to a syrup.

Add the tomato sauce or puree and the lentils and stir well, then add the bay leaf and enough water to barely cover the lentils (about 1 cup). Place the sausages and ribs on top of the lentils and bring to a boil.

Loosely cover the meat with a sheet of aluminum foil, cover with a lid and place in the oven. Cook until the lentils soften and most of the liquid has evaporated, about 1 hour 15 minutes.

Uncover the pot, add the vinegar and stir well to distribute the meat. Return to the oven for another 10 to 15 minutes, until most of the liquid has evaporated and any taste of raw vinegar is gone. Remove the bay leaf and serve.

8 to 10 servings

+ **Use potatoes,** winter squash and sweet potatoes as thickeners: to thicken soups, as binders for gratins and in fresh pastas, such as gnocchi.

+ **Baking potatoes have** much more starch than boiling potatoes. Use them when you want to thicken something or want a smooth puree. Use boiling potatoes when you want potatoes that will hold their shape.

+ **Be careful when pureeing** potatoes, or they'll develop a sticky, gluey texture. Always mash potatoes by hand or with a hand mixer.

+ **When using potatoes as a thickener,** make sure there is plenty of liquid to disperse the starch. It takes only about ¼ pound of cooked potato to thicken 2 cups of liquid. Be careful not to overwork the dish when using potato as a thickener. Its starch granules are very delicate and over-pureeing them can weaken their thickening ability.

+ **To make the lightest** mashed potatoes and gnocchi, get rid of as much excess moisture as possible. Puree the potatoes while they are still hot (a food mill or potato ricer is best) and spread them out to let them cool so the steam will evaporate. Reheat the puree if making mashed potatoes.

+ **Because squash** contains less starch than potatoes do, you can puree it in a food processor without developing its gluten.

+ **To vary the flavor** of a starchy vegetable that you will be pureeing, change the way you cook it. Boil it for a mild flavor. Steam it for a more intense flavor. Or roast it for the most intense flavor of all.

cream of cauliflower soup

Cauliflower has a bit of starch, but it's the addition of a baking potato that thickens this soup, with just a minimal amount of sour cream. Be generous with the salt; because of the amount of starch from the potato, which tends to flatten flavors, it will take more than you might think.

----

1 large leek

4 tablespoons (½ stick) butter

1 shallot, minced

2 cups dry white wine

1 (1½-pound) cauliflower, trimmed
and separated into small florets

1 (¾-pound) baking potato, peeled
and cut into small dice

4 cups water

2 cups chicken stock

1½ tablespoons Dijon mustard,
plus more to taste

¼ cup sour cream

2 teaspoons salt, plus more to taste

Freshly grated nutmeg

Trim the root end and tough green leaves from the leek. Quarter it lengthwise, leaving it attached at the root end. Wash well under running water, pulling the leaves apart to rinse away all the grime. Slice the leek thin.

Combine the leek and butter in a 4-to-6-quart soup pot, cover and cook over medium heat, stirring occasionally to keep the leek from sticking, for 10 minutes. Add the shallot and continue cooking, covered, stirring occasionally, until the leek is very soft, about 10 more minutes.

Increase the heat to medium-high and add the wine. Cook, stirring, until the wine has reduced by about half. Add the cauliflower and potato and mix well. Add the water and stock, cover and bring to a boil. Remove the lid, reduce the heat to a simmer and cook gently until the potato and cauliflower are very tender, about 30 minutes. You should be able to smash the cauliflower with a spoon.

Transfer half of the soup to a blender and add half of the mustard, sour cream and salt. Pulse to grind, then increase the speed to puree. Transfer the puree to a medium saucepan and repeat with the remaining cauliflower mixture, mustard, sour cream and salt.

Bring the soup back just to a simmer (don't boil, or the sour cream will curdle) and season to taste with additional salt and mustard. Ladle into bowls and sprinkle nutmeg over top.

8 servings

squash soup with moroccan spices

To get the squash pulp you need for this soup, cut a 2-to-3-pound winter squash in half and scoop out the seeds and veins. Then roast the two halves at 450 degrees, cut side down, in a baking pan with just enough liquid to cover the bottom. It'll take about 45 minutes to an hour to get good and soft. Once the squash has cooked and cooled, scoop out the pulp with a spoon.

- 1 cinnamon stick, broken in half
- ½ teaspoon coriander seeds
- ¼ teaspoon cumin seeds
- 4 whole cloves
- 2 cardamom pods
- ¼ teaspoon crushed red pepper
- 2 tablespoons butter
- 4 garlic cloves, minced
- 1 tablespoon minced ginger
- 4 cups roasted squash pulp (see above)
- 2½ cups water
- Salt
- ¾ cup plus 2 tablespoons yogurt
- Freshly grated nutmeg or New Mexican red chile powder

Toast the cinnamon, coriander, cumin, cloves, cardamom and red pepper in a small dry skillet over medium heat until fragrant and just beginning to darken, 3 to 5 minutes; stir to keep the spices from scorching. Cool, then grind the spices to a powder in a coffee grinder or mini-blender.

Combine the butter, garlic and ginger in a large soup pot and cook over medium heat, stirring, until the garlic is soft and translucent, about 3 minutes. Add the spice mixture and stir to combine well. Add the squash pulp and water, stir to combine well and cook over medium heat until heated through, 10 to 15 minutes.

Puree the soup in batches in a blender. Add salt to taste and stir in
½ cup of the yogurt.

Divide the soup equally among 6 soup bowls. Garnish each bowl
with 1 tablespoon yogurt and the nutmeg or chile powder.
Serve immediately.

6 servings

potato gratin

This gratin, which came from an idea of Richard Olney's, is a little different from most. The potatoes are shredded rather than sliced before cooking, which does two things: speeds up the process, because the potatoes are in smaller pieces, and frees more starch to create a firmer set.

- -

2   pounds boiling potatoes, peeled
3   cups milk
    Freshly grated nutmeg
    Salt
1   garlic clove
1   large egg
1½ cups freshly grated Gruyère or
    Parmigiano-Reggiano cheese
4   tablespoons (½ stick) butter

Shred the potatoes using the largest blade on a food processor, or grate them on the coarse holes of a grater, being careful to keep the strips as long as possible. As the potatoes are grated, place them in a bowl of cold water.

Drain the potatoes and pat dry with a kitchen towel. Combine the potatoes and milk in a large saucepan and place over medium heat. Add a grating of nutmeg and salt to taste, bring to a gentle simmer and cook until the potatoes are just tender, 10 to 15 minutes, depending on the thickness of the cut. Stir occasionally, being very careful not to break the potato strands and not to let the mixture boil or scorch. Drain the potatoes in a colander or a strainer placed over a large bowl to catch the milk.

Preheat the oven to 400 degrees.

Cut the garlic clove in half and rub the inside of a large gratin dish with the cut sides. Set the dish aside.

Beat the egg and half of the cheese and stir it into the hot milk. Season to taste with salt.

Butter the gratin dish generously and arrange the cooked potatoes in a uniformly thick layer in the dish. Pour the milk mixture over the potatoes. Sprinkle the remaining cheese over the top. Cut the remaining butter into thin slices and dot over the top.

Bake until the top is bubbling and browned, about 20 minutes. Serve immediately.

6 servings

potato gnocchi

Potatoes are starch, so why not make pasta with them? There aren't any special tricks to making gnocchi; you just need the right touch when you're kneading the potatoes and the flour. You want to add enough flour for the dough to hold together but not so much that it becomes heavy.

1½ pounds baking potatoes,
      unpeeled
1–1¼ cups all-purpose flour
4 tablespoons (½ stick) butter
2 sprigs fresh rosemary
½ cup freshly grated
      Parmigiano-Reggiano cheese

Steam the potatoes until a knife slips easily into the center, 40 to 45 minutes. While the potatoes are still quite hot, scrape off their peels, holding them in a tea towel and scraping with the back of a paring knife. Using a potato ricer, rice the potatoes onto a sheet of plastic wrap. Let cool completely.

Dump the riced potatoes onto a work surface sprinkled with ¼ cup of the flour. Sprinkle ¼ to ⅓ cup more flour over the top and gather the potatoes and flour together into a rough mass. Knead gently, adding more flour as necessary, until the surface is smooth, the in terior feels elastic and any cracks on the surface have rounded edges, 5 to 10 minutes.

Cut off a piece of the dough and roll it into a rope ½ to ¾ inch in diameter. Cut the rope into ¾-inch pieces and toss them in a mixing bowl with ¼ cup more flour. Shape the gnocchi, if desired, by indenting each one with your finger and/or ridging it with the tines of a fork. Repeat with the remaining dough.

Bring a large pot of salted water to a boil. Meanwhile, melt the butter in a small saucepan with the rosemary sprigs. Continue to heat over medium-low heat until the gnocchi are ready; do not let the butter color.

When the water has come to a rapid boil, add the gnocchi and cook until they float to the top, 30 to 45 seconds. Drain and place in a serving bowl.

Remove the rosemary sprigs from the butter and drizzle the butter over the gnocchi. Toss lightly, and dust with the cheese. Serve immediately.

6 servings

butternut squash puree
with balsamic vinegar

The balsamic vinegar cuts the luxuriousness of the puree while pointing up its sweetness.

- 2 tablespoons minced shallots
- 4 tablespoons (½ stick) butter
- 3 tablespoons balsamic vinegar
- 2 cups roasted butternut squash pulp (see page 207)
- 1 teaspoon salt
- Freshly grated nutmeg

Cook the shallots in 1 tablespoon of the butter in a large saucepan over medium heat until they soften, 3 to 5 minutes. Add the vinegar, increase the heat to high and cook until the vinegar is reduced to a syrup, another 3 to 5 minutes.

Add the squash pulp and salt and stir to combine. Reduce the heat to low and cook until the squash is heated through, about 5 minutes. Cut the remaining 3 tablespoons butter into small cubes and add them to the squash, beating vigorously to make a smooth puree. Serve immediately, dusted with nutmeg.

4 servings

gratin of sweet potatoes and bourbon

Most vegetable gratins need to be bound with a white sauce. This is not true of gratins made from starchy vegetables, which will release enough starch to thicken the liquid around them. Here the sweet potatoes are baked first to concentrate their sweetness and then cooked a second time with just enough cream to mellow them out. This dish is an ideal accompaniment to roast poultry or pork.

----

3 pounds dark orange sweet potatoes

4 tablespoons (½ stick) butter,
  plus butter for the baking dish

Salt

1 cup heavy (whipping) cream

1 tablespoon bourbon

Freshly grated nutmeg

Preheat the oven to 350 degrees.

Roast the potatoes on a baking sheet in the oven until they are easily pierced with a knife, about 45 minutes. Remove them from the oven and let cool. (The potatoes can be roasted up to 2 days in advance and refrigerated.) Leave the oven on.

Butter a gratin dish or baking dish.

Peel the potatoes and cut them into ¼-inch-thick slices. Arrange the slices in a single layer, overlapping them. Season to taste with salt.

In a small saucepan over medium heat, reduce the cream by one-third. Add the bourbon and whisk well.

Pour the cream over the potatoes. Dust the potatoes very lightly with nutmeg and dot with the butter. Bake until browned and puffy, about 30 minutes. Serve hot.

6 servings

puree of winter squash and apples

There are many different varieties of winter squash, ranging in flavor from green and vegetal to sweet and nutty and in texture from stringy to smooth. I like smooth, sweet, nutty squashes for this dish, such as butternut and acorn.

- -

4 cups roasted squash pulp
   (see page 207)

4 tablespoons (½ stick) butter

Salt

1 tart green apple, such as Granny Smith,
   peeled, cored and coarsely chopped

Combine the squash pulp and butter in a food processor and puree until smooth. Season to taste with salt. Add the apple and pulse just to finely mince the apple into the puree.

Spoon into a warmed serving bowl and serve immediately.

4 servings

meat and heat

Roasting meat is one of the most elemental acts of cooking. There is nothing simpler, yet at the same time there is little that is more complex, both in terms of symbolism and chemistry. We roast meats for all our most important holidays — turkey for Thanksgiving, prime rib for Christmas, leg of lamb for Easter. Roast chicken is the hallmark of simple home cooking. On one level, nothing could be easier: Season the meat; cook it until it's done. Cavemen could do it. It's so easy we rarely give a second thought to what is actually happening during roasting. Meat is, after all, just muscle or, even more essentially, protein. Yet good cooks know that every type of meat cooks a little differently. Pork is different from beef, which is different from chicken, which is certainly different from fish. It's even more complex than that: different muscles from the same animal can be dramatically different, and even different cuts from the same muscle can vary tremendously. And, of course, roasting is only one way of cooking meat.

Let's begin at the most basic level: when we say meat, what we mean is the muscle of an animal, a bird or a fish. For the most part, just like virtually everything else we cook, muscle is made up of water — depending on the animal and muscle, about 75 percent water. Another 5 percent is various minor constituents: fat, carbohydrates and minerals. The remaining 20 percent — the *defining* 20 percent — is protein. Proteins, of which there are many different kinds, are made up of amino acids joined by chemical bonds. They come in two forms: globular and fibrous. Having read that, you can now forget it. Globular proteins are found in blood and in egg whites. When we're talking about cooking meat, we're really only interested in the fibrous form, and the chemical makeup is only of borderline interest. Besides, the two behave similarly in the kitchen anyway.

All you really need to remember about protein in meat is that it is made up of fibers; actually, bundles of fibers. Or, even more accurately, bundles of bundles of fibers. Picture a telephone cord with all those brightly colored individual wires bound up into one big one. Now picture a telephone cable, made up of bundles of cords. Only it's even more complex than that. Think of an individual protein strand as being shaped like a wire. Now coil that wire like a spring and fold that spring back onto itself into an ellipse. That is the most basic structure of protein. Now take that fiber structure and bundle it with a bunch of others just like it. Take that bundle and bundle it again with even more groups of fibers. That is a muscle. You can see this last stage in certain raw cuts of meat, like a round steak. Try pulling on it at both ends and it will come apart. That's because what we call a round steak is actually made up of several different muscles — depending on the butcher, it may include parts of the rectus femoris, the vastus intermedius, the vastus lateralis, the vastus medialis, the rectus femoris, the semitendinosus and the semimembranosus, in addition to the two big muscles, the adductor and the biceps femoris. Take one of those muscles and cook it, then cut it open. What you're seeing is the next smallest division — what looks like a forest of tightly grouped fibers. Without a microscope, you can't see the smallest division — the spring coiled into the ellipse. The only reason you can see any of them, the reason meat doesn't appear to be a smooth sheet, is because each bundle of fibers, from the smallest to the largest, is wrapped in a thin sheet of connective tissue. Just like the plastic coating that wraps both the wires in our telephone cord and the cord itself.

To begin to understand what happens when meat is heated, let's concentrate first on these protein fibers. Apply heat, and the first thing that happens is that the bonds which hold those ellipses in shape weaken and the proteins begin to relax and straighten out so they resemble those coiled springs. This process begins at about 130 degrees. As they unwind, they bump into each other — we're talking about a very limited amount of space here, after all. When they bump into each other, they link up, bonding again. This process — both the relaxing of shape (denaturing) and the simultaneous linking up (coagulation) — can be caused by a surprisingly wide variety of things besides heat. Essentially, it can be triggered by anything that disrupts the relatively fragile bonds that hold the protein in its tightly wound original shape. Physical activity can do it (much the same thing happens when you beat egg whites). Acidity will do the same thing (this is the heatless "cooking" in ceviche). Even prolonged exposure to oxygen can do it (think about how meat left out of the wrapper for too long develops a hard skin). One might almost say it's in the nature of proteins to link up. Protein strands from meat that has been chopped — even finely ground — will continue to form bonds during cooking. That's why hamburgers don't fall apart on the grill, why sausages appear to come from a single piece of meat and why a slice of meat loaf or pâté doesn't crumble into a pile of its parts. Granted, sometimes this structure is achieved with the assistance of a couple of beaten eggs, but those are just adding more potential protein linkages to the mix.

As these muscle fibers link up, they shrink and become firmer, but not all at the same time. Ever notice how a pork loin roasted in a hot oven appears to bulge when it's cooking? It's because the outside, which is heated first, has shrunk, while the inside hasn't. As the fibers shrink, they begin to squeeze out water. For a while, this isn't that noticeable, because at the same time that the water is being squeezed out, water from within the protein cells is being squeezed out too and so is replacing the other water. Somewhere between 170 and 175 degrees, the losses begin to outstrip the conversions. As the cooking continues, the fibers shrink more and more and become harder and harder. Eventually, they will crack. This is why overcooked meat has a grainy, crumbly texture.

Protein isn't the only thing that changes during cooking. The connective tissue that wraps the fibers changes too. When raw, the collagen that forms the connective tissue is tough and stringy. Though it too is a protein, it is bound into a different shape from muscle protein, and that changes its texture. But heat, specifically moist heat, breaks up those bonds and softens the collagen into a kind of gelatin. This happens between 150 and 175 degrees, but it's not quite as simple as that. There are other variables that affect the process as well. In addition to the temperature itself, the amount of time the meat is held at that temperature will affect how much of the collagen is tenderized (the longer it is held, the more collagen will be softened). So will the acidity or alkalinity of any liquid in which it's cooked (a really concentrated stock is slightly alkaline, and meat cooked in it will be more tender than meat cooked in plain water). So will the age of the animal. The connective tissue of very young animals softens at lower temperatures than that of older animals (this is one reason for the popularity of veal stews). While stews and braises — moist cooking techniques — are best for cuts of meat with lots of collagen, this softening can also happen without added liquid, thanks to the water contained in the meat itself. That's the secret behind real pit barbecues — long cooking over a low fire. This tenderizing doesn't happen with all kinds of connective tissue. The really tough, rubbery, yellowish tissue that we commonly call gristle is slightly different and is unaffected by heat. The only solution is to cut it out.

Other parts of meat change with heat too: fat, for example. Fat occurs naturally in all meats, sometimes on the outside of the muscle, sometimes on the inside. The hardest, whitest fat can be found surrounding the vital organs, especially the kidneys. The softest fat is found within the muscles, between the fibers. This is what we call marbling. When this fat melts, it lubricates the protein fibers, making them seem more tender and contributing to that texture we call "juiciness." Of particular interest to cooks, the color of the water within the meat changes too. Though the red meat juices are frequently mistaken for blood, in reality they are simply watery solutions from within the protein cells and fibers. Real blood is removed from the veins of the animal at the slaughterhouse. These watery solutions look like blood because they contain hemoglobin and myoglobin, which are also components of blood. One very interesting quality hemoglobin and myoglobin share is that they change color when heated. At room temperature, they are bright red. Between 140 and 150 degrees, they turn gray or brown. That is just about the same temperature at which the collagen will have been fully converted, and it is just below the temperature range at which meat begins to lose moisture. It is also the temperature range that we call medium-rare to medium in beef. (Hemoglobin and myoglobin also turn color when exposed to oxygen for very long. When you buy meat, it should be brightly colored, no matter what animal it's from.)

Up to this point, almost everything that has been said applies equally to every kind of meat, however it is cooked — grilled fish, boiled chicken, roast beef. But it is obvious that there are major differences among different kinds of meat, among different cuts from the same species and among methods of cooking. The most fundamental differences are among the various species. They are all protein, but there is a difference between a fish and a fowl, to say nothing of a lamb and a cow.

Though there are important differences based on flavor, which have to do with the types of chemical components that make up the meat, we'll focus first on structure. The flavor difference between beef and swordfish is easy to discern, but the way their flesh is put together — which has just as much impact on how they are prepared — might be less obvious. The meat of land-based animals is high in connective tissue — it takes a lot of muscle to overcome gravity and stand upright — but fish, which live in a nearly gravity-free environment, have very little connective tissue. That is why there are no tough pieces of fish. Although there are dishes called fish stews, they're usually cooked in less than half an hour. That's also why fish dries out very quickly when cooked — there is very little collagen to melt and baste the meat. Another reason is that fat in fish is usually located in specific areas rather than throughout the muscle (usually just under the skin). Furthermore, since a fish's movement is basically restricted to a side-to-side waving of the tail, the muscle structure is much different from that of animals, consisting of sheets of very short muscle fibers separated by a thin wrap of collagen. Even fish differ, though: compare the flaky muscle structure of a lazy bottom feeder like sole with the meaty texture of a speed bomb like tuna.

As many dismayed shoppers will attest, fish differs from meat in one other important way: the speed with which it changes after it's been caught. All meats change, of course. Chemical changes within the muscles result first in rigor mortis — a stiffening of the muscles — and then in a gradual relaxation. In beef, this process can take so long that it may be weeks before the meat becomes inedible (indeed, aged beef is usually hung for as much as a month). With fish, the process happens within a matter of days. That's why good cooks look for fish with bulging eyes and firm flesh — the muscular deterioration following rigor mortis hasn't yet advanced very far. Fish are also the most problematic meat in terms of age because they come from a bacteria-rich environment, and spoilage progresses very rapidly. Other meats also vary in their ageability—pork, for example, should always be fresh, because the chemical makeup of its fat makes it extremely prone to rancidity.

Different types of meat taste different, though perhaps not as much as you might think. In fact, while there is a marked difference in flavor between fatty and lean meat from the same species, scientists have found that the pure lean raw protein of different mammals tastes remarkably similar. Even whale meat is only a little different from beef—presumably because of the chemical remnants of the crustaceans on which whales feed (it might be interesting to feed a cow nothing but shrimp and see what happens). So where does the flavor difference come from? In most cases, it is the fat that carries the flavor, whether it is distributed on the surface of the meat or between the fibers.

That is not the only reason to praise fat. One of the best things we can say about meat is that it is "juicy." But what exactly does that mean? On the surface, juiciness would seem to refer to the amount of moisture a piece of meat contains. It's not that simple, though. In fact, there are two types of juiciness. One does in fact refer to the meat's water-holding capabilities (in the prosaic language of scientists). The second, and more important, can be described best as "perceived juiciness," and it comes not from the meat being chewed, but from you, the chewer. When your mouth fills with juices as you're eating a great piece of meat, a good percentage of the moisture comes from your own saliva. And what prompts saliva? As anyone who has sat at a table loaded with good food can attest, many things, including sight and smell. Texture plays a part too—in fact, so does almost anything that we associate with that vague concept of deliciousness—including setting. But the most important factor in inspiring salivation (and, hence, juiciness) is fat.

While the most heavily worked muscles are those with the most connective tissue, they are generally also the ones with the most intramuscular fat. The combination of the two means that cuts taken from them have wonderful flavor but are full of tough, stringy fibers (at the same time, it explains why tender filets mignons cut like butter but don't really taste like much). We've learned how to solve the toughness problem. Those flavorful, heavily worked pieces of meat are sometimes referred to as "braising cuts." Cooked for a long time over moderate heat with moisture present, all that stringy connective tissue turns moist and jellied. The fat melts through the meat, and you wind up with an intensely meaty stew. (As a general rule of thumb, cattlemen say, the lower the animal part is to the ground, the tougher it will be.) Ever wonder why so many good cooks prefer meat cooked "on the bone," as opposed to filleted? It's the same thing — connective tissue fastens the muscles to the skeleton. When meat is cut from the bone, it loses a lot of flavorful connective tissue.

This difference between worked muscles and resting muscles is true for more than just beef and other hoofed animals, though they are the most extreme examples. It also explains the white and dark meat in chicken. Chickens and turkeys can't fly well. Their breast meat is there "for show" only; it is their legs that get the workout. In the case of these birds, though, the difference doesn't show up so much in connective tissue (poultry is generally extremely high in connective tissue throughout its body — that's one reason it's usually cooked to a higher temperature than other types of meat). Rather, you can see it in the distribution of our old friend myoglobin, which serves to store oxygen from the blood. Because the legs are worked so much more than the breasts, there is far more oxygen going to them, which gives them a darker color.

More than just determining tenderness, considering all of this information will tell you how a piece of meat should be cooked best: to what temperature and by what method. Remember reading about the temperature at which connective tissue melts? That's the key to much of meat cooking. Cuts that are low in connective tissue — again, those that do less work, such as the sirloin (which comes from the muscle that runs right along the spine) — will have a pleasing texture when cooked to very low temperatures or not cooked at all. Cuts that are harder-working, such as shanks, necks and tails, must be cooked more to ensure that the stringy bits are gone.

But there is more to temperature than tenderness. As meat is heated, complex chemical reactions are set in motion. Water within the cells heats and expands, and cell walls burst, mixing amino acids and other flavor-giving substances, with the result that the taste of the meat changes. Undercooked meat is actually more delicate in flavor — blander — than meat that has been cooked longer. Meat is, after all, 75 percent water. Heat is necessary to develop the flavors that we prefer. A piece of pork tenderloin is so tender that it could, theoretically, be eaten raw. But the taste of undercooked pork has an unpleasant edge, which food scientists describe as "serumy." It isn't until pork is cooked to around 160 degrees that the round, delicious flavors that we think of as "porky" emerge. The same is true to a certain extent of lamb, though in America we have become accustomed to eating our red meats rarer than people do in many other countries (rare or even medium-rare lamb is considered an abomination in much of the Mediterranean — outside of fancy restaurants, that is). It can be a revelation for rare-lamb lovers to taste a cut — even something as tender as a rack — that has been cooked a little further than normal, say, to 140 degrees. The same cut of beef, the sirloin, should be cooked to a slightly lower temperature: between 130 and 140 degrees is the best compromise for flavor, texture and juiciness. This is certainly not to say that meat tastes better the more it is cooked. Overcooked meat is no one's idea of pleasure. First, it is tasteless — the fat has been rendered into the pan, and all the juices have been squeezed out. There is the texture thing too — all those protein strands have cracked, leaving behind crumbly, grainy meat.

How do you know when meat is done? The surest way is with a thermometer, preferably one of those instant-read ones. Meat thermometers that stay in the roast while it is cooking are notoriously unreliable. However, because of these physical changes we've been talking about, you can learn to judge doneness pretty well without a thermometer — in some cases, you can do even better. A steak, for example, is too thin to measure accurately with a thermometer. Use your fingers: press the center of the steak and see how firm it is. What you're actually doing is feeling how coagulated, or set up, the protein strands are. Here's a good comparison: let your hand hang loosely, and pinch the muscle between your thumb and forefinger. That is approximately medium-rare. Form a loose fist and do the same thing. The muscle has flexed and is slightly firmer. That's medium. Finally, tighten the fist and try it again. That's well-done. And don't forget hemoglobin. Cut a slice in the center of the steak and check the color of the meat. Remember when we were talking about how the color of the juices changes when heated? This is a gradual process; it doesn't happen all at once. Meat cooked to 120 degrees (rare) will be redder than meat cooked to 140 degrees (medium). Pay attention.

With poultry, you can also test by making a small cut — at the hip — and judging the color of the juices that run out. With chicken, we want the temperature to be up past 160 degrees to make sure all the connective tissue has softened. At that point, the juices will run clear or a little golden. You'll also know the bird is done if, when you grasp and twist the drumstick, it moves quite easily — the softened connective tissue is no longer holding it so firmly in place. Remember, though, that chicken cooks unevenly because of its shape. The breast, which is exposed on top as it roasts, cooks more quickly than the hip, which is inside and on the bottom. Because the hip is dark meat and the breast white, the problem is exaggerated. Also, be aware that because of modern poultry-raising practices, you might find chicken that is still red at the bone despite being thoroughly cooked. This is because birds are slaughtered much younger than before — so young, in fact, that their bones have not finished building up calcium. That red is blood leaking from the bone and does not mean the meat is underdone.

Fish is a little troublesome, both because it is so thin and because it cooks so quickly. The old rule used to be to cook fish until it flaked (actually, that's the point when the last of the connective tissue between the muscle strands has softened). Today's taste is for fish that's a little moister. But you can still use the knife test: prod the fish with the tip of a knife; if it is just beginning to flake, it's done.

In all cases, remember that just because you've removed something from the heat doesn't mean it has finished cooking. Depending on the size of the piece of meat and the temperature at which it was cooked, it can gain as much as another 10 degrees because of the heat stored in the outer parts of the meat. Bigger pieces gain more because they retain more heat. Pieces that have cooked at higher temperatures will also gain more, because there is more heat retained. This is often called the "push," or carry-over cooking, and most of it takes place within 10 minutes or so of the meat being removed from direct heat. That final burst of cooking is one reason that it is a good idea to let meat sit, loosely blanketed in aluminum foil, for a little while before carving. There is another reason too. During the cooking process, the tightening of the protein drives some of the juices from the outer edges of the meat deep into the interior. A 10-minute rest is enough time for those juices to be redistributed evenly throughout the meat.

Obviously, the temperature at which you cook meat has a great effect on the finished dish. Cooks argue the relative merits of high-heat and low-heat roasting, but don't be fooled: there is no single correct answer. It depends on the kind of meat, its size and what you want it to taste like. Remember that it takes time for heat to transfer from the air to the meat and then from the outside of the meat to the interior. Cooking at a high temperature will give a very wide range of donenesses. The outside of the meat will be thoroughly browned while the inside may still be quite rare. The same cut of meat cooked at a low temperature might not be as well browned on the outside, but the interior will be more cooked. A good example is prime rib. It will come out very different when cooked at 450 degrees than when cooked at 300 degrees. At 450 degrees, the exterior will be browned and crusty while the interior will be rare, perhaps even barely firmed. Cook the same piece at 300 degrees, and by the time the exterior browns, the interior will be closer to medium. Which is better? You're the cook; you decide.

Remember, though, that it's the interior temperature you're thinking about. The larger the cut of meat, the longer it will take the heat to penetrate to the center, hence the lower the roasting temperature should be to avoid scorching the outside. The same is true for braising the more muscular cuts. Because of the higher desired interior temperature (to fully soften all the connective tissues), you should use a lower cooking temperature, lest the exterior part of the meat dry out before the interior is done. That's one main reason stews are cooked at a simmer (roughly 190 to 200 degrees) rather than a boil (212 degrees). There is a curious exception to this rule, however, though no one can really explain how it works. Meat can also be braised at high temperatures — 400 degrees and above. It takes a tightly sealed, very heavy pan and careful attention, and the results are markedly different from low-heat braises. Meat braised at high heat will have an almost buttery texture and will fall apart in chunks, rather than shredding the way most braises do. The reason that this happens is unclear, but the predominant theory is that the high heat deactivates the enzymes which help to turn meat crumbly when it is cooked to a high temperature.

Another part of your decision about what temperature to choose will be based on how well you like your meat browned. Browning is a key factor in the flavor of cooked meats. Although browning bears some resemblance to both burning and caramelization, it's neither. It's actually more closely related to what happens when bread bakes than to anything else (though some caramelization is occurring, and of course meat cooked for too long will definitely burn). The browning of the exterior of meat and the crust of bread are both attributed to something called the Maillard reaction, named after the nineteenth-century French scientist Louis-Camille Maillard. He found out that the brown of roasted meat and the brown of the crust of bread are both due to a chemical reaction that occurs when you heat amino acids and sugars (though it doesn't seem like it, meats do contain natural sugars). Depending on the type of protein, the type of sugars and the temperature to which they're heated, you get a wide range of smells and flavors. It's not important to remember which amino acids and which sugars result in which aromas. What is important to remember is that they occur within a specific range of temperatures and that they don't even begin to happen until around 185 to 195 degrees and don't really become noticeable until above 300 degrees. That explains why meat cooked with moisture will never brown. Because water boils at 212 degrees, the temperature of the surface of the meat won't get hot enough. If you want that deep-browned meat flavor in a stew or braise, you have to brown the meat before adding any liquid (not all stews are browned; in French cooking, there is a whole family of white stews, called blanquettes, that are appreciated for their delicate flavors). Furthermore, those temperatures also explain why you should always dry the surface of meat before you begin cooking it — it won't start browning until all the surface moisture has evaporated into steam, which could cook the surface in a way you don't want. There is even an extremist sect of roasters who insist that it is impossible to roast adequately in a modern oven because the space is so small that it creates an artificially moist environment. Real roasting, they insist, can be done only on an open spit.

How long does it take for meat to cook? It depends on several variables. The type of meat is one: chicken and pork are denser than lamb and beef and take longer. Obviously, the cooking temperature is another. Although it's not something many people think much about, the shape of the meat is important too: flat pieces cook faster than cylindrical pieces, and hollow rounds, such as an unstuffed chicken, cook faster than solid rounds, such as a stuffed chicken. The geometry gets even more confusing when you take size into consideration. The amount of time it takes for the center of a piece of meat to reach a certain temperature increases proportionately much more rapidly than the thickness of the meat. A steak that is the same shape as another one but twice as thick can take four times as long to cook to the same interior temperature. Another factor that is frequently overlooked is the beginning temperature of the meat. Meat taken directly from the refrigerator will take longer to cook to the same degree of doneness than meat that has first warmed to room temperature. For all these reasons, it is dangerous to make blanket statements about how many minutes per pound to allow. Though some home economists recommend 20 to 25 minutes per pound for a roast turkey, it takes only a little math to realize that with a 20-pound bird, you're talking about a potential time difference of more than 1½ hours.

Up until now, we've been talking about cooking meat by itself. Of course, that rarely happens in real life. Even at its simplest, meat usually comes with a seasoning, even if that seasoning is only salt and pepper (and with really good meat, that's actually quite enough). But sometimes you want to add more. That's where marinades come in. Some cooks seem to think of the art of meat cookery as mostly consisting of putting together a flavorful marinade. Garlic, vinegar, olive oil, rosemary . . . it sometimes can seem closer to aromatherapy than to cooking. And, actually, there's a lot of truth to that. The fact is, most marinades are of only limited use, no matter how much fun you may have putting them together. First of all, marinades have little, if any, effect on tenderness. While it is true that acids like wine, vinegar and lemon juice have a tenderizing effect on protein, that effect takes time. And even then, you might not like what you get. "Tenderness" is a vague word, and in this case it means softness. But as cooks, we know that's not what we want. Soak meat in an acid for long enough and the meat will become mealy—so mealy that it will almost crumble. That's not the tender we're looking for.

Providing flavor is something marinades do fairly well, but in most cases, that flavor is only skin-deep. It takes marinades a long time to penetrate much beneath the surface. That's even truer if the marinades are oil-based. Remember, meat is mostly water, and oil and water don't mix. But even if you're using a marinade without any oil at all, what you're doing is flavoring only the outer fraction of an inch of the meat. That's not necessarily a bad thing. Except for very large cuts of meat, you usually wind up eating a bit of the surface in every bite, so in effect the flavoring is working, though not nearly to the extent most people think.

The one type of marinade that really works is by far the simplest: brining. A brine is a combination of salt and water. Culinarily, the best for home use is about 7 percent salt (roughly ⅔ cup of salt per gallon of water). That's only faintly salty when you taste it, and there are no herbs, no oils, no exotic flavorings at all. Brining can have quite a positive effect on the flavor of meat—particularly poultry and pork—because of three factors. First, since it is mainly water, brine penetrates the meat fairly quickly—it contains no oils to slow it down. The salt causes the muscle fibers to swell, allowing even more water to penetrate. The salt also changes the fibers, causing them to retain more of the water during cooking. Finally, it seasons the meat, not just on the surface but all the way through. The difference is instantly visible, particularly with poultry. You know how a turkey breast usually collapses after it's removed from the oven and left to sit before carving? If you brine turkey, that won't happen. Furthermore, the breast meat, which tends to dry out no matter how you cook it, stays moist. And the turkey tastes fully seasoned, even without the addition of extra salt.

Brining is sometimes used on seafood as well. Salmon is brined before smoking, and the Chinese briefly soak shrimp in brine before stir-frying. In both cases, the brine both seasons the flesh and firms it. Beef is sometimes brined too; corned beef is brined ("corn" refers to the coarse salt used in the process), and so is pastrami.

Usually, though, a full-fledged brine is not used for beef and lamb. A simple sprinkling of salt a couple of minutes before cooking will be sufficient. Though it won't season all the way through, it will draw moisture to the surface. When that moisture is hit by intense heat, it sears the meat and forms a thin crust. It used to be said by old-time chefs that this crust "sealed in the juices," but you can easily see that this is not literally true. Sear one side of a steak, and when you turn it over, you'll still see moisture being driven through the seared side forming small drops right on top of what should have been the "seal." In another way, though, the old-timers were right: remember that juiciness consists of both moisture from the meat and moisture generated in your mouth. That seared crust is full of the delicious browned smells and flavors that are sure to start you salivating. The crust doesn't seal in the juices, but it sure can make the meat juicier.

The simplest way of all to add flavor to meat is by cooking it along with something else. To have much effect, though, this must be done in a moist environment. The flavors of the vegetables, herbs or spices that you add are absorbed by the liquid as the cells of those plants break down and spill their contents. As the meat cooks and its interior moisture is forced to the surface, nature's desire for balance takes over. To restore equilibrium in the moisture levels, the meat begins to absorb some of that flavored liquid. At the same time, the moisture from the meat spills out into the liquid, flavoring it. As a bonus, this exchange of liquids keeps the meat moister than it would be if cooked dry. Of course, there's a caveat: overcooked stewed meat will be dry; it just takes a higher temperature to become overcooked. Still, that means you can achieve more developed meat flavors than when cooked to a lower temperature. The flavors attained by stewing and braising are plainly more complex than those from any other kind of meat cookery.

+ **Because it is low in fat** and has little connective tissue, fish must be cooked carefully and usually for a fairly brief time.

+ **Choose a medium-oily fish,** such as salmon or halibut, if you are a beginning cook, since these are relatively high in fat and are more forgiving of mistakes than are lean fish. Meaty fish, such as tuna, shark and swordfish, are also a good choice for beginners, but be careful not to overcook them, or they will dry out.

+ **Never marinate fish for more** than 10 minutes in anything containing acid—it will begin to cook the flesh by itself.

+ **It's generally a good idea** to cook fish with the skin on so the fat will flavor the fish, though you should remove the skin before serving.

+ **If you're cooking a fillet,** you can watch its sides and see the color and texture change as the fish cooks. When it is a little more than halfway done, turn it over.

+ **Whole fish are best** grilled over high heat or roasted in a hot oven. Cut several slashes through the flesh, but not through to the bone, at least 2 inches apart, to allow the heat to penetrate. To keep the fish from sticking, oil it well before cooking and then don't move it until you're ready to turn it. Whole fish are done when you can pull out the dorsal fin (which runs along the back).

+ **Though the common rule** used to be to cook fish until it flakes, it's usually too done by that point. The trick is to cook the fish until just before it flakes, when you can see the muscle strands beginning to separate.

+ **Always undercook** rather than overcook fish. It will continue cooking after it has been removed from the heat.

ceviche with shrimp and avocado

In this recipe, the acidity from the lime juice "cooks" the shrimp without heat. Avocado is not traditional in ceviche, but its creaminess is a good foil for the slightly chewy shrimp. Serve this as an appetizer or a light lunch.

1½ pounds peeled small to medium shrimp (about 1¾ pounds in the shell)

Juice of 5 limes

2 tablespoons minced, seeded jalapeño chile

¼ cup minced red onion

Salt

1 cucumber, peeled, seeded and diced

2 avocados, halved, seeded, peeled and diced

1 bunch fresh cilantro leaves, chopped

Fried tortilla chips (optional)

Rinse the shrimp under cold running water and pat dry. Place them in a mixing bowl with the lime juice, 1 tablespoon of the jalapeño, 2 tablespoons of the onion and a sprinkling of salt. Toss well to coat. Spoon the mixture into a zipper-lock plastic bag, press out all the air and seal tightly. Refrigerate, turning from time to time to distribute the lime juice, until the shrimp are opaque, about 1 hour. Larger shrimp may take as long as 2 to 3 hours.

When ready to serve, toss the shrimp with the remaining 1 table-spoon jalapeño and 2 tablespoons onion, the cucumber, avocados and cilantro. Taste and adjust the salt. Serve with tortilla chips alongside, if desired.

8 to 10 servings

calamari salad

Calamari contains a tricky form of protein. Cook it very briefly, just until the flesh loses its pearly quality — any longer, and it will be tough. The alternative is to cook it for an extended period of time — 45 minutes to an hour. Serve as an appetizer or a light lunch.

- - - - - - - - - - -

1 pound cleaned calamari (squid),
   bodies cut into rings, tentacles halved

1 garlic clove, minced

1 teaspoon salt, plus more if needed

1 teaspoon crushed red pepper

½ cup fresh lemon juice, plus more if needed

1 tablespoon red wine vinegar

½ cup olive oil

½ pound celery (tender inner ribs only), sliced

⅓ cup chopped fresh parsley

Blanch the calamari very briefly in plenty of rapidly boiling water just until the color has lightened and the pieces have barely stiffened, 10 to 15 seconds. Drain immediately and plunge into an ice-water bath to stop the cooking.

In a large mixing bowl, combine the garlic, salt, crushed red pepper, lemon juice and vinegar and whisk to combine. Add the oil and whisk again to combine.

Pat the calamari pieces dry and add them to the dressing, along with the celery. Toss to mix well. Add the parsley and toss again. Season to taste with more salt and/or more lemon juice if necessary. Serve on chilled plates.

6 servings

crisp salmon salad

Here's a secret: some of the best parts of the salmon are usually thrown away. The belly, which is normally trimmed away to make a neater fillet, is full of flavorful fat. When you broil the belly, it turns crisp and tasty, almost like salmon bacon. Ask your fishmonger to set some aside for you. Serve this as a main course at lunch or as a light dinner.

1 pound salmon fillets, preferably belly cut
   Salt and freshly ground black pepper
2 tablespoons Dijon mustard
1 tablespoon red wine vinegar
¼ cup olive oil
½ pound mixed salad greens

Preheat the broiler. Cut the salmon lengthwise into strips about ½ inch wide. Salt and pepper them generously on both sides. Broil skin side up until the skin is crisp and dark brown, 7 to 10 minutes, depending on the thickness of the meat.

While the salmon is broiling, beat together the mustard and vinegar in a small bowl. Gradually add the oil, beating steadily until the dressing forms a smooth emulsion.

Add half of the dressing to the salad greens and toss well to mix. Add enough additional dressing so that the greens are lightly but thoroughly coated.

Divide the greens among 4 plates and arrange the salmon strips on top. Serve immediately, passing the extra dressing.

4 servings

dungeness crab coleslaw

After a lot of experimentation, I've found that it is very difficult to overcook Dungeness crab. Undercooking it, on the other hand, can be a real problem; the meat turns mushy—not at all tasty. And it would be a pity to waste one of the real treasures of the West Coast. If you can't find Dungeness crab, you'll need about 1¼ pounds of picked-over crabmeat from whichever varieties you can find.

3　(1½-to-2-pound) Dungeness crabs
　　(or see above)
1　large head napa cabbage
1　bulb fennel
1　bunch watercress
1　cup mayonnaise
1　tablespoon tarragon vinegar
　　Salt

Place the crabs in a large pot and cover with cold water. Cover and cook over high heat until the crabs turn bright red and white foam appears at the joints, about 20 minutes. Drain and rinse under cold water.

Clean the crabs: Remove the legs and claws. Remove the top shell and rinse off all the "jelly" and the soft lining. Remove the finger-like lungs. Cut the crab body into quarters and pick out the meat. Crack the legs and claws and pick out the meat. Reserve ½ cup of the crabmeat (preferably including the 6 big claws) for garnish.

Cut the cabbage into quarters and remove the core. Using a sharp chef's knife, shave the cabbage into thin strips. Cut the fennel lengthwise into quarters and remove the core. Using a mandoline, a Japanese vegetable cutter or the knife, shave the fennel into thin strips. Pick the leaves and tender stems from the watercress. Combine the cabbage, fennel and watercress in a large bowl.

Combine the mayonnaise and vinegar in a small bowl and beat until smooth. Add enough of the mayonnaise mixture, a little at a time, to the cabbage, tossing gently, to coat lightly but thoroughly. (You'll probably use about ⅔ cup.) Set aside for 20 minutes.

Add the crabmeat and salt to taste to the cabbage mixture and toss lightly to mix, being careful not to break up the chunks of crabmeat. Mound the coleslaw on chilled serving plates, garnish with the claws and the reserved crabmeat chunks and serve.

6 to 8 servings

fish soup with shellfish

Though some traditional fish soups come with specific formulas that dictate everything from what type of fish to use to how to serve it, there's nothing simpler or more adaptable. There are really only two requirements: a good flavorful stock and a mix of types of fish. Even the stock is easier than you might think. Though you can make it as elaborate as you want, simply simmering shrimp shells (and heads, if you have them) will give you a wonderful base.

- -

4 stalks celery, chopped

2 medium carrots, chopped

1 medium yellow onion, chopped

3 garlic cloves, minced

¼ cup olive oil, plus extra for drizzling

2 cups dry white wine

1 cup canned tomatoes, with juice

1 pound small clams, scrubbed

1 pound mussels, scrubbed and debearded

1 pound shrimp, preferably with heads

½ teaspoon saffron threads

1 pound firm oily fish steaks,
    such as swordfish or shark

1 pound white fish fillets,
    such as rock cod or red snapper

   Salt

1 teaspoon crushed red pepper

18 (½-inch-thick) slices baguette

In a large soup pot, cook the celery, carrots, onion and two-thirds of the garlic in 3 tablespoons of the oil over medium-high heat until softened, about 10 minutes. Add 1 cup of the wine and cook until reduced by one-third, about 5 minutes. Add the tomatoes and turn the heat to low.

In a large covered skillet, cook the clams in the remaining 1 cup wine over high heat for 3 minutes. Add the mussels and cook, shaking the pan occasionally to keep from scorching, until all the shellfish have opened, about 5 more minutes. Discard any that do not open. Transfer the shellfish to a bowl, cover tightly and refrigerate. Strain the remaining liquid into a large measuring cup and add enough water to make 4 cups.

Peel the shrimp, reserving the shells (and heads). Place the shrimp in a zipper-lock plastic bag, seal tightly and refrigerate until needed. Add the shrimp shells (and heads) and the shellfish cooking liquid–water combination to the soup pot and cook over medium heat for 25 minutes.

Ladle the contents of the soup pot into a food processor and grind for 5 minutes. Press through a strainer into a bowl. (This may need to be done in batches.) Add the saffron to the strained broth, cover tightly and refrigerate.

Cut the fish into chunks. Place in a zipper-lock plastic bag and add the remaining garlic, salt to taste, the crushed red pepper and the remaining 1 tablespoon oil. Seal tightly and massage the fish through the bag to distribute the ingredients evenly. Refrigerate for at least 30 minutes.

When you are almost ready to serve, bring the broth to a simmer. Add the fish and cook for 5 minutes. Add the shrimp and cook until opaque and firm all the way through, about 5 minutes more. Add the clams and mussels, in their shells, and heat through. Season to taste with salt.

Meanwhile, toast the baguette slices and drizzle lightly with oil.

Arrange 3 baguette slices in each of 6 wide soup bowls and ladle the fish soup over top. Serve immediately.

6 servings

salmon braised with leeks, prosciutto and mushrooms

> I call this a braise because there is very little liquid and that liquid is served along with the cooking vegetables.

3 small leeks

2 slices prosciutto

¼ pound small button mushrooms, cleaned

2 shallots, minced

4 tablespoons (½ stick) butter

2 cups dry white wine

¼ cup Champagne vinegar, or more to taste

Salt

6 (4-to-6-ounce) skinless salmon fillets

½ teaspoon fresh thyme leaves

Trim the green part of the leeks to 1 inch. Leaving the root ends whole, cut the leeks lengthwise into quarters and rinse them well. Slice thin crosswise. Slice the prosciutto into thin strips. Leave small mushrooms whole, and cut larger ones into quarters.

Combine the leeks, prosciutto, mushrooms, shallots and 2 tablespoons of the butter in a large sauté pan. Cook, covered, over medium-low heat until the leeks are tender, about 5 minutes. Add the wine and vinegar and cook until reduced by about half, 15 to 20 minutes. Season to taste with salt. Add more vinegar to taste. (The dish can be prepared several hours ahead up to this point and refrigerated.)

Increase the heat to medium. The liquid should just barely bubble, never boil. Place the salmon on the bed of leeks, sprinkle with the thyme, cover and cook gently until the fish is opaque on top, about 10 minutes. Test with the point of a sharp knife; the fish should just flake. Do not overcook.

Transfer the salmon to a platter, scraping away any leek mixture from the tops of the fillets. Cover and keep warm.

Raise the heat to high and reduce the liquid to several tablespoons. Add the remaining 2 tablespoons butter and cook, stirring, until the butter melts into the sauce. Place the salmon fillets on plates, top with the sauce and serve.

6 servings

oven-steamed salmon
with cucumber salad

This recipe is based on a technique I learned from Paula Wolfert. Salmon cooked this way comes out incredibly moist and flavorful, and because of the low heat, it retains its deep orange color even when completely cooked.

SALAD

5	cucumbers
	Salt
2	tablespoons snipped fresh chives
1	teaspoon sesame seeds, toasted
1	tablespoon rice vinegar, or more to taste
½	teaspoon toasted sesame oil, or more to taste
2	tablespoons chopped fresh cilantro

SALMON

1	(3-pound) salmon fillet
	Salt and freshly ground black pepper

Make the salad: Peel the cucumbers, cut them lengthwise in half and scoop out the seedy centers with the tip of a teaspoon. Cut each half lengthwise into 3 strips, then into 2-inch sections. Salt them and place in a colander to drain for 20 minutes.

When the cucumbers have drained, rinse them under cold running water and drain. Transfer the cucumbers to a bowl, add the chives, sesame seeds, rice vinegar and sesame oil and mix well. Taste and adjust the seasoning — the flavor of the sesame oil should be almost undetectable, the cucumbers should be slightly tart from the vinegar, and the herbs should be in balance. Refrigerate until ready to serve. Just before serving, add the cilantro and mix well.

Make the salmon: Preheat the oven to 300 degrees.

Remove the skin and pinbones from the salmon. Trim the sides to make a roughly rectangular shape that is fairly consistent in thickness (save the trimmings for chowder). Place the salmon on a baking sheet and salt and pepper liberally.

Place a roasting pan in the bottom of the oven and fill it with boiling water. Place the baking sheet with the salmon on the middle rack of the oven and cook until you see white fat begin to emerge on top of the fillet, about 20 minutes.

Carefully slide the salmon onto a serving platter, surround it with the salad and serve immediately.

6 to 8 servings

grilled salmon with chipotle-tequila butter

There's just enough chipotle in this recipe to add an earthy, spicy touch to the dish. If you want more, add more . . . up to another tablespoon.

- 1 garlic clove
- 1 tablespoon pureed canned chipotle chiles en adobo
- 8 tablespoons (1 stick) butter, at room temperature
- 2 teaspoons minced fresh cilantro
- 2 teaspoons tequila
- 2 teaspoons fresh lime juice

  Salt and freshly ground black pepper
- 6 (6-ounce) salmon fillets or steaks
- 2 tablespoons butter, melted

Drop the garlic through the feed tube of a food processor with the motor running. When the garlic is minced, scrape down the sides, add the chipotle puree and the butter and puree again. Add the cilantro, tequila and lime juice, and puree. Season to taste with salt and pepper (at least 2 grinds of pepper will be necessary to round out the flavor of the chipotle).

Mix well; then, with a plastic spatula, transfer the butter to a sheet of waxed paper. Spread the butter along one edge of the paper in a generous mound. Roll up the paper around the butter to form a sausage shape, pressing and patting the butter into a solid log. Twist the ends tightly and refrigerate for at least 2 hours or, even better, overnight.

Preheat the grill.

Lightly brush the salmon with the melted butter and season with salt and pepper on both sides. Grill over high heat, turning once, until the salmon just begins to flake when poked with the tip of a knife, 5 to 7 minutes. The salmon should be marked on the outside but still moist and pink inside. When the salmon is cooked, transfer it to a warm platter (it will cook a little bit more from its retained heat).

Unwrap the chipotle-tequila butter and slice it into 12 thin coins. Place 2 coins of butter on each piece of salmon and serve immediately, before the butter melts.

6 servings

grilled swordfish with salsa verde

Though swordfish is a meaty fish, it is usually cooked too much and winds up dry and chewy. Pay careful attention, and you'll have a nice, moist result. The sauce is a traditional Italian one that uses bread as a thickener. This was probably the first method used for thickening sauces (the Greeks wrote about it), but it's rarely used anymore, which is too bad.

SWORDFISH

- 1 garlic clove, minced

  Salt and freshly ground black pepper

- 4 (½-pound) swordfish steaks, about 1 inch thick

- 2 tablespoons olive oil

SALSA VERDE

- 1 (¼-inch-thick) slice country-style bread, trimmed of crusts and broken up

- ½ cup olive oil

- 2 tablespoons red wine vinegar

- 4 anchovy fillets

- 2 tablespoons capers

- 2 cups chopped fresh Italian parsley

  Dash of salt

- ½ lemon

Prepare the swordfish: Sprinkle the garlic and salt and pepper to taste over both sides of the swordfish steaks. Place the steaks in a zipper-lock plastic bag and add the oil. Press out as much air as possible and seal the bag. Massage the seasonings into the steaks through the bag, then marinate in the refrigerator for at least 1 hour and up to 4 hours.

Make the salsa verde: In a small bowl, combine the bread, oil and vinegar and stir to mix well. Set aside for at least 5 minutes to soften the bread.

In a food processor, combine the bread mixture, anchovies, capers and parsley and process until fairly smooth. Season to taste with salt. (The salsa can be made several hours ahead. Set aside at room temperature.)

Preheat the grill.

Remove the steaks from the plastic bag, reserving any marinade in the bag, and grill over medium heat until well marked on the first side, about 7 minutes. Brush with the reserved marinade and carefully turn over. Cook for another 5 minutes, or until the point of a small sharp knife can be easily inserted into the flesh.

Transfer the swordfish to a platter, squeeze the lemon juice over the top and smear each with about 1 tablespoon of salsa verde. Serve the remaining sauce on the side.

4 to 6 servings
(about 1 cup salsa)

baked fish with potatoes and artichokes

Most fish is cooked very quickly in order to keep it moist, but meaty fish like swordfish, tuna or shark is the exception. This cooking technique is similar to the way these fish are sometimes cooked in Morocco, and the result is moist fish and vegetables that are perfumed with juices from the fish and the spicing combination.

CALIFORNIA CHARMOULA

- 4 garlic cloves, coarsely chopped
- 2 green onions, coarsely chopped
- ¾ cup chopped fresh parsley
- ¼ cup chopped fresh mint
- 1 cup olive oil

  Juice of ½ lemon

  Salt

FISH

- 2 pounds swordfish, tuna or shark
  (or other oily fish) steak

  Salt and freshly ground black pepper

  Juice of 1 lemon
- 4 artichokes
- 4 baking potatoes, sliced ¼ inch thick

Make the charmoula: Place the garlic, green onions, parsley and mint in a blender and blend well. With the blender running, slowly add the oil in a thin stream. The mixture should form a thick emulsification. Add the lemon juice and season to taste with salt.

Prepare the fish: Rub the fish steaks on both sides with salt and pepper to taste. Pour the charmoula into a large bowl. Dip the steaks in the charmoula, then shake off any excess. Set the steaks aside on a plate, cover tightly and refrigerate for at least 45 minutes to marinate. Cover and refrigerate the remaining charmoula (leave it in the large bowl).

Preheat the oven to 400 degrees.

Fill a large bowl with cold water and add the lemon juice.

Trim the artichokes by pulling off any leaves clinging to the stem and the two outer rows of leaves around the base. Holding 1 artichoke in one hand and a sharp paring knife in the other, keeping the knife parallel to the stem, turn the artichoke against the knife, trimming away the outer leaves until only the pale green to yellow base remains. Lay the artichoke on its side and cut away the tops of the remaining leaves, roughly where the leaves swell out. With the paring knife, peel off the dark green skin of the artichoke heart from the base toward the stem, exposing the light green flesh underneath. Set the artichoke upside down on the work surface, and cut it into quarters. Trim away the hairy chokes and place the artichoke quarters in the bowl of lemon water. Repeat with the remaining artichokes.

Drain the artichokes, place the artichokes and potatoes in the bowl of charmoula and stir well to coat. Remove the artichokes and potatoes, leaving the remaining charmoula in the bowl, and scatter them over the bottom of a large oiled baking dish. Lay the fish steaks on top of the vegetables and seal the dish tightly with foil. Bake for 30 minutes.

Remove the foil, pour the remaining charmoula over all and return the pan to the oven until the vegetables begin to turn crusty and brown, about 20 minutes. Serve with sturdy bread to sop up the juices.

6 servings

broiled sand dabs (or sole)
with brown butter

Sand dab is a specifically West Coast fish. It is like a very small sole that is almost always sold with the fillets still on the bone. There is precious little meat, but what there is is choice —nutty and delicate. This is a classic treatment. You can substitute any sole with good results.

---

4 tablespoons (½ stick) butter
Salt
2 pounds sand dabs or sole fillets
½ lemon
1 tablespoon capers, with juice
1 tablespoon minced fresh parsley

Melt the butter in a small saucepan over medium-low heat and continue cooking until the butter is roughly hazelnut-colored and smells warm and nutty. Do not scorch the butter. (If black flecks appear, wipe the pan clean and start over with fresh butter.) Keep it warm.

Preheat the broiler and the broiler pan.

Lightly sprinkle salt on both sides of the sand dabs. Place the fillets skin side down on the preheated broiler pan and broil about 4 inches from the heat until the fish is firm, about 5 minutes. Brush the top of the fillets with some of the brown butter, raise the pan to within 1 to 2 inches of the broiler element and broil just long enough to brown the top of the fillets. Transfer the fillets to a warm platter.

Squeeze the lemon juice into the brown butter, add the capers and parsley and pour over the fillets. Serve immediately.

6 servings

+ **Because grilling is** done over relatively high heat, it is best used for relatively thin cuts of meat. Roasting is better for larger cuts.

+ **Always pat the meat dry** with paper towels before grilling or roasting. Any moisture left on the surface will steam the meat before it has a chance to brown.

+ **Season the meat well** before cooking. Seasonings for roasted or grilled meats can be as simple as salt and pepper or as complex as a marinade. Salt is the most important seasoning, because it draws some of the meat's juice to the surface, where it can caramelize and brown.

+ **While marinades** can contribute a lot of flavor, as a general rule, they affect only the very surface of the meat and do nothing for its texture. Be particularly careful with acidic marinades. If meat is left in them too long, the marinade will begin to break down the surface proteins, resulting in a mealy texture.

+ **When wine is used** in a marinade, cook it first to get rid of most of the alcohol and concentrate the flavor. The result is a much smoother, fuller-tasting marinade.

+ **When working with very lean meats,** it is important to use a marinade that adds fat. A paste of flavorings and oil pounded with a mortar and pestle or pureed in a blender or food processor works well.

+ **Made with nothing but salt and water** (though other, preferably dried, seasonings can be added as well), brine improves the flavor and the texture of close-grained meats—particularly poultry and pork. In general, do not brine beef and lamb.

+ **Bigger cuts take longer to cook.** Cook them with lower heat to get smooth cooking and even browning. If you want a contrast in doneness—say, medium-rare in the center and well browned on the surface—use a higher heat. Smaller cuts can be cooked at higher temperatures.

+ **If the meat to be cooked** is uneven in shape, such as a piece that has been cut away from the bone, like a leg of lamb, it will cook more evenly if you truss it or tie it into a more regular shape.

+ **Make sure there is room** for the hot, dry air to circulate around the meat. When roasting, use a rack to keep the meat off the bottom of the pan.

+ **Turn the meat occasionally** as it cooks so it browns evenly. This is important even with roasting.

+ **When roasting very small pieces** of meat, such as small birds or pork or lamb tenderloin, brown the meat first in a skillet, since the cooking time in the oven will be too short to do that.

+ **Basting adds some flavor** to the exterior of meat, but use only a melted pure fat, such as butter or pan drippings. Any liquid will result in steaming and softening the crust.

+ **Judging doneness** is very important with dry-heat cooking methods. The surest way is to insert an instant-read thermometer into the thickest or densest part of the meat.

+ **Generally, poultry should** be cooked to the highest temperature, about 160 to 165 degrees. Pork should be cooked to 155 to 160 degrees. Leg of lamb should be cooked to 140 to 145; chops and sirloins can be cooked to 130. Beef should be cooked to 130 to 140, depending on the desired doneness.

+ **All meats,** whether grilled or roasted, benefit from a 10-to-20-minute rest at the end of cooking to allow the moisture and the temperature to equalize inside the meat.

roast brined turkey

Brining results in roasted or grilled meats that are uniformly moist and flavorful. There are many different kinds of brines, and this is a good basic one that works well for both turkey and pork. Leaving the turkey uncovered in the refrigerator after it has been removed from the brine dries the skin thoroughly so that it will roast as crisp as possible. Turning the turkey from side to side during the early part of the roasting ensures that it browns evenly.

- ⅔ cup salt
- 1 gallon water
- 1 (12-to-14-pound) turkey

Combine the salt and water and stir until the salt dissolves. Pour the brine over the turkey in a stockpot just large enough to hold both. The turkey should be completely covered, but you may not need to use all the brine. Cover with aluminum foil and refrigerate for 6 hours, or overnight, turning two or three times to make sure all the turkey is submerged.

Remove the turkey from the brine (discard the brine) and pat it dry with paper towels. Refrigerate, uncovered, for 6 hours, or overnight, to air-dry the skin thoroughly.

Preheat the oven to 450 degrees.

Place the turkey on its side on a rack in a shallow roasting pan. Roast for 15 minutes. Turn the turkey onto its other side and roast for another 15 minutes. Turn the turkey breast side up and roast for another 15 minutes.

Reduce the heat to 325 degrees and roast until an instant-read meat thermometer inserted in the center of the thickest part of the thigh registers 160 to 165 degrees, about 2 hours.

Remove the turkey from the oven, cover loosely with foil and set aside for 20 minutes before carving.

10 to 12 servings

MEAT AND HEAT

turkey tonnato sandwich

Tonnato is a popular summertime sauce for cold veal in Italy. Veal is expensive here, so I tried the dish with turkey breast, which is plentiful and relatively inexpensive. Rolling and tying the boned turkey breast gives the meat a uniform shape so that it cooks more evenly and looks better when it's done. Instead of making sandwiches, you could serve the turkey and sauce on their own for a lunch or light dinner dish, along with a simply prepared vegetable.

Salt and freshly ground black pepper

1 (2-to-2$\frac{1}{2}$-pound) boneless turkey breast half, rolled and tied

$\frac{1}{3}$ cup olive oil, plus extra for cooking the turkey

1 (6-ounce) can tuna in olive oil, undrained

4–6 anchovy fillets, drained

Juice of 1 lemon, or more to taste

1 cup mayonnaise

$\frac{1}{4}$ cup capers, drained

1 large loaf ciabatta or other long rustic bread

1 small bunch arugula, trimmed and washed

Preheat the oven to 300 degrees.

Salt and pepper the turkey breast and rub it with oil to coat. Place the meat on a rack in a roasting pan and roast until an instant-read thermometer inserted in the center registers 160 degrees, about 1$\frac{1}{2}$ hours. Let the meat rest for 10 minutes.

Remove the breast from the rack and wrap it tightly in aluminum foil. Refrigerate for several hours, or overnight.

Puree the tuna and anchovies in a blender (you can use a food processor, but the sauce will be grainier). With the motor running, add the $\frac{1}{3}$ cup oil in a thin stream to make a smooth emulsion, scraping down the sides as necessary. Add the lemon juice and pulse to combine. The mixture should be very tangy; if necessary, add more lemon juice. If the anchovies aren't salty enough, add salt to taste.

Place the mayonnaise in a mixing bowl and pour the tuna mixture over it. Whisk to combine. Add the capers and whisk briefly just to mix. Pour half of the sauce onto a large platter and spread it evenly.

Remove the turkey from the refrigerator, unwrap it and cut away the strings. Cut it into 1/8-to-1/4-inch-thick slices, placing the slices on the platter, overlapping to make them fit. Spoon the remaining sauce evenly over the top. Cover tightly with plastic wrap and refrigerate for at least 2 hours, or overnight.

Cut the ends from the bread and split it horizontally in half, leaving the halves attached along one long side. Arrange the turkey slices on the bread and spoon over just enough sauce from the platter to moisten the meat. Scatter the arugula over the top and close the sandwich. Wrap tightly in plastic wrap and then in foil. Refrigerate until ready to serve, up to 4 hours. Slice and serve.

8 to 10 servings

real fajitas

Skirt steak is an extremely tough cut of meat (it's the muscle that supports the diaphragm, used in breathing). It has lots of flavor, but it needs to be sliced very thin so that it won't be too chewy.

- - - - - - - - - -

1   pound skirt steak
    Salt
1   jalapeño chile, seeded and minced
    Juice of 1 lime
12 corn tortillas, warmed
¾   cup salsa
¾   cup guacamole

Lay the skirt steaks on a work surface and check closely, removing any silverskin. Salt the steaks lightly on both sides. Put in a zipper-lock plastic bag with the jalapeño and lime juice and refrigerate for at least 1 hour, or overnight.

Preheat the grill.

Remove the steaks from the bag and pat dry with paper towels. Grill over a hot fire for 4 to 5 minutes. Turn and grill for 3 to 4 more minutes. Transfer the steaks to a cutting board, let rest for 5 minutes and slice against the grain into thin strips.

Divide the meat among the tortillas, garnish each with 1 tablespoon salsa and 1 tablespoon guacamole and serve.

12 tacos

umbrian-style pork roast

The spicing for this roast was inspired by Umbrian *porchetta*, or roast pig. Since the recipe uses the loin, you have to be very careful not to overcook it, or the meat will be dry. If you prefer, you can use pork butt, which will give you a much fattier, moister, more authentic and possibly more delicious roast. If using pork butt, you can push the internal temperature to 160 degrees, as the increased fattiness will keep the meat moist.

1 tablespoon black peppercorns
2 teaspoons fennel seeds
2 teaspoons kosher salt
1 (3-pound) bone-in pork loin roast
2 tablespoons olive oil

Grind the peppercorns, fennel seeds and salt with a mortar and pestle, spice grinder or coffee mill until fine. Set the pork loin on a plate to catch the excess and rub the spices over the meat, covering all sides thickly. Pour the oil over the meat and massage it to work in the spices and coat evenly. Set aside to marinate at room temperature for 2 hours.

Preheat the oven to 325 degrees.

Place the pork on a rack in a roasting pan and roast, turning every 30 minutes, until the interior temperature reaches 155 degrees, 2 to 2½ hours. Check the roast in several places with an instant-read thermometer, being careful not to touch the bone.

When the roast is done, remove it from the oven, tent it with aluminum foil and let it stand for 20 to 30 minutes to let the juices set.

To serve, carve the pork into thin slices.

6 servings

roast lamb with fresh peas and turnips

This is leg of lamb is traditional French cooking, not only in the manner in which it is roasted but also in the way flavors are layered and tied together. Trimmings and bones from the meat, peelings from the turnips and the pea pods all go into the stock, giving it a complex flavor from what are, essentially, scraps.

- -

1 (4-to-6-pound) leg of lamb,
   hipbone and trimmings removed
   (the butcher can do this) and reserved

2 garlic cloves, minced

3 sprigs fresh thyme, minced, plus
   ½ teaspoon fresh thyme leaves

Salt and freshly ground black pepper

1 (750-milliliter) bottle dry red wine,
   reduced over high heat to 3 cups

6 large turnips, peeled and cut into eighths, or
   24 small turnips, peeled (reserve the peelings)

4 medium carrots, cut into chunks

2 medium yellow onions, quartered

3 pounds fresh peas, shelled
   (reserve the pods)

6 tablespoons (¾ stick) butter

1 shallot, minced

2 coarse outer leaves romaine lettuce,
   cut into thin strips

Carefully trim away the tough outer layer of fat (fell) from the lamb. Rub the lamb all over with the garlic, thyme sprigs and salt and pepper. Place the lamb in a large zipper-lock plastic bag. Pour the reduced wine over and seal tightly. Marinate, refrigerated, for at least 8 hours, or overnight, turning occasionally to coat the lamb evenly with the marinade.

Preheat the oven to 450 degrees.

To make a lamb stock for cooking the vegetables and making the sauce, place the reserved hipbone and any lean trimmings in a roasting pan and roast, turning occasionally, until well browned.

Meanwhile, cook the turnips in rapidly boiling water just until a knife easily pierces the center, about 5 minutes. Drain the turnips and refresh them in ice water. Drain, cover and refrigerate.

Place the roasted hipbone and trimmings, half of the carrots and half of the onions in a medium saucepan. Cover with water and bring slowly to a simmer. Cook, keeping at a bare simmer, for at least 1 hour and up to 2 hours. Strain and chill.

When you are ready to roast the lamb, preheat the oven to 325 degrees. Grease a roasting pan.

Remove the lamb from the plastic bag, reserving the marinade, and pat the meat dry with paper towels. Place the lamb on a rack in a roasting pan and scatter the remaining carrots and onions over the bottom of the pan. Roast the lamb, turning it every 30 minutes, until the internal temperature reaches 135 degrees, about 20 to 25 minutes per pound.

While the lamb is roasting, remove the stock from the refrigerator and skim off the fat. Bring the stock, along with the reserved turnip peelings and a handful of the reserved pea pods, to a simmer. Cook for at least 30 minutes.

When the lamb is done, remove it from the roasting pan (set the pan aside) and place it on a serving platter or carving board loosely tented with aluminum foil to keep warm. Let rest for at least 30 minutes to allow the juices to set.

While the lamb is resting, in a large sauté pan, combine the peas, turnips, 4 tablespoons (½ stick) of the butter, the shallot, lettuce, thyme leaves and ¼ cup of the stock. Cook over medium heat just until the peas are no longer starchy, 5 to 7 minutes. Keep warm.

Meanwhile, remove the onions and carrots from the roasting pan and discard. Skim the fat from the meat juices left in the pan. To make the sauce, place the pan over high heat and add the reserved marinade. Cook, scraping up the browned bits from the bottom of the pan, until the marinade reduces to several tablespoons, 5 to 10 minutes. You should have about 1 cup lamb stock remaining; add it to the pan and cook until reduced to a thin sauce. Keep warm.

When ready to serve, carve the lamb (pour the juices into the warm sauce) and place on a platter. Bring the sauce to a boil and whisk in the remaining 2 tablespoons butter. Strain the sauce into a sauceboat and serve the peas and turnips alongside the lamb.

6 servings

+ **The difference among various** moist-heat cooking methods
  —braises, stews, daubes—is the amount of liquid used. Which
  method you choose depends on how much sauce you want.
  Braises are cooked with very little liquid—little more than
  enough to cover the bottom of the pan, really. Stews use more
  —the liquid will come halfway up the meat. Daubes use the
  most—the meat is nearly submerged.

+ **Use moist-heat cooking for tough cuts** of meat, such as the
  shank and other parts of the leg and shoulder. They are the
  only ones that have enough connective tissue to keep the
  meat moist after extended cooking. Tender cuts will break
  down and become grainy and dry.

+ **Try cooking whole cuts of meat** on the bone with moist heat.
  The connective tissue that attaches the meat to the bone will
  make the meat even moister.

+ **Usually you'll want to brown** the meat before adding the
  liquid. But there are exceptions—called blanquettes or fricassees—which are typically reserved for veal or chicken.

+ **Sometimes the meat is floured** before browning. In the case
  of moist-cooking methods, remember that although this flour
  will help to thicken the liquid later on, it will not thicken nearly
  so much as an equal quantity of raw flour. Because of the
  browning, its thickening ability will be substantially weakened.

+ **When browning the meat,** follow the procedure for sautéing:
  Be sure to use enough oil to amply cover the bottom of the
  pan. Season the meat. Make sure the oil is hot before adding
  the meat. Allow the meat to cook on the first side until thoroughly browned, without moving it about too much. To keep
  the aromatic vegetables (onions, garlic, etc.) from scorching,
  don't add them until after the meat has browned. Then be
  sure to pour off all excess oil before proceeding.

+ **Use a heavy pot** that is just big enough to hold the meat.

+ **Braises, stews and daubes** almost always include vegetables. Add some of them—onions, garlic, celery, carrots and peppers—early in the process, just after the meat has been browned, to flavor the liquid and the meat. Add a second group of vegetables shortly before the dish is done, to serve as accompaniments. Because the vegetables used for flavoring will almost certainly be too overcooked to serve, strain them out before adding the second batch of vegetables.

+ **Whatever type** of moist-heat cooking you're using, it is important to add no more liquid than is necessary, in order to keep the broth as concentrated as possible. A useful trick is to float a sheet of aluminum foil just on top of the meat, under the lid, which traps the moisture and keeps it from evaporating into the air space under the lid.

+ **When braising,** check the level of the liquid frequently, especially later in the cooking process. You'll want to maintain a level of at least 1/2 inch to keep the food from scorching.

+ **Usually, the heat used** for moist-heat cooking is "low and slow." Cook in the oven, at about 350 degrees, to keep the heat as even as possible. Meat cooked by low-heat braising can be separated into shreds.

+ **High-heat braises are delicious,** if a little tricky. For these, it is imperative that you use only heavy pots, such as cast-iron, with tight-fitting lids and that you check the liquid frequently. Meat cooked by high-heat braising separates into chunks.

+ **It's easy to tell** when a moist-cooked piece of meat is done—a knife or a carving fork can be inserted easily.

+ **Though it may seem unlikely,** you *can* overcook braises, stews and daubes. The meat will break down to the point that it is grainy. Test the meat at least every half hour for doneness.

+ **If, after cooking, the liquid** for your dish has not thickened enough, you can help it along by adding a beurre manié. Knead 2 tablespoons butter and 1 tablespoon flour together into a paste. Remove the meat and vegetables from the pot, increase the heat to high and whisk in the butter mixture, a bit at a time. Once the sauce is the desired thickness, return the meat and vegetables to the pot.

+ **Braises, stews and daubes** can be anything from homey to very refined. For a rustic dish, try removing the meat and pureeing the vegetables into the liquid. Cook a little longer, and they will thicken the sauce even more. For the most refined dish, strain out all the vegetables and meat, finish the sauce with a little butter, return the meat to the pot and serve with a fresh batch of accompanying vegetables on the side.

+ **Moist-cooked meats** are always better when allowed to stand, even briefly, then reheated. This allows for a more complete exchange of flavors among the meat, the flavorings and the liquid. Even a 20-minute rest after coming out of the oven will allow the flavors to mingle better.

+ **Although you should always season** the meat before browning, you must still season it again at the end of cooking. Always taste a bit of the liquid before serving.

chicken braised with green olives and thyme

We usually think of braising cuts of meat, but chicken braises well too, particularly dark meat. When braising white meat, which overcooks quickly, stack the pieces on top of the dark meat so they finish cooking without coming into direct contact with the hot liquid.

- - - - - - - - - - - - - - - -

3 (3-to-3½-pound) chickens

Salt and freshly ground black pepper

¼ cup olive oil

2 garlic cloves, unpeeled,
    plus 4 garlic cloves, sliced

2 medium yellow onions, chopped

1 large green bell pepper,
    cored, seeded and chopped

½ pound carrots, chopped

3 stalks celery, chopped

½ cup chopped fresh parsley,
    plus extra for garnish

3 cups dry white wine

1 (6-ounce) can tomato paste

2 pounds white boiling potatoes, peeled

½ pound green olives, preferably unpitted

1 tablespoon chopped fresh thyme

1 teaspoon chopped fresh mint

Rinse the chickens well and disjoint each into 2 drumsticks, 2 thighs, 2 wings and 2 breasts. Cut each breast crosswise in half. Reserve the backs, wing tips and necks for another use, if desired. Pat the chicken pieces dry with paper towels. Salt and pepper them well.

Heat the oil in a wide skillet over medium-high heat. Add the unpeeled garlic cloves. When the garlic begins to sputter and color, begin browning the chicken in batches: drumsticks and thighs first, then wings, then breast pieces. Cook each until lightly browned, 10 to 15 minutes per side. As each batch is finished, transfer the chicken pieces to a large Dutch oven, beginning with a layer of the drumsticks and thighs on the bottom, then the wings, then the breast pieces. Remove and discard the garlic if it begins to scorch.

Preheat the oven to 350 degrees.

When all the chicken is browned, pour off all but about 1 tablespoon of the rendered fat from the pan. Return the skillet to the stovetop and increase the heat to high. When the browned bits begin to sizzle, add the onions, green pepper, carrots, celery, sliced garlic and ¼ cup of the parsley. Let the vegetables sit for 1 minute or so, until they begin to soften, then stir them, scraping the bottom of the skillet to get up as many of the sticky browned bits as possible. When the vegetables are brightly colored and beginning to wilt, pour them over the chicken in the Dutch oven.

In a small bowl, mix 1 cup of the wine with the tomato paste until smooth. Return the skillet to high heat. Add the remaining 2 cups wine to the skillet, then add the wine-tomato paste mixture, and stir, scraping the bottom and sides of the pan to free all the browned bits, until the wine no longer smells of alcohol. Pour the mixture over the chicken and vegetables. Gently stir to distribute the vegetables and wine around the chicken pieces, but be careful not to disturb the layers. Place a sheet of aluminum foil loosely over the chicken. Cover and bake for 30 minutes.

While the chicken is cooking, cook the potatoes in plenty of rapidly boiling salted water until a knife can easily be inserted, about 20 minutes. Drain and, when just cool enough to handle, cut into quarters.

Remove the chicken from the oven and add the potatoes, the olives, thyme, mint and the remaining ¼ cup parsley. Gently stir again to distribute without disturbing the layers of chicken. Return to the oven and cook until the chicken is very tender, about 30 more minutes.

Season the broth to taste with salt and pepper. Serve in broad pasta bowls, garnished with plenty of parsley.

8 to 10 servings

chicken in the pot

This is a version of the French classic *poule au pot*. Notice that the chicken is not browned before cooking, which keeps the flavor delicate. Notice also the large amount of aromatics that lend their perfume to the broth and the chicken. Talk about exchange of flavors! Notice that the chicken is cooked in two layers—the white meat above the dark—to keep the breast meat from overcooking.

----

3 medium carrots

1 medium leek, trimmed and washed

1 medium yellow onion, quartered

1 stalk celery

¼ medium parsnip

2 garlic cloves

1 bunch parsley, leaves chopped,
   stems reserved

2 bay leaves

2 (3½-pound) chickens, quartered

2 cups dry white wine

2 cups chicken stock

1 pound small boiling potatoes,
   quartered

1 pound sugar snap peas,
   trimmed and stringed

1 pound brown mushrooms, cleaned

Coarse salt, preferably sea salt

Combine the carrots, leek, onion, celery, parsnip, garlic, parsley stems and bay leaves in a large soup pot. (It is not necessary to chop the vegetables.) Place the chicken pieces on top of the vegetables, the leg quarters on the bottom, the breasts on top. Pour the wine and stock over, then add enough water to barely cover the chicken.

Bring to a simmer over medium heat. Place a sheet of aluminum foil loosely over the chicken. Cover and cook at a bare simmer, using a flame-tamer if necessary, for 1 hour.

While the chicken is cooking, boil or steam the potatoes until barely soft, about 20 minutes. Boil or steam the peas until bright green but still crisp, about 5 minutes.

In a nonstick skillet, cook the mushrooms over high heat, tossing them to keep them from burning, until browned, about 5 minutes. Salt lightly.

When the chicken is cooked, transfer the pieces to a warmed oven-proof platter, cover with aluminum foil and keep warm in a low oven. Ladle the chicken cooking liquid through a cheesecloth-lined strainer into a saucepan. Bring the liquid to a boil. Season with salt to taste. The broth should be somewhat undersalted, as more salt will be added later.

Place 1 chicken quarter in the middle of each of 8 shallow soup or pasta bowls and arrange some potatoes, peas and mushrooms around it. Spoon over the hot broth, being careful not to disturb the vegetables. Sprinkle lightly with the chopped parsley, sprinkle some salt over the chicken and serve.

8 servings

mushroom pot roast

Although we usually braise meat at low temperatures, it can also be cooked in a very hot oven, as long as you keep an eye on it. Meat cooked this way has an almost buttery texture and falls apart in chunks. Use a heavy cast-iron casserole with a tightly fitting lid and monitor the level of the liquid carefully, particularly in the last hour of cooking.

1 (3½-to-4-pound) chuck roast,
    either 7-bone or round-bone

Salt

1 (750-milliliter) bottle dry red wine

3 tablespoons olive oil

1 pound yellow onions, sliced

½ pound carrots, sliced

6 garlic cloves, smashed

1 stalk celery

1 bay leaf

Stems from 1 bunch parsley, plus
    ¼ cup finely chopped fresh parsley

1 whole clove

½ cup red wine vinegar

2 tablespoons butter

1 pound button mushrooms,
    cleaned and quartered

Freshly ground black pepper

Sprinkle the roast with salt on both sides and place in a 1-gallon zipper-lock plastic bag. Add the wine, seal the bag and refrigerate for 8 hours, or overnight, turning occasionally to make sure all the meat is covered with wine.

Preheat the oven to 450 degrees.

Heat the oil in a Dutch oven over medium-high heat. Remove the roast from the bag, reserving the wine, and pat it dry with paper towels. Place the roast in the Dutch oven and brown well on both sides, 5 to 10 minutes per side.

Transfer the roast to a plate. Pour off all but 1 tablespoon of the rendered fat from the Dutch oven and reduce the heat to medium. Add the onions, carrots and 4 of the garlic cloves and cook until the vegetables are slightly softened, about 5 minutes.

Cut the celery in half. Tie both stalks together with the bay leaf and parsley stems using kitchen twine and insert the clove in a celery stalk, to make a bouquet garni. Add the bouquet garni and the reserved wine to the vegetables and simmer for 5 minutes.

Add the meat and vinegar and place a sheet of aluminum foil loosely over the meat. Cover the Dutch oven with a tight-fitting lid, place it in the oven and cook until the meat is easily pierced with a sharp fork and is falling off the bone, 2 to 2½ hours. Every 30 minutes, turn the meat and stir the liquid and vegetables. If the level of the liquid gets too low, add up to 1 cup water, a little at a time, to prevent the meat and vegetables from scorching.

Transfer the meat to a plate and cover it with aluminum foil to keep warm. Pour the liquid and vegetables into a strainer over a bowl, pressing on the vegetables to get as much liquid as possible; discard the vegetables. Set the liquid aside until the fat floats to the top.

Wash out the Dutch oven. Skim off the fat from the settled liquid and return the meat and liquid to the Dutch oven. Keep warm over low heat.

Melt the butter in a large skillet over medium-high heat. When the butter has foamed and subsided, add the mushrooms and the remaining 2 garlic cloves and cook, tossing, until the mushrooms are lightly browned, about 5 minutes.

Add the mushrooms to the pot roast and cook for 15 minutes over low heat to marry the flavors. Season to taste with salt and pepper, garnish with the chopped parsley and serve.

6 to 8 servings

lamb and lentils to eat with a spoon

This recipe sounds impossible: the lamb is cooked at high heat for more than five hours. Not only does it work, but the results are superb. When I talked to meat scientists about it, no one could tell me why it works the way it does. A thin pan or an insufficiently tight lid will result in dry, overcooked meat. I learned the method from Patricia Wells. The distinctive use of vinegar, which cuts so wonderfully through the richness of the lamb, comes from Michael Roberts, cookbook writer and former chef at Trumps and at Twin Palms. I put the whole thing together, added the lentils and then wondered a lot.

1½ pounds onions, sliced

½ pound carrots, sliced

6 garlic cloves, sliced

1 (5-to-6-pound) leg of lamb, hipbone removed
     (the butcher will do this)

   Salt and freshly ground black pepper

5 cups water

3 tablespoons tomato paste

2 cups red wine vinegar,
     plus more to taste

1 (750-milliliter) bottle dry red wine

2 cups lentils, preferably lentils du Puy,
     picked over and rinsed

2 teaspoons minced fresh herbs,
     preferably thyme and rosemary

Preheat the oven to 425 degrees.

Scatter the onions, carrots and two-thirds of the garlic across the bottom of a large, heavy Dutch oven. Place the lamb skin side up on top. Roast, uncovered, for 15 minutes. Turn the lamb so the skin side is down and roast, uncovered, for another 15 minutes. Remove the pot from the oven, but leave the oven on.

Season the lamb generously with salt and pepper, then turn and season the other side (the skin side should again be up). Mix 1 cup of the water and the tomato paste until smooth. Pour over the lamb, along with the vinegar and the wine. Bring to a boil on top of the stove.

Place a sheet of aluminum foil over, but not touching, the surface of the meat. Cover the pot tightly and return it to the oven. Roast until the meat begins to fall off the bone and a fork penetrates it very easily, 5½ to 6 hours. Baste the lamb every hour to start, then every 30 minutes as the liquid reduces. By the end, you should check every 15 minutes; it will want to scorch. Do not turn the lamb, but occasionally push it from side to side to keep it from scorching.

About 1 hour before serving, combine the lentils, the remaining 4 cups water, 1 teaspoon salt and the remaining garlic in a large saucepan. Bring to a boil, reduce the heat and simmer until the lentils are tender, about 45 minutes. Drain.

When the lamb is done, add the lentils to the pot along with the herbs, stirring to combine the cooking juices and the lentils. Do not turn the lamb, and stir carefully to avoid breaking up the meat. Return the pot to the oven and roast, covered, for 5 minutes longer.

Remove from the oven and adjust the seasonings. The lentils should be tart; if they are not, add 1 to 2 tablespoons vinegar. Serve immediately.

8 servings

braised lamb shanks with green olives

Be careful to brown the lamb shanks slowly, or the outside will dry out during the braising.

-- --

4 lamb shanks (about 4 pounds)

Salt

2 tablespoons olive oil

2 medium carrots, chopped

1 stalk celery, chopped

1 medium yellow onion, chopped

1 green bell pepper, cored,
    seeded and chopped

2 garlic cloves, chopped

¼ cup tomato paste

2 cups dry red wine

1 cup unpitted green olives

Freshly ground black pepper

1 tablespoon chopped fresh rosemary

2 teaspoons grated lemon zest

2 tablespoons minced fresh parsley

Pat the lamb shanks dry with paper towels and salt them liberally on all sides. Heat the oil in a large cast-iron Dutch oven over medium heat. When the oil is hot enough so that the meat instantly sizzles when it is added to the pan, brown the shanks on all sides. You may need to do this in 2 batches, depending on the size of the pan. As the shanks are browned, transfer them to a plate and keep warm. It should take about 30 minutes to brown all 4 shanks in 2 batches.

Preheat the oven to 350 degrees.

Drain all but a film of fat from the pot. Add the carrots, celery, onion and green pepper and cook, stirring, until the vegetables begin to soften, about 10 minutes. Add the garlic and cook, stirring, until it becomes very fragrant, about 5 minutes. Add the tomato paste and cook, stirring, until you see dark streaks across the bottom of the pan where the paste is browning, about 5 minutes. Add the wine and stir to combine well.

Place the shanks on top of the vegetables. Loosely cover with aluminum foil, cover tightly with a lid and bake for 45 minutes.

Remove the lid and aluminum foil and add the olives and a good grinding of pepper. Stir to mix well. Turn the shanks and check the level of liquid: it should just cover the vegetables and the bottoms of the shanks. Add some water if necessary. Cover, return to the oven and bake until the lamb is tender enough to fall off the bone, another 45 to 60 minutes.

Remove from the oven, turn the shanks again and add the rosemary. Cover and set aside for 5 to 10 minutes, then season to taste with salt.

Chop together the lemon zest and parsley. Serve the shanks with some sauce and with the lemon-parsley combination sprinkled over the top.

4 servings

ragù napoletano

This is old-fashioned Italian cooking. After five hours of cooking, the ragù tastes of neither tomatoes nor meat but of something else entirely. For a real treat, serve the sauce with fresh pasta; then serve the sliced pork afterward (or later in the week) with a bitter green such as broccoli rabe. This recipe will serve a crowd, and the leftovers freeze well.

¼ pound pancetta, cubed

4 medium yellow onions, coarsely chopped

4 garlic cloves, peeled

1 bunch fresh parsley

2 tablespoons olive oil

Salt and freshly ground black pepper

1 (4-to-5-pound) pork butt roast,
     trimmed of any bones and tied

3 cups hearty dry red wine

2 (6-ounce) cans tomato paste

2 (16-ounce) cans crushed tomatoes

1 pound Italian sausage meat, crumbled

6 pounds fresh or dried fettuccine

4 tablespoons (½ stick) butter, cut up

Freshly grated pecorino Romano cheese
     for serving

Grind together the pancetta, onions, garlic and parsley in a meat grinder or a food processor.

Warm the oil in a Dutch oven over low heat and add the ground pancetta mixture. Cook, stirring frequently, until the onions soften and become fragrant, about 20 minutes.

Liberally salt and pepper the pork and add it to the pot. Cover and cook, turning once, for about 1 hour; do not scorch.

Add the wine, cover and cook until the wine reduces to about one-fourth, about 1 hour.

Add the tomato paste, 2 to 3 tablespoons at a time, stirring between additions, until the sauce is smooth. Cover and cook until the sauce is dark and savory, about 1 hour.

Add the tomatoes and cook until the pork is falling-apart tender, about 1 more hour. Remove the pork and reserve for another meal.

Add the sausage and cook for 1 more hour.

Shortly before serving, cook the pasta in plenty of rapidly boiling salted water until tender, about 5 minutes for fresh pasta and 10 minutes for dried, or according to package instructions. Drain and transfer to a large mixing bowl.

Add the butter and 10 cups of the sauce to the pasta. Toss well to combine, adding more sauce if necessary, just to coat the pasta. Serve in individual bowls, each topped with another ¼ cup of the sauce and a sprinkling of cheese.

10 servings

+ **Starchy fillers** (bread or cracker crumbs) not only function as extenders but also absorb and hold in flavorful juices.

+ **Using a combination** of meats in meat loaf gives you a fuller-flavored, moister dish. Try a mixture of half ground beef and a quarter each of pork and veal (by weight).

+ **Making sausages at home** is a simple process, especially if you have a good meat grinder with a sausage-stuffer attachment. Sausage can also be served as a fried patty.

+ **Sausage meat should contain** about 30 percent fat to keep it moist. The simplest way to ensure this is to use pork butt, which has approximately that proportion.

+ **Cold is the key** to making a sausage with good texture. Keep the meat well chilled until just before you're ready to start (stick the cubed meat in the freezer for 15 to 20 minutes). Since the mechanical action of the grinding will heat the meat up, return the meat to the refrigerator between grindings. Chill the meat thoroughly before stuffing the sausage skins.

+ **Grind the meat well** to break down any tough fibers and to emulsify the lean and the fat into a smooth paste.

+ **Make sure the meat is well seasoned** before you put it in the sausage casings or form it into a meat loaf. To test, take a small amount, flatten it into a patty and sauté it; then correct the seasonings if necessary.

+ **Remember that the meat will swell** from the heat when sausages are cooked. Cook them gently to keep them from splitting and losing all the flavorful fat. Poach them in well-seasoned liquid (water, wine or beer) until they feel firm. Then fry or grill, if you like.

---

wild mushroom meat loaf

A combination of meats (half beef, one quarter each pork and veal) gives meat loaf the most complex flavor and the most pleasing texture. Cracker crumbs are the best extender — they have a better texture than oatmeal or bread crumbs. Allow ¼ cup per pound of meat. You can alter the basic combination of meat, crackers and eggs by adding many different flavorings — even plain old-fashioned ketchup on top.

3 ounces dried wild mushrooms,
    preferably morels

1 cup dry red wine

1 tablespoon olive oil

2 medium carrots, coarsely chopped

1 stalk celery, coarsely chopped

1 medium yellow onion, coarsely chopped

1 garlic clove, minced

2 pounds ground beef,
    preferably 15% fat

1 pound ground pork

1 pound ground veal

2 teaspoons fresh thyme leaves

1 teaspoon minced fresh rosemary

2 large eggs

1 cup cracker crumbs

1 tablespoon salt

Freshly ground black pepper

Simmer the mushrooms and wine in a small saucepan over low heat until the mushrooms soften, 15 to 20 minutes; drain. When the mushrooms are cool enough to handle, chop them and set aside.

Preheat the oven to 350 degrees.

Heat the oil in a medium sauté pan over high heat. When it is very hot, add the carrots and cook, without stirring, for 2 to 3 minutes, until they begin to darken. Toss and stir to prevent them from sticking and cook for 2 to 3 minutes more. Reduce the heat to medium, add the celery and stir and cook for 2 to 3 minutes. Add the onion and stir and cook for 2 to 3 minutes. Finally, add the garlic, stir and remove from the heat. Let cool.

In a large mixing bowl, thoroughly mix the beef, pork and veal, squeezing the meat mixture between your fingers to make sure no clumps remain. Add the cooked vegetables, mushrooms, thyme and rosemary; stir well to combine. Add the eggs and mix lightly but thoroughly, using your hands. Sprinkle in the cracker crumbs and mix, again by hand, until all the crumbs are absorbed. Add the salt and add pepper to taste.

Form the meat into a rough loaf shape in a shallow baking pan. Bake until the outside is browned and the interior temperature reaches 150 degrees, about 1½ hours. Transfer to a platter, slice and serve.

10 to 12 servings

spicy garlic sausages

This is one of my favorite sausages. It's wonderful by itself or in other dishes. Sausage casings can be found at specialty butchers. If you don't have them, you can form the sausages into patties and cook them that way.

2 pounds boneless pork butt,
   coarsely ground
½ cup dry white wine
3 garlic cloves, pressed or minced
1 teaspoon crushed red pepper
1 tablespoon salt
   Sausage casings (optional)

Combine the meat, wine, garlic, crushed red pepper and salt in a bowl and stir well to mix thoroughly. Refrigerate for at least 1 hour, until well chilled.

Stuff the mixture into casings, if desired, or form it into patties.

Prick the sausages and poach them in simmering water until cooked through, about 10 minutes, or panfry the patties. They can be finished on the grill or in a tomato sauce, if you like. Serve hot.

8 servings

lamb, orange zest and rosemary sausages

I prefer this sausage stuffed into narrow casings. It makes a nice presentation if you stuff it into a 2-to-3-foot length and then form it into a coil. A couple of skewers inserted at right angles will hold the coil together during cooking. If you can't find casings, this makes a nice patty sausage as well. Serve it with a Moroccan-style carrot slaw.

1 pound lamb stew meat, coarsely ground
1 pound boneless pork butt, coarsely ground
½ cup dry red wine
Grated zest of 1 orange
1 tablespoon minced fresh rosemary
4 garlic cloves, pressed or minced
2 teaspoons salt
1 teaspoon crushed red pepper
Sausage casings (optional)

Combine the lamb, pork, wine, orange zest, rosemary, garlic, salt and crushed red pepper in a bowl and stir well to mix thoroughly. Refrigerate for at least 1 hour, until well chilled.

Stuff the spiced meat into sausage casings, if desired, or form it into patties.

Prick the sausages and poach them in simmering water until cooked through, about 10 minutes, or panfry the patties. They can be finished on the grill, if you like. Serve hot.

8 servings

smokerless smoked bratwurst

I love smoked bratwurst, but not having a smokehouse, I thought making them was impossible. Then I decided to use a little of the smoked pork loin found in many supermarkets.

¾ pound boneless pork butt, finely ground
½ pound veal stew meat, finely ground
¼ pound sliced smoked pork loin, finely ground
Freshly grated nutmeg
¼ teaspoon caraway seeds, ground
Pinch of dried marjoram
1½ teaspoons salt
½ cup ice water
Sausage casings (optional)

Combine the ground pork butt, veal and smoked pork and finely grind together a second time. Place in a bowl, add a grating of nutmeg, the ground caraway, marjoram, salt and water and stir well to mix thoroughly. Refrigerate for at least 1 hour, until well chilled.

Stuff the meat into casings, if desired, or form it into patties.

Prick the sausages and poach them in simmering water until cooked through, about 10 minutes, or panfry the patties. They can be finished on the grill, if you like. Serve hot.

6 servings

fat, flour and fear

Fear is a natural part of cooking. After all, there are all those hot pans and sharp knives. And, oh yes, let's not forget the piecrusts. In fact, in the hierarchy of kitchen phobias, who's to say that piecrusts aren't the worst? We deal with burners and knives almost every time we cook something, but it is precisely because we make piecrusts so rarely that they have the power to inspire dread disproportionate to their actual difficulty. A piecrust ain't nothin' but flour, fat and water, right? That, of course, is disingenuous. It is *because* the ingredients are so basic that piecrusts are so difficult. They are almost totally dependent on technique, and technique is not something that you can pick up on a quick trip to the grocery store. The only way to learn how to make a good piecrust is to make enough bad ones that you finally acquire both an understanding and a feel for how a good one is made. No one can help you get the feel without standing beside you for every motion. But the understanding part is different.

There are two basic types of piecrust. For want of better names, we'll call them American and European. Most people start with the American. They want to make an apple pie in the fall or a cherry pie in the spring. It would never occur to them to try to make one of those fancy fruit tarts. That's a mistake: fruit tarts are actually much easier to make — at least, the crust is. In the language of pastry people, American pie doughs are flaky, and European tart doughs are short, meaning they have a texture that's closer to a cookie than to puff pastry. The quest for that all-American flakiness is at the heart of most people's problems with pastry. To get it right, you have to mix the three key ingredients — flour, water and fat — together in just the right way. As far as the crust is concerned, one of those glittering fruit tarts in the pâtisserie's window is easier than pie.

At the heart of any crust is flour and water. The fat is there to mediate the relationship between the two. When flour and water are mixed together, a couple of proteins — glutenin and gliadin — link up and form gluten. If you've made bread, you know what this is. It's the long, stringy sheets that provide the structure for the bread — they form the balloons that the yeast then inflates. Different flours contain different amounts of protein, depending upon the variety of wheat, the climate it's grown in and how it is milled. Hard winter wheats from the northern plains contain the highest amount of protein (about 12.5 percent) and will produce the greatest amount of gluten. In stores, this flour is usually sold as bread flour, though a good deal of it winds up in dried Italian pastas as well. Semolina, which is familiar from pasta packages, is milled from durum wheat — one of the highest in protein — and has a percentage of greater than 13 percent. All-purpose flour, the kind that is most commonly available, is made from either all hard wheat or a blend of hard and soft wheats to produce a protein content of about 10.5 percent. This is the flour used for most kinds of baking. Unbleached flour is simply all-purpose flour that has not been treated to whiten it. It has about the same percentage of protein as all-purpose. Cake flour and pastry flour come from soft wheats and are finely milled. They have protein contents of about 7.5 percent. Whole wheat flour is only a little stronger than cake or pastry flour — the bits of hull left behind in the milling inhibit the formation of gluten.

While it might seem that a flour with a high protein content is desirable for making piecrusts (after all, it's the gluten sheets that trap the air and create the puff), this is a case of more not necessarily being better. Too much protein, and the gluten sheets are too strong. Then you've got a piecrust that's tough enough to deflect bullets. This is not to say that bread flour should never be used for pastries. It's great for strudel, where the dough is stretched thin enough to read through — you need a lot of gluten to avoid winding up with a pastry sheet full of holes. In general, though, the best flour to use for pastries is either all-purpose or pastry flour. Since pastry flour can be hard to find in supermarkets, pastry-queen author Rose Levy Beranbaum came up with an acceptable substitute: a mixture of two-thirds all-purpose flour and one-third whole wheat flour. The average of the protein contents is low enough to work.

Gluten is tough stuff. Roll out a sheet of pasta, and it will literally shrink back underneath your rolling pin. It's almost like fighting something alive. In fact, if you simply mix flour and water, without any fat, you wind up with something like dried pasta. That's nobody's idea of a good piecrust. So we add fat, which works to prevent those long gluten strings from forming. Added to the flour before the water goes in, it coats the flour granules, essentially waterproofing the starch so that when the water is added and the dough is worked, those gluten strands have a much harder time developing. That is true for both American and European doughs.

Where the two differ is in the way the fat is added. In European doughs, the fat is thoroughly cut into the flour before the water goes in. In making one of these, you want the flour-and-fat combination to resemble coarse cornmeal before you begin adding the water. You should not be able to see any bits of fat at all. In American doughs, you want to stop working the fat in at about the halfway mark. The flour-and-fat combination should become pea-sized bits, with little clumps of fat remaining unmixed. American doughs are all about compromise. You want enough gluten to form the flaky framework, but you don't want enough to make the piecrust tough. The flakiness comes from those little chunks of fat that are wrapped up in the thin gluten framework. When the crust bakes, the fat melts, leaving air-filled gaps in the framework. Furthermore, any water that the fat contains converts to steam, puffing the gaps even bigger. Those airy gaps in the delicate gluten sheets are the secret to a flaky pastry.

Obviously, we're calling for fat to do two fairly contradictory things here — cover the starch granules thoroughly yet remain intact enough to create steam pockets during baking. The first is a function of the fat's shortening power — its ability to cover a surface and block water. The more unsaturated the fat, the better it does this. Oil is very effective. But if you've ever made a piecrust with just oil, you know that the results are far from flaky. In fact, they're usually tough and grainy. For piecrust, you need a solid fat —butter, margarine, shortening or lard. Each has its strengths and its drawbacks. Lard can be the best fat for a piecrust because its fat crystals are larger and will create greater flakiness. Unfortunately, most commercially rendered lard tastes bad (if you ever get a chance to try a piecrust made with good-quality lard, jump at it). Shortening and margarine are good choices for piecrusts because they have the unusual ability to maintain the same texture at a wide range of temperatures. There is little melting or softening in the early stages of heating. Furthermore, shortening and margarine are 100 percent fat — they contain no water, so there is less chance of the crust toughening. Butter is weaker in all these desirable qualities. It is highly saturated, so its shortening power is lower. It is highly changeable in texture. It must be chilled after rolling in order to maintain its structure in the oven. And it contains as much as 15 percent water, which can make the crust tough. On the other hand, it has absolutely superb flavor.

Some bakers recommend a blend of butter and shortening to get the best of both worlds. But there is no comparing the flavor of that blend with a pure-butter pastry. Most bakers feel that using all butter is worth the extra effort.

You can get a little clearer understanding of how all these things work by examining the different ingredients used in other types of doughs. For example, the difference between a sheet of pasta and a loaf of bread is that the bread is leavened. In one way or another, air has been incorporated to make the dough lighter (in the case of most breads, the leavener is the organism yeast, which digests sugar and produces carbon dioxide). But aside from bread's being lighter and airier because of the leavener, the gluten structures of the two are about the same. The difference between pasta and pastry is that the pastry contains far more fat, shortening the gluten strands and slightly leavening the dough. The difference between a pastry dough and a cookie is that the cookie is usually leavened and contains far more sugar, which robs water from the gluten strands, shortening them even further and creating a texture that is crumbly rather than flaky. Cakes are delicate because they are made with fat and sugar as well as another leavener — just beating the fat and sugar together to create air pockets provides some leavening.

While you want to develop some gluten in a flaky piecrust, you want only so much. Too much, and the crust will be tough, so hard you can't cut it with a knife. The first secret to limiting the development of gluten is to work the dough as little as possible. Remember: gluten is formed by water and flour combined with mechanical action. Handle the dough lightly and gently. Roll it out in as few strokes as possible — and don't reroll flaky dough unless it's absolutely necessary. You can further reduce the gluten development by adding some sugar to the flour before adding the water — the sugar will rob water from the flour, limiting the development of the gluten. Adding a bit of vinegar or lemon juice will also work, since an acid environment discourages gluten development. Resting the dough periodically helps too. When the dough has been worked, the gluten strands tighten, making them harder to stretch. If the dough begins shrinking back while you're rolling it out, pop it into the refrigerator for 10 or 15 minutes and the gluten will relax. Then you can proceed much more easily.

Of course, a crust is no more a pie than a house is a home. To make it complete, a crust needs a filling. These fillings take myriad forms, from the simplest jam tart to the fanciest custard. The type of filling will dictate to a certain extent the type of crust you use. Flaky pie doughs are best when you want top crusts, as with fruit pies. Use a short crust for custard pies and for tarts that don't have a top crust. Short crusts are especially good with moist fillings — the waterproofing ability of the fat works in more ways than one.

Though sweet piecrusts are the most basic combination of sugar, flour and butter, they are far from the only ones. In fact, those three ingredients define just about every kind of pastry known to man — from the lightest, most delicate cake to the crunchiest cookie. Obviously, that is too big a chunk of cooking to cover comfortably. Instead, let's concentrate on doughs, which we can loosely define as those pastries in which the solid ingredients outweigh the liquid. To put it more simply, those pastries that start out solid rather than liquid.

The most obvious connection is between piecrusts and cookie doughs. When you look at recipes for cookie doughs, the first thing that may strike you is their similarity to pie doughs. In fact, many cookie doughs could work as pie doughs. In the reverse, what could be better — or more cookie-like — than freshly baked scraps of pie dough dusted with cinnamon sugar? The next thing you'll probably notice is the addition of either baking powder or baking soda. These leaveners introduce carbon dioxide gas into doughs by chemical reaction, making them lighter. This is important if a dough is going to be very thick. A cookie dough baked without leavener, such as shortbread, will still taste pretty good, but it will be as hard as a brick. More is not better, of course. Too much leavener can puff a cookie to ridiculous heights, giving it a texture more like that of a cake. No crunch there.

Baking soda — technically bicarbonate of soda — is the original chemical leavener. When it is added to an acidic batter — one that contains something like buttermilk, for example — a chemical reaction occurs that produces air bubbles. (Remember the elementary school science project where you combined baking soda and vinegar?) These air bubbles are then caught in the gluten network of the batter. When heated, they expand, making the batter lighter. The most common acidifiers are dairy-based, like sour cream, yogurt and buttermilk. But there are other ingredients that will work as well. Honey, for example, is more acidic than any of the daily-based products. Molasses, regular cocoa and chocolate are almost as acidic. So are bananas, as long as they aren't overripe. As you can see, the necessity of including one of those acidifiers narrows the range of possibilities when it comes to baking cookies. That's where baking powder comes in.

Invented a little more than 100 years ago, baking powder is baking soda combined with a chemical acidifier, so you don't need to add any acid ingredients. Most baking powders today are "double acting." This means that they begin to form air bubbles both when they are first combined with a liquid and then again when they are heated. Baking powder will lose its leavening power rather quickly (within a matter of, say, six months, depending on storage conditions). To test your baking powder, simply put some in a bowl with a little water. It should bubble and foam, kind of like that elementary school experiment.

There is another way to get those air bubbles into a dough, but it's a lot trickier and hence is only occasionally used by itself anymore. However, many recipes still begin by having you "cream" butter and sugar together before you add a leavener.

What exactly does creaming mean and why is it so important? Creaming butter and sugar means to beat them together until they are thoroughly mixed. While the obvious effect of this is to soften the butter and make it spreadable and capable of absorbing the flour when it is added, there is another purpose as well, only it's a little harder to see. If you were to look at creamed butter and sugar under a magnifying glass, you would see that the sharp edges of those sugar grains have created gaps in the butter — holes, really — filled with air. Again, when that air is heated during baking, it will expand, making the baked dough lighter.

The other difference you'll notice is that in general, there are simply *a lot more* ingredients in cookie doughs than in pie doughs. While the basic piecrust is often nothing more than flour, fat, sugar and a little liquid, cookies are jazzed up with all kinds of things, from chopped or ground nuts and fruit to chocolate chips. In reality, you could add any of these things to a pie dough as well. The only restriction is one of good taste. Nuts can be added to especially good effect, as long as they are rather finely ground. For a basic 9-inch pie, you can add as much as ⅓ to ½ cup of ground nuts without removing any flour or having to make any further substitutions or changes to the recipe. A little of the bitterness of cocoa can be nice too, depending on the filling. Add up to ¼ cup for the same-sized pie.

Whatever you're doing to that piecrust, though, do it carefully and with confidence. Remember, pastry senses fear.

✦ **The easiest type of piecrust** for a beginner to make is a tart, or short, crust. For this crust, the fat is thoroughly worked into the flour before the water is added. Usually the base for open-faced, European-style tarts, this pastry can be used for any type of tart or pie.

✦ **Using all or part** pastry, or soft, flour will produce a tenderer crust.

✦ **Adding an acid,** such as vinegar, and a little sugar can make a piecrust shorter and more tender. It doesn't take much of either ingredient—2 to 3 teaspoons of acid or up to 2 table-spoons of sugar for a double-crust pie.

✦ **Butter has the best** combination of flavor and the physical qualities that contribute to flakiness, but it is more difficult to work with than other fats. You can substitute any solid fat—such as lard or vegetable shortening—for part or all of the butter.

✦ **Take your time** when making piecrust. Be sure all the ingredients are well chilled beforehand, and stop from time to time to chill the dough if it starts to get warm. This is especially important after both the kneading and the rolling, when all the physical action is most likely to develop gluten.

✦ **For a short-crust dough,** work the fat in well enough so that you do not see any flecks of it. For a flaky crust dough, leave the pieces of fat in small chunks. These will melt, creating steam pockets and making the pastry flaky. You should be able to see pieces of fat in the dough when it is rolled out.

✦ **Because the moisture content** of butter and flour can vary, add the water a little bit at a time. Stop when you see the dough start to form largish clumps. Press a piece of the dough in your hand. The dough should have the texture of modeling clay and should not crack at the edges. If it does crack, add just a little more water and test again.

✦ **Once the dough** has begun to come together, remove it from the bowl and gather it into a loose ball. Knead it lightly only one or two times with your hand—the dough should be smooth, not grainy. Then form it into a disk, wrap it and refrigerate it until you're ready to roll it out.

✦ **If a chilled dough** is too hard to roll out when you remove it from the refrigerator, soften it by whacking it across the top several times with a rolling pin. This should restore some plasticity without melting the fat.

✦ **When rolling out** a pie dough, be sure to move the rolling pin across the dough rather than pressing down on it. Keep rotating the dough and keep it well floured to prevent sticking. When you finish rolling it out, brush away any excess flour.

✦ **To place rolled-out dough** in a pie plate or tart pan without cracking the dough, roll it up onto the pin and then unroll it into the plate or pan. Form the rim, then chill it in the freezer for 10 to 15 minutes to allow the gluten to relax, to prevent shrinking.

✦ **If, despite** your best efforts, the dough still cracks and breaks apart, don't worry. Almost any piecrust can be mended simply by patching and pressing the pieces of dough together.

✦ **Cover the dough** with a sheet of aluminum foil and fill the foil with some kind of heat-conducting material, such as copper pennies or beans or rice, which will hold the dough in place and help it to brown. Bake the shell until the dough has browned, about 10 minutes, then remove the weights and aluminum foil and continue baking until the interior of the shell has browned, 10 to 15 minutes more.

✦ **For fruit tarts,** the filling is usually cooked separately or used raw. For fruit pies, the fruit is normally cooked in the crust.

✦ **When using cooked fruit,** make sure that it is well drained so you don't get a soggy crust. For raw fruit, sugar it in advance, then drain away any juices that are drawn out. If using a raw fruit filling, you'll usually include a layer of some kind of melted jelly, either as a liner for the pastry or as a glossy topping for the fruit itself.

✦ **Fruit that is cooked** in the piecrust needs some kind of thickener to absorb the liquid that will be cooked out. Flour is the easiest to use and gives a nice firm set, but it will make the filling cloudy and can impart a pasty taste. Cornstarch is crystal-clear, but it can make the filling too firm. Tapioca is the happy medium and has the added advantage of being thoroughly cooked at a lower temperature. Whatever the thickener, you need a top crust to seal in the heat, or you'll have raw starch in the pie.

✦ **There is no firm rule** for how much sugar and how much thickener to use for a given amount of fruit. Different fruits vary in the amount of water they contain, and even the same kind of fruit will vary with the season and with how long it has been stored. As a general rule, allow 4 to 5 cups fruit, about ½ cup sugar and 3 tablespoons thickener for a 9-inch pie.

✦ **Always bake a fruit pie** immediately after filling, to keep the bottom crust from absorbing too much liquid and becoming soggy.

✦ **Cobblers and crisps** are by far the easiest baked fruit desserts to make, since neither has a bottom crust to get soggy. Because of this, getting the proper ratio of fruit to thickener is not as critical. A cobbler is simply an inverted pie—cooked fruit on the bottom, flaky pastry crust on top. Crisps are even easier, because the topping is so simple to put together: For an 11-X-8-inch baking dish, mix together ½ cup flour or ground nuts and ¼ cup each of butter and sugar until clumps form, then scatter the topping over the fruit. Bake at 400 degrees until the fruit is thickened and bubbling and the topping is crisp and brown.

---

short-crust pastry

Thoroughly mixing the butter and the flour is the hallmark of short-crust pastry. This is the dough to use with open-faced tarts.

- - - - - - - - - -

1¼ cups all-purpose flour, plus extra for rolling

1 tablespoon sugar

Pinch of salt

8 tablespoons (1 stick) cold unsalted butter, plus extra for greasing

2–3 tablespoons ice water

Combine the flour, sugar, salt and butter in a food processor or large bowl and cut them together until the mixture resembles coarse corn-meal. Add the water 1 tablespoon at a time, stirring constantly or processing until the mixture just begins to come together. Remove the dough from the bowl and knead it lightly and briefly to make a smooth mass. Wrap it in plastic wrap and refrigerate for at least 30 minutes.

On a well-floured work surface, roll out the dough into a circle roughly 11 inches in diameter. Roll the dough back onto the rolling pin and transfer it to a buttered 9-inch tart pan with a removable bottom. Unroll the dough and gently press it into the pan. Trim the excess dough to 1 inch from the pan edges and fold the extra dough over itself between the pan and the dough rim to make a sturdier, taller edge. Refrigerate for 30 minutes.

Preheat the oven to 425 degrees.

To prebake the tart crust: Bake the crust until it is firm and the rim begins to brown, about 10 minutes.

Enough for one 9-inch tart

flaky piecrust

For a flaky crust, take care not to cut the butter too fine and not to overmix the dough. The butter should be left in relatively large chunks, about the size of peas. This is the dough to use with American fruit pies.

1¼ cups all-purpose flour, plus extra for rolling

¼ teaspoon salt

⅛ teaspoon baking powder

8 tablespoons (1 stick) unsalted butter, well chilled, cut into 8 pieces

2–3 tablespoons ice water

To mix by hand: Combine the flour, salt and baking powder in a large bowl and stir well. Add the butter and toss once or twice to coat with flour, then use your fingertips, two knives or a pastry blender to cut the butter into the dry ingredients, continuously pinching and squeezing the butter into the dry ingredients, or use a pastry blender. Be careful to keep the mixture uniform by occasionally reaching down to the bottom of the bowl and mixing all the ingredients evenly together.

Continue the process until the pieces of butter and flour are no bigger than peas. Scatter 2 tablespoons of the water over the mixture and stir gently with a fork. The dough should begin to hold together. If it still appears dry and crumbly, add some or all of the remaining water, 1 teaspoon at a time, until the dough holds together easily.

To mix in a food processor: Combine the flour, salt and baking powder and pulse 3 times to mix together. Add the butter and process, pulsing about 15 times at 1-second intervals, until the pieces of flour and butter are no bigger than peas.

Scatter 2 tablespoons of the water over the mixture and pulse 5 or 6 times. The dough should begin holding together. If it still appears dry and crumbly, add some or all of the remaining water, 1 teaspoon at a time, until the dough holds together easily.

Scrape the dough onto a lightly floured surface and form it into a disk. (If you are doubling the recipe, form the dough into 2 equal-sized disks.) Place the dough between 2 pieces of plastic wrap and press into a 6-inch disk. Refrigerate until firm, at least 1 hour, or until ready to use.

Enough for a one-crust 9-inch pie

rustic tart crust

This unusual recipe is adapted from Nancy Silverton, the pastry genius at Los Angeles' Campanile restaurant. It breaks many of the rules of pastry making, yet it is the easiest dough I've ever found to work with. It makes a fairly coarse, short crust that is perfect for galettes — free-form fruit pies that are made simply by mounding fruit in the middle of a circle of dough and then folding the edges over. It can also be made in the food processor, but be careful not to overmix.

- 1 cup cake flour, plus extra for rolling
- ½ cup bread flour
- 2 tablespoons sugar
- Dash of salt
- 8 tablespoons (1 stick) unsalted butter, well chilled, cubed
- 4 teaspoons ice water
- 2 teaspoons vanilla extract

Combine the cake flour, bread flour, sugar and salt in a large bowl with an electric mixer. Distribute the butter evenly over the top and mix on low speed until the mixture resembles coarse cornmeal. Do not overmix.

Alternatively, the butter can be worked in by hand. Toss the cubes with the dry ingredients and then rub the cubes quickly and lightly between your thumbs and forefingers until the mixture resembles coarse cornmeal. Do not overmix.

Combine the water and vanilla and sprinkle all of it over the dough. Mix on low speed or by hand with a fork until the dough forms a rough ball that pulls cleanly away from the sides of the bowl. (This takes much longer than you might expect, 3 to 4 minutes.)

Transfer the dough to a well-floured work surface or pastry board and gently but firmly knead it until it is smooth and no longer shaggy at the edges, 2 to 3 minutes. Form the dough into a ball and flatten it into a disk. Wrap tightly with plastic wrap and refrigerate until very cold, at least 30 minutes, before rolling out.

Enough for one 9-inch tart

rustic peach tart

Don't roll the pastry too thin; it's a prime attraction, not just a container for fruit.

- - - - - - - - - - - - - - - -

2 cups sliced peeled peaches
3 tablespoons sugar
1 tablespoon cornstarch
⅛ teaspoon ground cloves
   Rustic Tart Crust (page 299), chilled

Preheat the oven to 375 degrees.

Combine the peaches, sugar, cornstarch and cloves in a medium bowl, and toss well until the cornstarch is no longer visible.

Let the dough soften slightly, if necessary. On a well-floured surface, roll out the tart dough into a circle roughly ⅛ inch thick. Transfer it to a greased baking sheet. Spoon the peach mixture into the center, leaving a 2-inch border.

Fold the edges of the dough over the peaches to form a five-sided tart, with the peaches showing in the center: Fold one edge over, then fold the second edge over, pleating the dough as necessary and pressing firmly on the pleat. Repeat three more times to enclose the filling.

Bake for 10 minutes. Reduce the heat to 350 degrees and bake until the crust is light brown, 45 to 50 minutes. Check every 10 minutes to make sure the crust is not burning on the bottom, and reduce the heat to 300 degrees, if necessary. Cool briefly to let the juices set, then cut into wedges and serve.

8 servings

nectarine and almond tart

I love the combination of almonds and stone fruit. That would not surprise a botanist, since they are first cousins, both members of the drupe family. Almonds come in a thick fruit-like husk that is removed during processing.

¼ cup slivered almonds

1 pound nectarines

1 tablespoon sugar, plus more for dusting

1 tablespoon fresh lemon juice

Rustic Tart Crust (page 299), chilled

½ cup fresh raspberries

Preheat the oven to 375 degrees.

Toast the almonds on a small baking sheet in the oven until aromatic, about 5 minutes. Leave the oven on. Cool the almonds slightly, then coarsely grind them in a food processor. Set aside.

Slice the nectarines thin and toss them in a mixing bowl with the sugar and lemon juice until thoroughly mixed.

On a well-floured surface, roll out the pastry dough ⅛ inch thick. Transfer the dough to a greased baking sheet or jelly-roll pan.

Scatter the ground almonds over the dough. Mound the nectarine slices in a rough pile in the center. Scatter the raspberries over the top. Fold the edges of the dough over the nectarines to form a five-sided tart, with the nectarines showing in the center: Fold one edge over, then fold the second edge over, pleating the dough as necessary and pressing firmly on the pleat. Repeat three more times to enclose the filling. Dust lightly with sugar.

Bake for 10 minutes. Reduce the heat to 350 degrees and bake until the crust is light brown, about 45 minutes. Check every 10 minutes to make sure the crust is not burning on the bottom, and reduce the heat to 300 degrees if necessary. Cool briefly to let the juices set, then cut into wedges and serve.

6 servings

lavender-fig tart

This dessert is the essence of late summer/early fall in Los Angeles. The raspberry jam should just cover the bottom of the shell, accenting the figs rather than dominating them. The same caution is true for the lavender, which tastes like cheap perfume if used in excess.

----

  1 pound fresh figs
1–1½ cups raspberry jam
  1 tablespoon water
     Juice of ½ lemon
     Short-Crust Pastry (page 296), baked
  3 tablespoons sugar
  1 tablespoon chopped fresh lavender leaves
        or 1 teaspoon fresh thyme leaves
     Barely sweetened whipped cream for serving

Preheat the oven to 425 degrees.

Trim the stems from the figs and cut crosses in their tops, going down nearly to the bottom, so the figs will open like flowers. Set aside.

Combine the jam, water and lemon juice in a small nonreactive saucepan over medium-high heat and heat, stirring, until the jam is smooth and flowing. Then cook until the jam is slightly thickened, about 5 minutes. Pour the mixture through a strainer into the baked tart crust and spread it evenly across the bottom.

Place the figs in the tart, pressing them open first and arranging them to cover as much of the bottom as possible. Combine the sugar and lavender or thyme in a small bowl and stir roughly to combine. Strain out the pieces of herb and sprinkle the flavored sugar over the top of the figs.

Bake until the figs soften, about 10 minutes. Cool slightly on a rack. Remove the rim of the pan, cut the tart into wedges and serve with whipped cream.

6 to 8 servings

apple crisp

You can use this crisp mixture for all different kinds of fruits — anything from peaches to rhubarb and strawberries. It's so easy to make that I bake it much more frequently than I make pies or tarts. This is great with vanilla ice cream.

- 4 apples (preferably Granny Smiths), peeled, cored and cut into eighths
- 1 quince, quartered, cored and coarsely grated
- ¼ cup dark or golden raisins, plumped in brandy or warm water and drained
- ¾–1 cup sugar
- ¼ cup finely ground walnuts
- ¼ cup all-purpose flour
  Dash of salt
- 3–4 tablespoons unsalted butter, well chilled, cut into tablespoons, plus extra for greasing

Preheat the oven to 350 degrees. Butter a 13-x-9-inch baking dish.

Combine the apples, quince and raisins in a large mixing bowl. (There should be about 8 cups of fruit.) Add sugar to taste, ¼ to ½ cup, depending on the sweetness of the fruit. Do not oversweeten.

To make the topping, combine the remaining sugar, the walnuts, flour and salt in a food processor or a small mixing bowl. Pulse or stir to mix well. If using a food processor, add 2 tablespoons of the butter and pulse briefly to mix. Add another tablespoon and pulse again. If the combination takes on the consistency of moist sand, do not add additional butter. If not, add the remaining 1 tablespoon butter and pulse again. If making by hand, add the butter following the same procedure, rubbing the flour mixture and butter between your fingertips.

Pour the fruit into the baking dish and spread it evenly. Sprinkle the topping over the top, breaking up any large clumps.

Bake for 45 to 50 minutes, or until the fruit is tender and the topping is browned. Cool briefly to let the juices set, then spoon onto serving plates.

8 servings

✦ **Because the ratio** of the ingredients has to be just right, cookie recipes tend not to be very friendly to improvisation. Stick to the recipe.

✦ **It's a good idea** to sift together all the dry ingredients except the sugar. This will ensure that they will be evenly distributed through the cookie dough.

✦ **When butter and sugar** are properly creamed, the combination should be light and fluffy and nearly white in color. This usually takes 2 to 3 minutes of beating. If using a stand mixer, though, don't walk away while the butter is creaming. Overbeating the butter will deflate the air bubbles you just achieved.

✦ **Add the flour** a bit at a time, beating constantly to make sure it is well distributed.

✦ **Chill cookie doughs** that are to be rolled out.

✦ **In general, cookie doughs** can be worked much more than pie doughs. After you've rolled and cut out one batch of cookies, you can reroll the scraps as many as two or three times without loss of quality.

---

snickerdoodles

This is one of my mom's recipes, and it is the bane of my existence. No matter what I serve of my own for dinner, these always get the most praise.

- 2¾ cups all-purpose flour
- 2 teaspoons cream of tartar
- 1 teaspoon baking soda
- ½ teaspoon salt
- 1 cup shortening
- 1¾ cups sugar
- 2 large eggs
- 1 tablespoon ground cinnamon

Sift together the flour, cream of tartar, baking soda and salt into a bowl; set aside.

Cream the shortening and 1½ cups of the sugar in a large bowl with an electric mixer until light and fluffy. Add the eggs 1 at a time, beating thoroughly after each addition. Reduce the mixer speed and gradually add the flour mixture, beating well. Gather the dough into a ball, wrap it in plastic wrap and refrigerate until firm, about 30 minutes.

Preheat the oven to 350 degrees.

Combine the remaining ¼ cup sugar and the cinnamon.

Tear off pieces of dough about the size of a walnut, roll them into balls, roll them in the cinnamon sugar and place them about 2 inches apart on ungreased baking sheets.

Bake until the cookies are light brown and firm on top, 10 to 15 minutes. The tops will be deeply cracked and the centers still somewhat soft.

Cool on the baking sheets for 5 minutes, then transfer to a rack to cool completely. Repeat with the remaining dough. Store in an airtight container.

About 4 dozen cookies

new mexican christmas cookies (biscochitos)

The flavor of these cookies may be a little surprising because of the combination of anise seeds and brandy. But once you get attached to them, it won't be the holidays without them. The texture is that of a crisp butter cookie.

- 6 cups all-purpose flour
- 1 tablespoon baking powder
- ¼ teaspoon salt
- 1 pound lard, at room temperature, or 2 cups shortening
- 1¾ cups sugar
- 2 teaspoons anise seeds
- 2 large eggs
- ¼ cup brandy
- 1 tablespoon ground cinnamon

Sift together the flour, baking powder and salt into a bowl and set aside.

Cream the lard or shortening and 1½ cups of the sugar in a large bowl with an electric mixer until light and fluffy. Beat in the anise seeds, then add the eggs 1 at a time, beating well after each addition. Beat in the brandy. Reduce the mixing speed to low and gradually add the flour mixture and beat until the dough pulls cleanly away from the sides of the bowl. Cover and chill for 1 hour.

Preheat the oven to 350 degrees.

Combine the remaining ¼ cup sugar and the cinnamon and set aside.

Remove the dough from the refrigerator at least 20 minutes before rolling out.

Roll out the dough ¼ to ½ inch thick on a lightly floured surface and cut into desired shapes. Place cookies 1 inch apart on ungreased baking sheets and dust with cinnamon sugar.

Bake until lightly browned, about 10 minutes. Cool on a rack. Repeat with the remaining dough. Store in an airtight container.

About 6 dozen cookies

gingersnaps

These are thin, flat and flexible, kind of like the cookies the French call "cat's tongues." This recipe comes from the southern California artist Annie Stromquist.

- -

2 cups all-purpose flour

2 teaspoons baking soda

1 teaspoon ground ginger

1 teaspoon ground cinnamon

1 teaspoon ground cloves

¼ teaspoon salt

¾ cup shortening

1 cup packed light brown sugar

1 large egg

¼ cup molasses

Sugar for rolling

Sift together the flour, baking soda, ginger, cinnamon, cloves and salt into a bowl; set aside.

Cream the shortening and brown sugar in a large bowl with an electric mixer until light and fluffy. Add the egg and molasses and beat well. Reduce the mixer speed to low and gradually add the dry ingredients, beating well. Gather the dough into a ball, wrap it in plastic wrap and refrigerate until firm, about 30 minutes.

Preheat the oven to 350 degrees. Grease 2 baking sheets.

Tear off pieces of dough about the size of a walnut, roll them into balls, roll them in sugar and place them about 2 inches apart on the baking sheets.

Bake the cookies until they flatten, 10 to 15 minutes. The tops will be deeply cracked and the centers still somewhat soft.

Cool the cookies on the baking sheets for 5 minutes, then transfer to a rack to cool completely. Repeat with the remaining dough. Store in an airtight container.

About 3 dozen cookies

grandma smith's christmas cookies

This is an old favorite of my family's. Crisp and somewhat neutral in flavor, these cookies are perfect for cutting into elaborate holiday shapes and smothering with colored icing and sparkly colored sugar.

5½ cups all-purpose flour, plus more if needed

2 teaspoons baking powder

1 cup shortening or margarine (2 sticks),
   at room temperature

2 cups sugar

2 large eggs

½ cup milk

Colored sugars and/or icing

Sift the flour and baking powder together into a bowl. Set aside.

Cream the shortening or margarine and sugar in a large bowl with an electric mixer until light and fluffy. Add the eggs 1 at a time, beating well after each addition, then beat in the milk. Reduce the mixer speed to low and beat in the dry ingredients 1 cup at a time. Continue beating until the mixture pulls cleanly away from the sides of the bowl, 30 to 45 seconds. If necessary, add a little more flour.

Cover the dough and chill for 1 hour.

Remove the dough from the refrigerator at least 30 minutes before rolling out.

Preheat the oven to 350 degrees.

On a lightly floured work surface, roll out one-quarter of the dough ¼ to ½ inch thick. Cut into shapes and transfer to ungreased baking sheets. Sprinkle with colored sugar, if not using icing.

Bake the cookies until light brown, about 10 minutes. Cool briefly on the baking sheets, then transfer to a rack and decorate with icing, if desired. Repeat with the remaining dough. Store in an airtight container.

About 6 dozen cookies

sour cherry–stuffed almond cookies

This macaroon is made without starch or fat (aside from that in the nuts). Instead, it relies on the binding power of beaten egg whites to hold the dough together and on the air pockets left between the irregularly ground chunks of nuts for leavening. The recipe is based on the cookbook author Mary Taylor Simeti's version of an old Sicilian one. The main difference is that the macaroons are stuffed with dried sour cherries rather than the traditional, somewhat bitter jam.

- 1 pound blanched whole almonds (about 3 cups)
- 2 cups sugar
- ½ teaspoon vanilla extract
- 3 large egg whites
- 2 cups dried sour cherries, soaked in warm water until soft, and drained

Preheat the oven to 300 degrees. Grease and flour a baking sheet.

Grind the almonds and sugar fine in a food processor. Add the vanilla extract and pulse to mix. Pour in the egg whites, distributing them evenly across the top of the mixture. Process until a ball of dough forms on the blade.

Remove the dough from the food processor. Tear off a walnut-sized piece of dough and roll briskly between your palms into ball. Use your finger to poke a hole into the middle of the ball. Stuff 1 or 2 cherries into the center and press the dough together to seal the hole. If desired, form into a rough pyramid, using three fingers and your thumb. Repeat with the remaining dough.

Place 1 inch apart on an ungreased baking sheet and bake for about 25 minutes, or until delicately browned. Cool briefly on the pan before transferring to a rack to cool completely. Store in an airtight container.

About 2 dozen cookies

Page numbers in **boldface type** denote recipes.

Acids (acidic ingredients)
  cooking beans with, 159
  cooking fruits with, 59, 94
  cooking vegetables with,
    52, 53, 61
  in custards, 131
  in doughs, 291
  green vegetables and, 62
  in piecrusts, 293
  in starch-thickened sauces,
    152–53
Acidulated water (water with
    lemon juice), for pre-
    venting browning owing
    to enzymes, 53, 93
Acrolein, 13
Alkaline substances, cooking
    vegetables with, 52, 53
All-purpose flour, 286
Almond
  -apricot clafoutis, **114**
  cookies, sour
    cherry–stuffed, **310**
  and nectarine tart, **301**
Amaretti, in peach fritters, **30**
Amino acids, crust of fried
    foods and, 22
Amylopectins, 149, 151, 156,
    161
  in rice, 156–57
Amylose, 149, 150, 156

Anchovies, in pasta with
    broccoli rabe, **168**
Animal fats, 11, 12
  crispest crusts obtained
    with, 23
Anthocyanin, 50, 58
Anthoxanthin, 50
Apple(s), 56, 59, 93
  crisp, **303**
  puree of winter squash and,
    215
  refrigeration of, 59
  ripening stone fruit and
    pears and, 93
  vanilla-baked, with bourbon
    sauce, **112**
Applesauce, quince, **98**
Apricot(s), 56, 57, 59, 93
  -almond clafoutis, **114**
  dried
    in cornmeal waffles with
      winter fruit compote,
      110
    in fall fruit compote, **97**
Arrowroot, 151, 154
Artichoke(s)
  baked fish with potatoes
    and, **250**
  browning owing to
    enzymes, 53, 61
  risotto, **184**

Artichoke(s) (*cont.*)
  spring vegetable stew of
    snap peas, lettuce, new
    potatoes and, **80**
Arugula salad, pork schnitzel
  with, 44
Asparagus
  in green goddess salad, **136**
  roasted, free-form lasagna
    of, **175**
  scrambled eggs with morels
    and, **141**
Avocado(s), 56
  ceviche with shrimp and,
    235
  in green goddess salad, **136**

Bacon, brussels sprouts
  and, **36**
Baked fish with potatoes and
  artichokes, **250**
Baked tomatoes stuffed with
  mozzarella, **73**
Baking (baked foods),
  tomatoes, 73
Baking powder
  in batters, 22
  as leavener, 291
  testing, 291
Baking soda
  in batters, 22
  cooking beans with, 159
  cooking vegetables with,
    53
  as leavener, 291
Balsamic vinegar, butternut
  squash puree with, **213**
Bananas, ripening of, 56, 58
Basting, roasting meat and,
  254
Batter for clafoutis, 114
Batters (batter-coated fried
  foods)
  beer in, 18, 22
  fried little fish, **29**
  keeping ice-cold, 22
  leaveners in, 22
  peach fritters, **30**
  salt and, 23
  serving, 24
  stuffed zucchini flowers, **27**
  water in, 22
Bean(s), 155–60
  age of, 160
  cooking in the oven, 160
  cranberry, stew of charred
    tomatoes, pasta and, **82**
  fava, ragout of shrimp
    and, **84**
  flatulence (gas) caused by,
    158, 159
  lima, California succotash
    of squash, corn and, **68**
  myths about, 158
  pinto
    puree, **192**
    and squash stew, **196**
  pork and, . . . and endive,
    198
  refried, 162
  salting before cooking,
    158–59, 190
  serving cold, 190
  soaking before cooking,
    158, 160, 190
  testing for doneness, 190
  white
    crostini, **191**
    and Swiss chard stew, **194**
Beard, James, 30
Bearnaise sauce, 139
Béchamel, 152
Beef. *See also* Meat(s)
  brining, 232
  corned, 232
  pastrami, 232
  pot roast, mushroom, **270**

skirt steak, in real
fajitas, **258**
temperature for cooking,
254
Beer, in batters, 18, 22
Beet and orange salad,
roasted, **78**
Belgian endive, braised with
cream, **65**
Bell peppers
in grilled vegetable
sandwich, **86**
red, in ratatouille, **76**
Beranbaum, Rose Levy, 287
Berry(-ies), 56, 93
ice cream, **115**
Betalain, 50
Beurre manié, 163, 265
Bicarbonate of soda. *See*
Baking soda
Biscochitos (New Mexican
Christmas cookies), **307**
Blackberry ice cream, **115**
Blanching vegetables, 52
before shallow-frying or
sautéing, 32
Blanquettes, 229, 263
Blender, making mayonnaise
in a, 128–29, 134
Blood, 221
Blue cheese, celery salad
with walnuts and, **135**
Blush of fruits, 51
Bocconcini, stuffed zucchini
flowers with, **27**
Boiling point of water versus
oil, 10
Boiling vegetables, 53, 54
Bourbon
gratin of sweet potatoes
and, **214**
sauce, vanilla-baked apples
with, **112**
Braised duck and lentils, **200**

Braising (braises)
meat, 233, 263–65
chicken braised with
green olives and
thyme, **266**
duck and lentils, **200**
lamb shanks with green
olives, **274**
level of liquid in, 264
mushroom pot roast, **270**
salmon braised with
leeks, prosciutto and
mushrooms, **242**
temperature for, 228–29,
264
vegetables in, 264
vegetables, 62
Belgian endive braised
with cream, **65**
butter-braised spinach,
64
Bratwurst, smokerless
smoked, **283**
Bread crumbs, crust of fried
foods and, 22
Bread flour, 286, 287
Breads, 289
Brined turkey, roast, **255**
Brining, 231–32, 253
Broccoli, 50
blanching, 52
Broccoli rabe
lasagna, **172**
pasta with, **168**
Broiled foods
crisp salmon salad, **237**
rajas (grilled peppers and
cream), **74**
sand dabs (or sole) with
brown butter, **252**
Broiled sand dabs (or sole)
with brown butter, **252**
Brown butter, sand dabs (or
sole) with, **252**

Browning. *See also*
    Caramelization
  by cooking, 17
    eggs in batters and, 18
    flouring meats before
      browning, 263
    meats, 6, 229–30, 263
    meats in braises, stews
      and daubes, 263
    onions, 19–20
    starches for sauces, 153
    vegetables, 54
  enzymatic, 53, 59, 93
Brussels sprouts and
    bacon, **36**
Bubbles, frying and, 15
Butter
  beurre manié, 163, 265
  -braised spinach, **64**
  brown, broiled sand dabs
    (or sole) with, **252**
  chipotle-tequila, grilled
    salmon with, **246**
  clarified, 126
  creaming sugar and,
    292, 305
  in hollandaise sauce, 130
  in hot emulsion sauces, 139
  for piecrusts, 288–89
  in piecrusts, 293
  in risottos, 183
  in scrambled eggs, 140
Buttermilk, in doughs, 291
Butternut squash puree with
    balsamic vinegar, **213**

Cabbage
  blanching, 52
  crisp-skinned salmon on
    creamy leeks and, **38**
  odor of, 54
Cajun roux, 153
Cake flour, 286

Cakes, 289
Calamari (squid)
  salad, **236**
  in seafood rice salad, **188**
California charmoula, **250**
California succotash of
    squash, lima beans and
    corn, **68**
Candied citrus peel, **100**
Canning jams and jellies, 118
Canola oil (rapeseed oil), 11
Caramelization (carameliz-
    ing), 17. *See also*
    Browning, by cooking
  browning meats and, 229
  onions, 20
  of vegetables, 55
Caramelized onions and
    green olives, goat
    cheese tart with, **34**
Carotenoids, 50, 52
Carrots, 50, 52
Casserole, eggplant and goat
    cheese, **91**
Cauliflower
  blanching, 52
  soup, cream of, **205**
Celery salad with walnuts and
    blue cheese, **135**
Cellulose, 48–49, 51, 53
Cell walls of fruits and
    vegetables, 53–56, 59
Cereal starches, 151, 154. *See
    also* Cornstarch; Flour
Ceviche, 219
  with shrimp and avocado,
    235
Charmoula, California, **250**
Charred tomatoes, stew of
    pasta, cranberry beans
    and, **82**
Cheese(s)
  blue, celery salad with
    walnuts and, **135**

cotija, in pinto bean
    puree, **192**
goat
    and eggplant casserole, **91**
    roasted tomatoes with, **63**
    tart, with caramelized
        onions and green
        olives, **34**
    macaroni and, with green
        onions and ham, **170**
    mozzarella, baked tomatoes
        stuffed with, **73**
    mozzarella, stuffed zucchini
        flowers with, **27**
Cherry(-ies), 56, 93
    -almond clafoutis, **114**
    dried sour, in fall fruit
        compote, **97**
    sour, -stuffed almond
        cookie, **310**
Chicken. *See also* Poultry
    braised with green olives
        and thyme, **266**
    breasts, pan-fried, with
        fresh tomatoes, green
        olives and rosemary, **42**
    country fried, **40**
    in the pot, **268**
    white and dark meat in,
        224
Chickpeas (garbanzo beans),
    160
Chiles
    chipotle meco, in pinto
        bean puree, **192**
    poblano, in rajas (grilled
        peppers and cream), **74**
Chinese fried rice, 157
Chipotle, -tequila butter,
    grilled salmon with, **246**
Chlorophyll, 50–52
Chocolate, pots de crème,
    144
Cholesterol, 12, 127

Christmas cookies
    Grandma Smith's, **309**
    New Mexican (biscochitos),
        307
Citrus fruits, 56, 93
Citrus peel, candied, **100**
Clafoutis, apricot-almond,
    114
Clarified butter, 126
Classic Home Desserts
    (Sax), 144
Clumping of starch-thick-
    ened sauces, 153
Cobblers, 295
Cocoa, in piecrusts, 292
Coleslaw, Dungeness crab,
    238
Collagen, 220, 222
Compote
    fruit, fall, **97**
    spiced plum, cornmeal
        crepes with, **108**
    winter fruit, cornmeal
        waffles with, **110**
Conduction, 10
Connective tissue, 220,
    222, 224, 225
Cookie(s), **305**
    amaretti, in peach
        fritters, **30**
    Christmas, Grandma
        Smith's, **309**
    doughs, 290–92, **305**
    gingersnaps, **308**
    leaveners in, 291
    New Mexican Christmas
        (biscochitos), **307**
    snickerdoodles, **306**
    sour cherry–stuffed
        almond, **310**
Corn
    California succotash of
        squash, lima beans
        and, **68**

Corn (*cont.*)
  soup, smoky cream of
    corn, **165**
Corned beef, 232
Cornmeal
  crepes with spiced plum
    compote, **108**
  polenta with ragù, soft, **180**
  waffles with winter fruit
    compote, **110**
Cornstarch, as thickener
  for custards, 132
  for pie fillings, 295
  for sauces, 151–52, 163
Cotija cheese, in pinto bean
    puree, **192**
Country fried chicken, **40**
Crab, Dungeness,
    coleslaw, **238**
Cranberry beans, stew of
    charred tomatoes, pasta
    and, **82**
Cream
  Belgian endive braised
    with, **65**
  Mexican, 74
    mango crepes with, **106**
Creamed onions with shiitake
    mushrooms, **70**
Creaming butter and sugar,
    292, 305
Cream of cauliflower
    soup, **205**
Cream of corn soup,
    smoky, **165**
Crepes
  cornmeal, with spiced plum
    compote, **108**
  mango, with Mexican
    cream, **106**
Crisp(s), 295
  apple, **303**
Crisp salmon salad, **237**
Crisp-skinned salmon on

  creamy leeks and
    cabbage, **38**
Crostini, white bean, **191**
Crust(s). *See also* Piecrust(s);
    Tart(s), crust for
  of fried foods, 12, 15, 17
  deep-frying, 22
  sautéing, 32
  short-, pastry, **296**
Cucumber salad, oven-
    steamed salmon
    with, **244**
Curdling of eggs, 130–32
Custards, 131–32
  baked, 132, 139
  drops of liquid on top
    of, 140
  starches in, 132
  stirred and cooked on the
    stove, 132

Dal Pescatore (restaurant),
    186
Daubes, 263–65
Deep-frying (deep-fried
    foods), 9, 18, 22–24.
    See also Batters (batter-
    coated fried foods);
    Frying
  flour dusting for, 22
  fried little fish, 29
  peach fritters, **30**
  size of pieces of food for, 22
  stuffed zucchini flowers, **27**
  temperature for, 23, 24
  thermometer for, 23
  Tuscan potato chips, **25**
Doughs, 289. *See also*
    Piecrust(s); Tart(s),
    crust for
  acidifiers in, 291
  creamed butter and sugar
    in, 292

for pies, 290–94
Dreamsicle oranges, **99**
Duck and lentils, braised, **200**
Dungeness crab coleslaw, **238**

Echo (restaurant), **96**
Egg(s), 123–47
  air pocket in, 124–25
  in batters, 18, 22
  in custards, 131–32
  fried, 140
  hard-boiled, 124–25
  overcooked, 140
  parts of, 123–24
  in puddings, 130–31
  in sauces, 125–27
  scrambled, 140
    with morels and aspara-
      gus, **141**
  whites, in batters, 22
  yolk, 123–24
    as emulsifier, 127–29
    in hollandaise sauce,
      129–30
    in hot emulsion sauces,
      139
Eggplant(s)
  and goat cheese casserole,
    91
  in grilled vegetable sand-
    wich, **86**
  in ratatouille, **76**
Emulsifier(s), 126
  egg yolk as, 127–29
Emulsions (emulsified
    sauces), 123, 125–27
  hollandaise sauce, 129–30
  hot, 139–40
  mayonnaise as, 125
  physically induced, 125–26
  puddings as, 130–31
  vinaigrettes as, 125–26,
    133

Endive
  Belgian, braised with
    cream, 65
  pork and beans . . . and, **198**
Enzymes
  browning owing to, 53,
    59, 93
  in fruits, 59
    ripeness and, 55
Epicurean, The
    (Ranhofer), 65
Ethylene gas, 58

Fajitas, real, **258**
Fall fruit compote, **97**
Fat(s). *See also* Oil(s)
  for basting, 254
  chemical composition
    of, 11
  in fish, 222
  highly saturated, 11
  in meats
    flavor differences and,
      223
    heat, effect of, 221
    marbling, 221
  in piecrusts, 293
  piecrusts and, 286–88
  shortening power of
    different types of, 288
Fava beans, ragout of shrimp
    and, **84**
Fennel, in market mix, **72**
Fiber, in beans, 158
Fig(s), 56, 93
  tart, lavender-, **302**
  and white peach ice
    cream, **117**
Fish
  baked, with potatoes and
    artichokes, **250**
  deterioration after being
    caught, 222–23

Fish (*cont.*)
fillets, 234
fried little, **29**
grilling, 234
marinating, 234
meat compared to, 222
salmon. *See* Salmon
sand dabs (or sole) with
  brown butter,
  broiled, **252**
sautéing, 32
soup with shellfish, **240**
swordfish, grilled, with salsa
  verde, **248**
techniques for cooking, 234
testing for doneness,
  227, 234
trout mousse, **142**
Flaky piecrust, **297**
Flatulence (gas), caused by
  beans, 158, 159
Flour(s)
all-purpose, 286
bread, 286, 287
cake, 286
in custards, 132
dusting of, for deep-frying
  foods, 22
pastry, 286, 287, 293
for piecrusts, 286–87
protein content of, 286
semolina, 286
as thickener
  for pie fillings, 295
  for sauces, 151–52, 163
unbleached, 286
Flouring meat before
  browning, 263
Food processor, making
  mayonnaise in a,
  128–29, 134
Free-form lasagna of roasted
  asparagus, **175**
French fries, 12

baking potatoes as best for,
  161–62
potatoes for, 16–17
stages in the life of oil and,
  14–15
Fricassees, 263
Fried little fish, **29**
Fried rice, Chinese, 157, 182
Fritters, peach, **30**
Fruit(s), 47
cobblers, 295
colors of, 50, 51
compote, 93
  fall, **97**
  winter, cornmeal waffles
    with, **110**
cooking, 58–59
crisps, 295
for jam making, 118
picking, 57
pie fillings, 294–95
refrigeration of, 59, 93
ripeness of, 55–58, 93
softening with sugar, 93
stone, 57, 58, 93
  ice cream, **116**
  ripening at room
    temperature, 93
storage of, 59, 93
sugar's effect on, 59
sweetening, 59
sweetness of, 57
tart fillings, 294–95
temperature for storing, 58
vegetables compared to, 55
washing, 59
Frying (fried foods). *See also*
  Deep-frying; Oil(s), frying in; Shallow-frying
  (panfrying and
  sautéing); *and specific
  types of fried foods*
coatings for, 17–18
crust of, 12, 15, 17

as a drying process, 14, 15
as efficient cooking
    method, 11
fear of, 9–10
as one of hottest forms of
    cooking, 9–10
panfrying, 18–19
roasting compared to, 10
serving, 24
soaps created by, 14
steam and, 15–16
water and, 15–16

Garbanzo beans
    (chickpeas), 160
Garlic
    sausages, spicy, **281**
    sautéed green beans with
        sage and, **37**
    sautéing onions and, 19
Gelatinization, 150–52
Gingersnaps, **308**
Glaze, from braising
    vegetables, 62
Glazed zucchini, **67**
Gliadin, 286
Gluten
    in pasta, 155, 156
    piecrusts and, 286–90
Glutenin, 286
Gnocchi, 155, 204
    potato, **211**
Goat cheese
    and eggplant casserole, **91**
    roasted tomatoes with, **63**
    tart, with caramelized
        onions and green
        olives, **34**
Grandma Smith's Christmas
    cookies, **309**
Grapes, 56, 93
Gratin
    potato, **209**

potatoes, 162
    of sweet potatoes and bour-
        bon, **214**
Gravy, flour-thickened, 150
Green beans, with garlic and
    sage, sautéed, **37**
Green goddess salad, **136**
Green onions, macaroni and
    cheese with ham
    and, **170**
Grilled salmon with chipotle-
    tequila butter, **246**
Grilled vegetable
    sandwich, **86**
Grilling (grilled foods)
    fish, 234
    meats, 253, 254
    rajas (grilled peppers and
        cream), **74**
    salmon with chipotle-
        tequila butter, **246**
    swordfish with salsa
        verde, **248**
    vegetables, 54
    vegetable sandwich, **86**
Gristle, 221

Halibut, 234
Ham, macaroni and cheese
    with green onions
    and, **170**
Hard water, cooking beans
    and, 159
Hard wheat, 286
Heart disease, saturated fats
    and, 12
Heat, frying and, 9–10
Hemoglobin, 221, 226
Herbs, cooking beans
    with, 159
Highly saturated fats, crispest
    crusts obtained with, 23
Hirtzler, Victor, 136

Holland, Adams, 96
Hollandaise sauce, 129–30, 139
Homogenization, 126
Honey, in doughs, 291

Ice cream
  berry, **115**
  fruit-flavored, 59
  stone fruit, **116**
  white peach and fig, **117**
Instant puddings, 153
Italian sausage(s)
  in pork and beans . . . and endive, **198**
  in ragù napoletano, **276**
  and ribs with red wine–braised lentils, **202**
  in soft polenta with ragù, **180**

Jam, 56, 59, 118. *See also* Preserves
  nectarine and rose geranium, 120
Jam jar lids, 118
Jam jars, 118
Jellies, 118

Kamman, Madeleine, 142
Keller, Thomas, 38
Kitchen Garden Cookbook, The (Thompson), 119
Kiwis, 56
Kramer, Matt, 157

Lamb, 225
  and lentils to eat with a spoon, 272

orange zest, and rosemary sausages, **282**
  roast, with fresh peas and turnips, **260**
  shanks with green olives, braised, **274**
  temperature for cooking, 254
Lard, in piecrusts, 288, 293
Lasagna, 166
  broccoli, **172**
  of roasted asparagus, free-form, **175**
  wild mushroom, **177**
Lavender-fig tart, **302**
Leaveners, 289, 291. *See also* Baking soda
Lecithin, as emulsifier, 127
Leeks
  and cabbage, creamy, crisp-skinned salmon on, **38**
  salmon braised with prosciutto, mushrooms and, **242**
Lemon
  curd tart, **147**
  juice
    in piecrusts, 290
    in starch-thickened sauces, 152–53
  Meyer, marmalade, 121
  sponge pudding, **146**
Lentil flour, 155
Lentils, 160, 190
  braised duck and, **200**
  lamb and, to eat with a spoon, **272**
  red wine–braised, sausages and ribs with, **202**
  serving cold, 190
Lettuce, spring vegetable stew of snap peas, new potatoes, artichokes and, **80**

index

Lima beans, California
succotash of squash,
corn and, **68**
Lime-mint syrup, sliced
melons in, **96**

Macaroni and cheese with
green onions and
ham, **170**
Maillard reaction, 229
Mango(es), 56, 93
crepes with Mexican
cream, **106**
refrigeration of, 59
Marbling, 221
Margarine, for piecrusts, 288
Marinades (marinating)
fish, 234
for meats, 231, 253
Market mix, **72**
Marmalade, Meyer
lemon, 121
Mayonnaise
as emulsion, 125
in green goddess salad, **136**
proportion of oil to yolk
in, 128
in smoked tuna salad in
tomatoes, 137
technique for making,
127–29, 133–34
Meat(s). *See also* Beef;
Chicken; Lamb; Pork;
Poultry; Turkey
on the bone, 224, 263
braising. *See* Braising
(braises), meats
browning, 6, 229–30, 263
color changes in, 221
cooking methods for,
224–26
differences among kinds of,
221–22

dry-heat cooking methods
for, 253–54
fat in
flavor differences
and, 223
heat, effect of, 221
marbling, 221
fish compared to, 222
flavor differences in, 223
flouring before
browning, 263
grilling, 253, 254
heat's effect on, 219–21
juiciness of, 223
marbling, 221
marinades for, 231
moist-heat cooking meth-
ods for, 263–65. *See
also* Braising; Stew(s)
beurre manié as
thickener, 265
browning meats for, 263
chicken in the pot, **268**
lamb and lentils to eat
with a spoon, **272**
liquids, 264
mushroom pot roast, **270**
resting and then
reheating, 265
rustic versus refined
approaches, 265
seasoning, 265
temperature for, 264
testing for doneness,
264
vegetables, 264
"push" or carryover
cooking, 227
resting before carving,
227, 254
roasting, 217, 253, 254
brined turkey, **255**
lamb with fresh peas and
turnips, **260**

Meat(s) (*cont.*)
    pork roast, Umbrian-
      style, **259**
    resting at the end of
      cooking, 254
    searing (seared crust)
      of, 232
    seasoning before
      cooking, 253
    shallow-frying (panfrying
      and sautéing), 21,
      32, 33
    stews, 233
    temperatures for cooking,
      224–25, 227–29,
      253, 264
    tenderizing, 220
    tenderness of, 220, 221,
      225, 231
    testing for doneness,
      226–27, 254
    time needed to cook, 230
    tough cuts of, 224, 263
    trussing or tying, 254
Meat loaf
    combination of meats
      for, 278
    starchy fillers for, 278
    wild mushroom, **279**
Meat thermometers, 226,
    254
Melons, 56, 93
    in lime-mint syrup,
      sliced, **96**
    refrigeration of, 59
Meringue baskets, perfumed
    strawberries in, **104**
Mexican cream, 74
    mango crepes with, **106**
Meyer lemon marmalade,
    121
Milk, in custards, 131
Mint-lime syrup, sliced
    melons in, **96**

Moist-heat cooking methods
    for meats. *See also*
    Braising; Stew(s)
beurre manié as
    thickener, 265
browning meats for, 263
chicken in the pot, **268**
lamb and lentils to eat with
    a spoon, **272**
liquids, 264
mushroom pot roast, **270**
resting and then
    reheating, 265
rustic versus refined
    approaches, 265
seasoning, 265
temperature for, 264
testing for doneness, 264
vegetables, 264
Molasses
    in Boston baked beans, 159
    in doughs, 291
Morels
    scrambled eggs with
      asparagus and, **141**
    in wild mushroom
      lasagna, **177**
Moroccan spices, squash
    soup with, **207**
Mousse, trout, **142**
Mozzarella
    baked tomatoes stuffed
      with, **73**
    stuffed zucchini flowers
      with, **27**
Mung bean flour, 155
Muscles. *See also* Meat(s)
    worked versus resting, 224
Mushroom(s)
    browning owing to
      enzymes, 53
    in market mix, **72**
    morels, scrambled eggs
      with asparagus and, **141**

porcini, and zucchini
    risotto, **186**
pot roast, **270**
salmon braised with leeks,
    prosciutto and, **242**
shiitake, creamed onions
    with, **70**
wild
    lasagna, **177**
    meat loaf, **279**
Mustard
as emulsifier, 126–27
in vinaigrettes, 126–27, 133
Myoglobin, 221, 224

Nectarine(s), 56, 57, 59, 93
and almond tart, **301**
ice cream, **116**
and rose geranium jam, 120
New Mexican Christmas
    cookies (biscochitos),
    307
Nuts, in piecrusts, 292

Oil(s)
frying in. *See also* Frying
    (fried foods)
    adding a little old oil, 23
    amount to use, 23
    bubbles, types of, 15
    changes in oil, 12–14
    heat transfer and, 10
    panfrying, 18–19
    sautéing, 19
    smoking point of, 13
    temperature of oil, 16
    thermometer, 23
    very fresh oil, 13–15, 23
in mayonnaise, 127–28, 133
rancidity of, 12
soaps as by-products of the
    breakdown of, 14

stages in the life of, 14
white truffle, 191
Olives, 56
green
    braised lamb shanks
        with, **274**
    chicken braised with
        thyme and, **266**
    goat cheese tart with
        caramelized onions
        and, **34**
    pan-fried chicken breasts
        with fresh tomatoes,
        rosemary and, **42**
Olney, Richard, 209
Onion(s)
browning (caramelizing),
    19–20
chemical reactions caused
    by cutting or
    smashing, 1
creamed, with shiitake
    mushrooms, **70**
crying caused by, 2
sautéing garlic and, 19
sweetness of, 2–3
Orange(s), 50, 58
blood, 51
dreamsicle, **99**
and roasted beet salad, **78**
Orecchiette, with prosciutto
    and peas, **167**
Oven-steamed salmon with
    cucumber salad, **244**

Palm oil, 11
Panfrying, 18–19. *See also*
    Shallow-frying
Papain, 117
Papayas, 56
Pasta, 155–56
adding cooking water to the
    sauce, 166

Pasta (*cont.*)
  with broccoli rabe, **168**
  cooking, 166
  heating along with
      the sauce, after
      cooking, 166
  lasagna, 166
      broccoli, **172**
      of roasted asparagus,
          free-form, **175**
      wild mushroom, **177**
  macaroni and cheese with
      green onions and
      ham, **170**
  orecchiette with prosciutto
      and peas, **167**
  with potatoes, **179**
  resting dough for, 166
  shape of, 166
  stew of charred tomatoes,
      cranberry beans and, **82**
  Tuscan potato chips, **25**
Pastrami, 232
Pastry, 289. *See also*
      Piecrust(s)
  short-crust, **296**
Pastry flour, 286, 287, 293
Peach(es), 56–59, 93
  fritters, **30**
  ice cream, **116**
  to peel, 94
  tart, rustic, **300**
  white, and fig ice
      cream, **117**
Pears, 56, 59, 93
  in cornmeal waffles
      with winter fruit
      compote, **110**
  refrigeration of, 59
  ripening at room
      temperature, 93
Peas
  fresh, roast lamb with
      turnips and, **260**

orecchiette with prosciutto
    and, **167**
  split, 160
Pectic acid, 56
Pectin(s), 48, 49, 51, 53,
    55, 56
  in potatoes, 161
Peeling, peaches, 94
Pelargonidin, 51
Perfumed strawberries
    in meringue baskets,
    104
Persimmons, 56, 93
Photosynthesis, 48
Pie(s)
  fillings, 290
    sugar in, 154
    thickeners for, 154
  open-topped, 154–55
Piecrust(s) (pie doughs),
    285–99
  American versus European,
    285–88
  baking the shell, 294
  chilling ingredients and
      dough for, 293
  cocoa in, 292
  difficulty of making, 285
  doughs for, 290–94
      cookie doughs compared
          to, 290
  fat in, 286, 287
  fillings for, 290, 295
  flakiness of, 286, 288–90,
      293
  flaky, **297**
  flour for, 286–87
  gluten and, 286–90
  kneading and rolling, 294
  nuts in, 292
  patching cracks and
      breaks, 294
  placing dough in a pie plate
      or tart pan, 294

types of, 285
water in, 293
Pilaf, 157, 182
Pinto bean
   puree, **192**
   and squash stew, **196**
Plum(s), 57, 59, 93
   compote, cornmeal crepes
      with spiced, **108**
   ice cream, **116**
Poblano chiles, in rajas
      (grilled peppers and
      cream), **74**
Polenta with ragù, soft, **180**
Polymers, 13, 14
Porcini and zucchini
      risotto, **186**
Pork
   and beans . . . and
      endive, **198**
   brining, 231, 253
   butt
      in ragù napoletano, **276**
      as sausage meat, 278
   ribs
      in pork and beans . . . and
         endive, **198**
      sausages and, with
         red wine–braised
         lentils, **202**
      in soft polenta with
         ragù, **180**
   roast, Umbrian-style, **259**
   sausage, Italian. *See* Italian
      sausage(s)
   schnitzel with arugula
      salad, 44
   temperature for cooking,
      225, 254
Potato(es), 48, 160, 204
   baked fish with artichokes
      and, **250**
   baking, 160–62, 204
   boiling, 161, 204

browning owing to
      enzymes, 53, 61
   french fries, 12
      potatoes for, 16–17,
         161–62
      stages in the life of oil
         and, 14–15
   gnocchi, 155, **211**
   gratin, 162, **209**
   in market mix, **72**
   mashed, 161
   new, spring vegetable stew
      of snap peas, lettuce,
      artichokes and, **80**
   pasta with, **179**
   storage of, 60
   as thickeners, 162, 204
      in cream of cauliflower
         soup, **205**
   types of, 160
Potato starch, 151, 154, 163
Pot roast, mushroom, **270**
Pots de crème, chocolate, **144**
Poule au pot, **268**
Poultry. *See also* Chicken;
      Turkey
   brining, 231, 253
   redness at the bone, 227
   temperature for
      cooking, 254
   testing for
      doneness, 226–27
Preserves, strawberry, 119
Prosciutto
   orecchiette with peas
      and, **167**
   salmon braised with leeks,
      mushrooms and, **242**
Protein(s), 217–23
   fibers of, 218
   in flours, 286
Prunes, in cornmeal waffles
      with winter fruit
      compote, **110**

Pudding(s), 130–31
  chocolate pots de
    crème, **144**
  instant, 153
  lemon sponge, **146**
Puree
  butternut squash, with
    balsamic vinegar, **213**
  of winter squash and
    apples, **215**

Queso ranchero, 74
Quince(s)
  applesauce, **98**
  in fall fruit compote, **97**

Radicchio, al forno, **66**
Ragout of shrimp and fava
    beans, **84**
Ragù
  napoletano, **276**
  soft polenta with, **180**
Raisins, in fall fruit
    compote, **97**
Rajas (grilled peppers and
    cream), **74**
Rancidity of oils, 12
Ranhofer, Charles, 65
Rapeseed oil (canola oil), 11
Raspberry ice cream, **115**
Ratatouille, **76**
Real fajitas, **258**
Refried beans, 162
Refrigeration of fruits, 59, 93
Retrogradation, 157
Rhubarb, 59
Rice, 155, 156
  fried, Chinese, 157, 182
  long-grain, 156, 157, 182
  pilaf, 157, 182
  risotto, 156, 182, 183
    artichoke, **184**

zucchini and porcini, **186**
salad, 182
  seafood, **188**
as thickener, 162
types of, 156
Rice flour, 154, 155
Rigor mortis, 222
Ripeness of fruits, 55–58, 93
Risotto, 156, 182, 183
  artichoke, **184**
  zucchini and porcini, **186**
Roasted beet and orange
    salad, **78**
Roasted tomatoes with goat
    cheese, **63**
Roasting (roasted foods)
  frying compared to, 10
  meats, 217, 253, 254
    brined turkey, **255**
    lamb with fresh peas and
      turnips, **260**
    pork roast, Umbrian-
      style, **259**
    resting at the end of
      cooking, 254
  vegetables, 54
    beet and orange salad,
      roasted, **78**
    market mix, **72**
    radicchio al forno, **66**
Roast lamb with fresh peas
    and turnips, **260**
Roberts, Michael, 272
Robuchon, Joel, 38
Root starches, 151, 154
Rose geranium, and
    nectarine jam, 120
Rosemary
  lamb, and orange zest
    sausages, **282**
  pan-fried chicken breasts
    with fresh tomatoes,
    green olives and, **42**
Roux, 163

Cajun, 153
Rustic peach tart, **300**
Rustic tart crust, **299**
Rutabaga, 52

Sage, sautéed green beans
    with garlic and, **37**
Salad
  arugula, pork schnitzel
    with, 44
  calamari, **236**
  celery, with walnuts and
    blue cheese, **135**
  cucumber, oven-steamed
    salmon with, **244**
  green goddess, **136**
  rice, 182
    seafood, **188**
  roasted beet and orange, **78**
  salmon, crisp, **237**
  smoked tuna, in tomatoes,
    137
Salad dressing. *See*
    Vinaigrette
Salmon
  braised with leeks,
    prosciutto and
    mushrooms, **242**
  brining, 232
  crisp-skinned, on creamy
    leeks and cabbage, **38**
  grilled, with chipotle-
    tequila butter, **246**
  oven-steamed, with
    cucumber salad, **244**
  salad, crisp, **237**
Salsa verde, grilled swordfish
    with, **248**
Salt(ing). *See also* Brining
  batters and, 18, 23
  beans before cooking,
    158–59, 190
  in mayonnaise, 128

meat before sautéing, 32
  meats, 253
Sand dabs (or sole), broiled,
    with brown butter, **252**
Sandwich
  grilled vegetable, **86**
  turkey tonnato, **256**
Saturated fats, 11–12
Sauce(s)
  bourbon, vanilla-baked
    apples with, **112**
  eggs in, 125–27
  hollandaise, 129–30
  ragù napoletano, **276**
  after sautéing, 33
  starch-thickened, 150–53,
    163–64
    avoiding clumping, 153
    browning the starch be-
      fore adding liquid, 153
    holding before
      serving, 164
    ingredients added after
      a sauce has
      thickened, 164
  tomato, for broccoli
    lasagna, **172**
  white
    ratios of fat, flour and
      liquid for, 164
    in wild mushroom
      lasagna, **177**
  zabaglione, 130
Sausage(s), **278**
  casings, 281
  cooking technique for,
    278
  grinding meat for, 278
  Italian. *See* Italian
    sausage(s)
  lamb, orange zest and
    rosemary, **282**
  seasoning meat for, 278
  spicy garlic, **281**

index

Sausage(s) *(cont.)*
  temperature of meat for
    making, 278
Sautéed green beans with
    garlic and sage, **37**
Sautéing. *See* Shallow-frying
Sax, Richard, 144
Science of cooking, 6–7
Scrambled eggs, 140
  with morels and
    asparagus, **141**
Seafood
  brining, 232
  rice salad, **188**
Searing (seared crust) of
    meats, 232
Semolina, 286
Shallow-frying (panfrying
    and sautéing), 18–21,
    32
  amount of oil to use for, 32
  brussels sprouts and bacon,
    36
  chicken breasts with fresh
    tomatoes, green olives
    and rosemary,
    pan-fried, **42**
  country fried chicken, **40**
  crisp-skinned salmon on
    creamy leeks and
    cabbage, **38**
  as final step in cooking, 20
  fish, 32
  goat cheese tart with
    caramelized onions and
    green olives, **34**
  green beans with garlic and
    sage, **37**
  keeping food from
    sticking, 32
  meaning of, 19
  meats, 21, 32, 33
    for braises, daubes, and
      stews, 263

pork schnitzel with arugula
    salad, 44
sauce you can make
    after, 33
temperature of oil for, 32
vegetables, 53
Shellfish, fish soup with, **240**
Shiitake mushrooms,
    creamed onions
    with, **70**
Shortcake, ultimate
    strawberry, **102**
Short-crust pastry, **296**
Shortening, 11
  crispest crusts obtained
    with, 23
  for piecrusts, 288, 289
  in piecrusts, 293
Shrimp
  and avocado, ceviche
    with, **235**
  brining, 232
  and fava beans, ragout
    of, **84**
  in green goddess salad,
    136
  in seafood rice salad, **188**
Silverton, Nancy, 299
Simeti, Mary Taylor, 310
Skirt steak, in real fajitas,
    258
Sliced melons in lime-mint
    syrup, **96**
Smoked tuna salad in
    tomatoes, 137
Smokerless smoked
    bratwurst, **283**
Smoking point of oils, 13
Smoky cream of corn
    soup, **165**
Snap peas, spring vegetable
    stew of lettuce, new
    potatoes, artichokes
    and, **80**

Snickerdoodles, 306
Soaps, as by-products of the
    breakdown of oil, 14
Soft polenta with ragù, 180
Sol, 153–54
Sole (or sand dabs), broiled,
    with brown butter, 252
Soup
    cream of cauliflower, 205
    fish, with shellfish, 240
    smoky cream of corn, 165
    squash, with Moroccan
        spices, 207
    strawberry, 95
Sour cherry–stuffed almond
    cookies, 310
Sour cream, in doughs, 291
Spiced plum compote, corn-
    meal crepes with, 108
Spicy garlic sausages, 281
Spinach, butter-braised, 64
Split peas, 160
Spring vegetable stew of snap
    peas, lettuce, new pota-
    toes and artichokes, 80
Squash(es), winter, 160, 162
    butternut, puree with
        balsamic vinegar, 213
    California succotash
        of, lima beans, corn
        and, 68
    with Moroccan spices, 207
    and pinto bean stew, 196
    pureeing, 204
    puree of apples and, 215
    as thickeners, 204
Squid (calamari)
    salad, 236
    in seafood rice salad, 188
Starch(es)
    composition of, 149
    in custards, 132
    gelatinization of, 150–52
    "pure," 151

quick-thickening, 153
root, 151, 154
sauces thickened with,
    150–53, 163–64
    avoiding clumping, 153
    browning the starch be-
        fore adding liquid, 153
    holding before
        serving, 164
    ingredients added after
        a sauce has
        thickened, 164
    thickening properties
        of, 152–54
Steam, frying and, 15–16
Steaming vegetables, 54
Steingarten, Jeffrey, 56
Stew(s) (stewing), 228,
    263–65
    of charred tomatoes, pasta
        and cranberry beans, 82
    meats, 233. See also
        Meat(s), moist-heat
        cooking methods for
    testing for doneness, 264
    vegetables in, 264
    pinto bean and squash, 196
    spring vegetable, of snap
        peas, lettuce, new pota-
        toes and artichokes, 80
    white (blanquettes), 229,
        263
    white bean and Swiss
        chard, 194
Sticking, keeping foods
    from, 32
    grilled fish, 234
    lasagna, 166
Stone fruit(s), 57, 58, 93
    ice cream, 116
    ripening at room
        temperature, 93
Storage of fruits, 59, 93
Strawberry(-ies), 58, 59

Strawberry(-ies) (*cont.*)
  ice cream, **115**
  in meringue baskets,
      perfumed, **104**
  preserves, 119
  shortcake, ultimate, **102**
  soup, **95**
Stromquist, Annie, 308
Stuffed zucchini, **88**
Stuffed zucchini flowers, **27**
Succotash of squash, lima
    beans and corn,
    California, **68**
Sugar(s)
  creaming butter and,
      292, 305
  crust of fried foods and, 22
  in custards, 131
  in fruits, 56
  fruit softened by, 59, 93
  in pie fillings, 154
  in starch-thickened
      sauces, 152
Sugar syrup, for fruit
    compotes, 93
Sulfenic acids, 1, 2
Sulfur, in eggs, 124
Sulfuric (sulfurous)
    compounds
  in cabbage, 54
  in onions, 1–3
  in vegetables, 52
Sweating, 20
Sweet potatoes, 162
  and bourbon, gratin of, **214**
  as thickeners, 204
Swiss chard stew, white bean
    and, **194**
Swordfish, grilled, with salsa
    verde, **248**
Syrup
  for fruit compotes, 93
  lime-mint, sliced melons
      in, **96**

Tapioca, as thickener
  for pie fillings, 295
  for sauces, 151, 154
Tarragon, in bearnaise, 139
Tart(s)
  crust, rustic, **299**
  crust for, 293. *See also*
      Piecrust(s)
    goat cheese tart with
        caramelized onions and
        green olives, **34**
  fruit, fillings for, 294
  goat cheese, with
      caramelized onions and
      green olives, **34**
  lavender-fig, **302**
  lemon curd, **147**
  nectarine and almond, **301**
  peach, rustic, **300**
Tea, 53
Tenderizing of meats,
    220–21
Thermometers
  deep-frying, 23
  meat, 226, 254
Thickener(s). *See also* Corn-
    starch, as thickener;
    Starch(es)
  beurre manié, 265
  flour as
    for pie fillings, 295
    for sauces, 151–52, 163
  pasta cooking water as,
      166
  for pie fillings, 295
  potatoes as, 162
  rice as, 162
Thompson, Sylvia, 119
Thyme, chicken braised
    with green olives and,
    266
Tomato(es), 58
  baked, stuffed with
      mozzarella, **73**

charred, stew of pasta, cranberry beans and, **82**
pan-fried chicken breasts with green olives, rosemary, and fresh, **42**
roasted, with goat cheese, **63**
sauce, for broccoli lasagna, **172**
smoked tuna salad in, 137
storage of, 59, 61
Tonnato sandwich, turkey, **256**
Tradition of home cooking, 4
Trout mousse, **142**
Truffle oil, white, 191
Trussing meats, 254
Tuna
smoked, salad in tomatoes, 137
in turkey tonnato sandwich, **256**
Turkey. *See also* Poultry
brining, 232
roast brined, **255**
tonnato sandwich, **256**
white and dark meat in, 224
Turnips, roast lamb with fresh peas and, **260**
Tuscan potato chips, **25**
Tying meats, 254

Ultimate strawberry shortcake, **102**
Umbrian-style pork roast, **259**
Unbleached flour, 286

Vanilla, -baked apples with bourbon sauce, **112**
Vegetable(s), 47–91. *See also specific vegetables*
acids given off by cooking, 53
blanched, 62

blanching, 52
boiling, 53, 54
in braises, stews and daubes, 264
braising, 62
cellulose walls of, 48–49
colors of, 50–53
cooked with acidic ingredients, 52
cooking methods for, 54–55
cooking times for, 61
cutting, 61
defined, 47–48
flavor changes from cooking, 53–54
fruits compared to, 55
green, cooking, 61
grilled, sandwich, **86**
grilling, 54
leafy, 51–52
peeling, 61
roasting, 54
beet and orange salad, roasted, **78**
market mix, **72**
radicchio al forno, **66**
selecting, 49, 61
spring, stew of snap peas, lettuce, new potatoes and artichokes, **80**
steaming, 54
storage of, 61
storing, 49
Vegetable fats, 11
Vegetable oils, 11
Vegetable shortening. *See* Shortening
Velouté, 152
Vinaigrette
for blanched vegetables, 62
as emulsion, 125–26, 133
Vinegar
balsamic, butternut squash puree with, **213**

Vinegar (*cont.*)
  in hollandaise, 139
  in mayonnaise, 128
  in piecrusts, 290
  in piecrusts and cookie
    doughs, 291, 293
  rinsing onions in, 2–3
  in starch-thickened sauces,
    152–53

Waffles, cornmeal, with
    winter fruit compote,
    110
Walnuts, celery salad with
    blue cheese and, **135**
Washing, fruits, 59
Water
  as heat conductor, 10
  in piecrusts, 293
  sautéing vegetables
    and, 53–54
Water bath (*bain-marie*)
  custards baked in, 131,
    139
  to hold a hot hollandaise or
    other emulsion sauce
    before serving, 139
  for lemon sponge
    pudding, 146
Watermelon, 56
Wells, Patricia, 38, 272
Whale meat, 223
Wheat flour. *See also* Flour(s)
  pastas, 155
Whitebait, fried, **29**
White bean
  crostini, **191**
  and Swiss chard stew, **194**
White peach and fig ice
  cream, **117**
White sauce, 152
  ratios of fat, flour and liquid
    for, 164

in wild mushroom
    lasagna, **177**
White truffle oil, 191
Whole wheat flours, 286–87
Wild mushroom lasagna, **177**
Wild mushroom meat loaf,
    279
Wild rice, 156
Wine
  in hollandaise, 139
  in marinades, 253
  in starch-thickened
    sauces, 152–53
Winter fruit compote, corn-
    meal waffles with, **110**
Winter squash, 160, 162
  butternut, puree with
    balsamic vinegar, **213**
  California succotash of,
    lima beans, corn
    and, **68**
  with Moroccan spices, **207**
  and pinto bean stew, **196**
  pureeing, 204
  puree of apples and, **215**
  as thickeners, 204
Wolfert, Paula, 244
Woods, Tim, **96**

Yeast, batters with, 22
Yogurt, in doughs, 291

Zabaglione, 130
Zucchini
  California succotash of
    lima beans, corn and,
    68
  flowers, stuffed, **27**
  glazed, **67**
  and porcini risotto, **186**
  in ratatouille, **76**
  stuffed, **88**

© Anacleto Rapping

Russ Parsons is a staff writer and the former food editor of the *Los Angeles Times* and has been writing award-winning articles about food for more than fifteen years. This is his first book.